Stan Woollams, M.D., is a fellow of the American Group Psychotherapy Association and treasurer and teaching member of the International Transactional Analysis Association. He is coauthor, with Michael Brown, of *Transactional Analysis* and *Transactional Analysis in Brief,* and he has twenty years of experience in the treatment of adults, adolescents, and families and in the training of professionals in the practice of psychotherapy.

Michael Brown, Ph.D., is the author of *Psychodiagnosis in Brief* and *NoTAtions: A Guide to TA Literature.* He is a teaching member of the International Transactional Analysis Association, a practicing clinical psychologist, and an internationally known trainer in Transactional Analysis, group therapy, and other disciplines.

Acknowledgement is made to "The International Transactional Analysis Association" for permission to reprint Egogram (Figure 2-6) from Dusay, "Egogram and the Constancy Hypothesis" (*TA Journal,* vol. 2, no. 3, July 1972; also note the expanded work *Egograms* by John M. Dusay, New York: Harper and Row, 1977); OK Corral (Figure 6-3) from Ernst, "Psychological Rackets and the OK Corral" (*TA Journal,* vol. 3, no. 2, April 1973); OK Miniscript and Not-OK Miniscript (Figures 10-1 and 10-2) from Kahler with Capers, "The Miniscript" (*TA Journal,* vol. 4, no. 1, January 1974); and Drama Triangle (Figure 7-2) from Karpman, "Fairy Tales and Script Drama Analysis" (*TA Bulletin,* vol. 8, no. 2, April 1968).

A SPECTRUM BOOK   Prentice-Hall, Inc., Englewood Cliffs, NJ 07632

TA

THE TOTAL HANDBOOK OF TRANSACTIONAL ANALYSIS

STAN WOOLLAMS
MICHAEL BROWN

Library of Congress Cataloging in Publication Data

Woollams, Stan.
  TA, the total handbook of transactional analysis.

  (A Spectrum Book)
  Includes index.
  1. Transactional analysis. I. Brown, Michael,
1947-   joint author. II. Title.
  RC489.T7W65   158   79-1028
  ISBN 0-13-881920-3
  ISBN 0-13-881912-2 pbk.

© 1979 by Prentice-Hall, Inc., Englewood Cliffs, N.J. 07632

A SPECTRUM BOOK

Printed in the United States of America

10 9 8 7 6 5 4 3 2 1

To Kristy, with my love and appreciation.
(S.W.)

And to my family and friends, who share their lives with me.
(M.B.)

Editorial/production supervision and interior design by Maria Carella
Manufacturing buyer: Cathie Lenard

PRENTICE-HALL INTERNATIONAL, INC., *London*
PRENTICE-HALL OF AUSTRALIA PTY., LIMITED, *Sydney*
PRENTICE-HALL OF CANADA, LTD., *Toronto*
PRENTICE-HALL OF INDIA PRIVATE, LIMITED, *New Delhi*
PRENTICE-HALL OF JAPAN, INC., *Tokyo*
PRENTICE-HALL OF SOUTHEAST ASIA PTE., LTD., *Singapore*
WHITEHALL BOOKS, LIMITED, *Wellington, New Zealand*

Contents

Preface

This book is for anyone who wants to know about Transactional Analysis (TA)—therapists, ministers, counselors, teachers, businesspersons, physicians, students, . . . anyone, really, who wishes to use TA to better understand and improve their interactions with themselves and others.

This book is also for those who want to know about people. Transactional Analysis has become popular both among professional people-helpers and the public because of its clear analysis of how people function internally as well as interpersonally. Besides providing a general theory of personality and psychotherapy, TA can also be used as a framework to integrate other methods and techniques. Thus, TA practitioners tend to be eclectic, drawing widely from other sources for information about personality development, psychodynamics, and treatment techniques. Conversely, therapists, social scientists, and business consultants who are trained in other theories and styles comfortably add TA to their frameworks.

A major reason TA has proven to be so useful is because it responds to all three parts of a person. First, TA appeals to the child part of each person (the *Child* ego state) by providing an easily understandable theory and language—understandable even to an eight-year-old. Furthermore, the creativity and energy of the eight-year-old in each of us is invited to be an active participant in the learning or therapy process in as comfortable a way as possible. While TA jargon is designed to appeal to the person's Child, its orderly, commonsense approach to integrating theory with practice simultaneously appeals to the person's logical and rational thinking part (the *Adult* ego state). And although the basic TA concepts are simple and straightforward, advanced TA theory is more complex and intricate, providing plenty of food for thought for the hungry theorist. Transactional Analysis also appeals to the part of the personality which specializes in opinions, morals, and values (the *Parent* ego state). Transactional Analysis theory provides a basic value structure which defines people as OK, accepts human fraility, and invites professional helpers, clients, and laypersons to assume personal responsibility by taking charge of their lives. Throughout this book the positive, humanistic philosophy of TA will permeate the presentation of theoretical concepts and their effective application.

In the last few years the body of TA literature has grown immensely as many individuals, including ourselves, have added their contributions. This book, though it is not exhaustive, brings together what we consider the major techniques of TA theory and practice. The result is *our version of TA.*

Our Outline

While doing workshops and lectures we consistently find that when presentations of TA theory are interspersed with its practical applications an impressive flow of ideas and insights are stimulated in the listener. We follow that same style in this book. A chapter is devoted to each major aspect of theory with accompanying discussions of how these concepts can be applied. Then, the main body of the book is concluded with several chapters devoted to the philosophy, process, and techniques of therapy. An Appendix provides a list of exercises which may be used to enhance the learning of the various concepts. Finally, there is a Reference List listing major sources for further reference. The bracketed reference numbers throughout the chapters refer to them.

Our Style

We will capitalize the words *Transactional Analysis* or use the abbreviation *TA* to represent the entire field, while using *transactional analysis* in lower-case letters to denote the analysis of transactions between two or more people. In general, capitalized words refer to specific TA terms (such as *Parent, Adult, Child, Victim, Rescuer, Persecutor*) and not to their ordinary meanings, which remain uncapitalized. The word *stroke* (a unit of attention) will mean a positive stroke unless otherwise specified. The words *treatment* and *therapy* will be used interchangeably to describe the process of one person helping another become more successful at managing his or her life. Next, we choose to refer to those individuals who receive the services of TA practitioners as *clients* rather than *patients.* We do this for two reasons. First, most people who receive TA services do so in nonmedical settings. Second, the term *patient* has an unfortunate connotation for many people, since its common usage in the medical profession invites a sense of being one-down and not a full partner in the change process. We believe the term *client* connotes a more cooperative relationship. Finally, we intermix the use of feminine and masculine pronouns throughout the book.

Some Strokes

We want to thank many people for their contributions to this book. The numerous footnotes in each chapter and the Bibliography are a measure of our indebtedness to the innovators within TA as well as to some from other fields. We have learned from most of them personally as well as through their writings, and we extend to them our profound thanks and respect. A big thank you goes to our trainees and clients, who told us when we were not clear and stimulated us to write this book. We particularly thank Steve Lankton and Taibi Kahler who provided valuable feedback on early drafts. Our heartfelt appreciation is given to Sherry Hutchins and Jan Meyers who typed our manuscript and in the process showed talent for the interpretation of hieroglyphics. Lastly, many warm furries and fuzzies to Susan Greenlick for her excellent illustrations.

1

Introduction to Transactional Analysis

*"No Sigmund,
it has nothing to do with Transcendental Meditation."*

Transactional Analysis (TA) is many things. First, it is a *philosophy*—a point of view about people. Second, it is a *theory* of personality development, intrapsychic functioning, and interpersonal behavior. Third, it is a system of *techniques* designed to help people understand and change their feelings and behaviors. All these aspects are thoroughly interconnected—even though we occasionally discuss each of them separately.

Before we proceed further we want to emphasize that the material in this book is our version of TA theory and practice. As in any developing field there are areas of disagreement as well as some hazy aspects of theory. What follows is our present idea of what makes the most sense and what works best.*

Philosophy of TA

To really appreciate both the theory and the techniques you must first understand the framework which the philosophy provides for them. Transactional Analysis espouses a positive, humanistic philosophy which not only provides a foundation for its many applications, but also directly promotes change by allowing the process to be safe, exciting, and often even fun.

The overall philosophy of TA begins with an assumption that we are all *OK*. This means that each of us, regardless of our behavioral

---

*For a more advanced and expanded treatise see our book *Transactional Analysis* (Huron Valley Institute Press, Box 123, Dexter, Michigan).

style, has a basic core which is lovable and has the potential and desire for growth and self-actualization. All our parts have a positive intention and are therefore important and useful to us. Since we believe that these parts exist and have positive intentions, we search for them diligently, and we find them. Once we have established contact with these parts, we pay attention to them (*stroke them*), nurture them, and invite them to flourish. This philosophy leads to what is probably the most basic assumption in TA theory and practice: *I'm OK and You're OK.*

It follows, then, that whatever the relationship—wife-husband, father-daughter, employee-employer, student-teacher, therapist-client—both parties enter as equal partners. Both have needs, wants, and feelings which are important and should not be discounted. To foster cooperation and mutuality in relationships, TA emphasizes the use of *contracts* which delineate and protect each person's rights and responsibilities.

Since all people are basically OK, each of us deserves *positive strokes* just because we exist. It is beautiful to see a person come alive and glow with the positive strokes from acceptance, love, and caring. They recharge our battery and provide us with new energy. Even though everyone needs these strokes, most of us do not learn efficient methods for obtaining them. Instead, we tend to stroke only those parts of ourselves or others which we believe to be worthwhile, choosing to ignore or to put down those parts which we dislike. Whether in or outside our awareness, these rejected and unresolved parts demand our attention, depriving us of useful energy. If these rejected parts of the personality are accepted and appropriately stroked, they are more willing to change and cooperate with the accepted ones. Positive stroking invites more OKness and solves more problems than any other type of therapeutic intervention.

Transactional Analysis theory is based on a *decisional* model. Each of us learns specific behaviors and decides upon a life plan as we are growing up. Although our childhood decisions are strongly influenced by parents and others, we ourselves make these decisions in our own unique style. Since we decided our life plan, we also have the power to change it by making new decisions at any time. Thus each of us is responsible for our own growth, as we alone exercise the choice to retain our old decisions or make new ones. No one can *make* us change. Each of us is ultimately responsible only for himself, and not for others. No matter how much we may try, we cannot blame our behavior on anyone other than ourselves.

However, we do *influence* each other, sometimes profoundly. And since we are both OK, we want those influences to be positive, thus increasing the likelihood that each of us will make growth-enhancing decisions. That is what TA is all about!

History of Transactional Analysis

Eric Berne (1910–1970) is the originator, primary developer, and euhemerus* of Transactional Analysis. Like many other creative innovators, he had a great capacity for work, writing a total of eight books and publishing many articles. He liked words—especially words that were unusual and elegant like *euhemerus* and *palimpsest,* or words that were short and snappy like *racket* and *script.* Berne enjoyed cutting through the circumlocutions and excess verbiage of many in our field; once, to satirize the problem, he gave a talk entitled "Away from a Theory of the Impact of Interpersonal Inter-action on Non-Verbal Participation" [3] .†

Berne was trained as a psychiatrist and psychoanalyst, but because of his predilections he never became a card-carrying analyst. He was simultaneously attracted to the brilliance and profundity of psychoanalysis and bothered by its slowness, overcomplexity, and rigidity. The psychoanalytic community also had difficulty accepting Berne, and in 1956, after many years of training, his psychoanalytic institute turned down his application for membership. Nevertheless, psychoanalysis greatly influenced him, and its ideas are evident throughout his writings.

Berne's first TA theories appeared in 1949; by 1958 they were mostly laid out. In 1958 Berne started the first TA seminar—the San Francisco Social Psychiatry Seminar, attended by a grand total of six people. By the next year the seminar had grown and was split into an introductory course (called a 101) and an advanced seminar. Membership quickly increased, and soon TA was being discussed and used all around the country. In order to keep members up to date on organizational developments and advances in theory

*A departed, highly revered leader.

†Bracketed numbers refer to entries in the References at the end of the book.

and practice, the quarterly *Transactional Analysis Bulletin* was begun in 1962. In 1971 it was expanded into the *Transactional Analysis Journal*. The first annual TA summer conference was held in 1963. By 1964 there were already members in many of the fifty states as well as Canada, Costa Rica, and England. By now the San Francisco Social Psychiatry Seminar was too parochial a title. A new name was needed, and the International Transactional Analysis Association (ITAA) was formed. In addition to publishing a journal, the ITAA puts out a newsletter (*The Script*) for its members, holds two annual conferences, and in general promotes TA as an area of specialization. The ITAA also performs two other very important functions. First, and perhaps foremost, it sponsors fun. Time, space, and energy are made available for the Child at conferences, seminars, and in the *Journal*. Second, the ITAA is very active in the training and certification of its members. Membership categories and standards have been clearly established for the protection and education of the public, as well as for the guidance of professionals who desire training. The ITAA office in San Francisco (1772 Vallejo Street) is available to inquiries about any member's qualifications and about specific educational and training standards and opportunities.

During the 1960s and until his death in 1970, Berne continued his development of TA theory. His books on groups (*The Structure and Dynamics of Organizations and Groups*, 1963), games (*Games People Play*, 1964), and scripts (*What Do You Say After You Say Hello?*, 1972) are landmarks [4, 7, 9]. Eric Berne's contributions were primarily in the areas of theory and philosophy. Those who have followed him have added breadth and depth to these areas, and only one fundamental change has occurred. Berne once declared that "anyone who touches their patients is not doing transactional analysis." This was probably a reflection of his psychoanalytic background, plus his concern that TA therapists might become sexually involved with their clients. Most TA therapists today believe and behave differently—although they still refrain from sex, they often do touch their clients in the process of helping them. We will discuss this issue in depth in the chapter on strokes. Contemporary TA writers have especially sparkled in the development of techniques and the amalgamation of TA with other therapeutic systems. Today, Berne might not easily recognize the many different ways TA is put into practice, but he would appreciate the verve, skill, and fun with which it is done.

2

Ego States

*"How about if you and I get together—
the six of us will have a great time."*

Ego states are the building blocks of TA. All the various ways that each of us behaves, thinks, and feels may be put into three large categories of ego states called *Parent, Adult,* and *Child.* *The *Parent* ego state is a collection of attitudes, thoughts, behaviors, and feelings which a person has taken in from outside sources who served as her parent figures. The *Adult* ego state is a data processor which functions like a computer as it organizes information, estimates probabilities, and makes logical statements. The *Child* ego state consists of feelings, thoughts, and behaviors which are typical of children and spontaneous adults.

These building blocks may be organized and divided in different ways to produce different understandings. The *personality diagram,* illustrated in Figure 2-1, shows the three basic ego states of one

FIGURE 2-1. THE THREE EGO
STATES OF A PERSON.

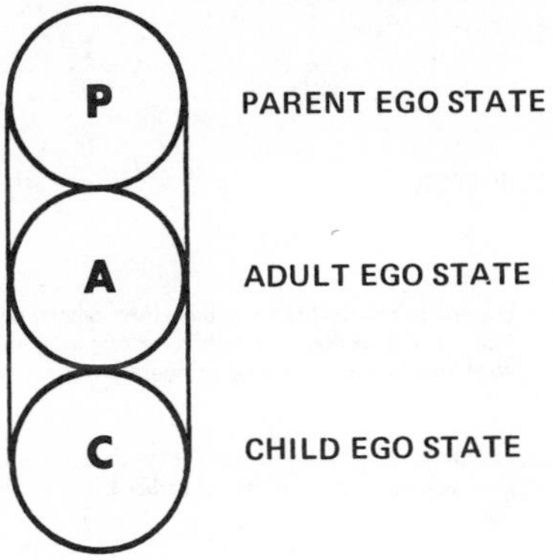

P — PARENT EGO STATE

A — ADULT EGO STATE

C — CHILD EGO STATE

*When capitalized, *Parent, Adult,* and *Child* refer to ego states; lower-case *parent, adult,* and *child* refer to persons.

9

person. The outer "skin" which encloses the three circles indicates that they all function as a unit to form one personality. This is called a *first-order diagram*, since the ego states are not broken down into smaller parts.

To better understand the smaller building blocks that make up the three ego states, we will do what is called a *second-order analysis*. (see Figures 2-2 and 2-3). This analysis is both *structural*, representing the biological and historical components of ego states, and *functional*, referring to how they are used. *Structural analysis* deals with each ego state's developmental history and innate capacity for expression—in other words, the *content* of the ego state. *Functional analysis* describes how a person uses her ego states to relate to herself and to others—in other words, the *process* of the ego state. The ensuing discussion of ego states will examine the various divisions in detail, first structurally and then functionally.

FIGURE 2-2. SECOND-ORDER STRUCTURAL DIAGRAM.

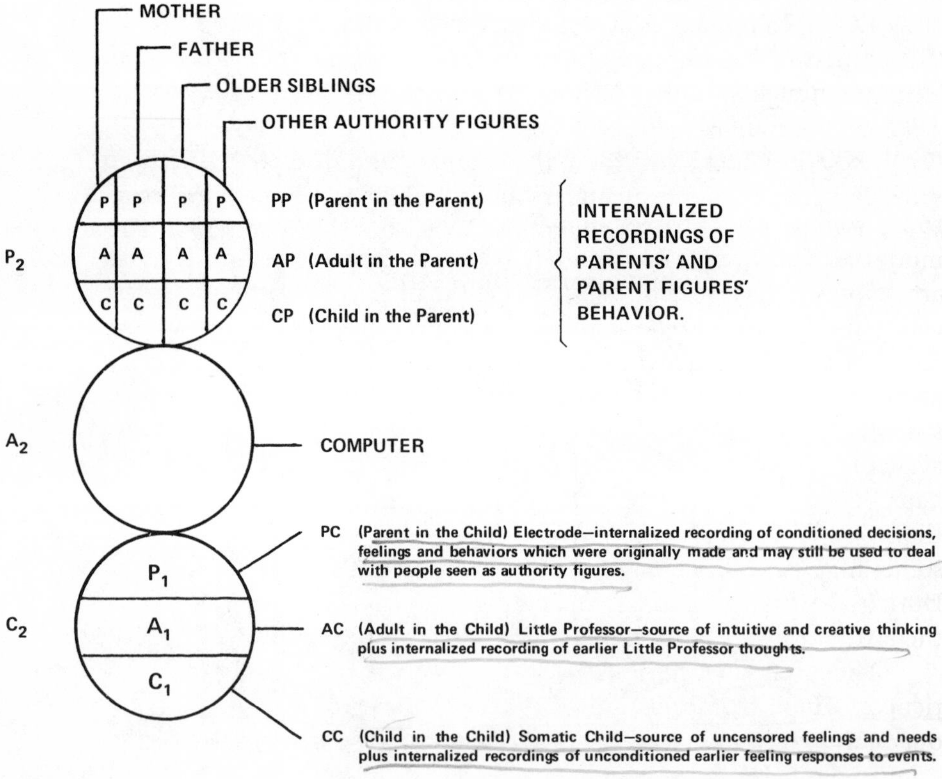

MOTHER
FATHER
OLDER SIBLINGS
OTHER AUTHORITY FIGURES

P_2

PP (Parent in the Parent)

AP (Adult in the Parent)

CP (Child in the Parent)

INTERNALIZED RECORDINGS OF PARENTS' AND PARENT FIGURES' BEHAVIOR.

A_2 — COMPUTER

C_2

P_1
A_1
C_1

PC (Parent in the Child) Electrode—internalized recording of conditioned decisions, feelings and behaviors which were originally made and may still be used to deal with people seen as authority figures.

AC (Adult in the Child) Little Professor—source of intuitive and creative thinking plus internalized recording of earlier Little Professor thoughts.

CC (Child in the Child) Somatic Child—source of uncensored feelings and needs plus internalized recordings of unconditioned earlier feeling responses to events.

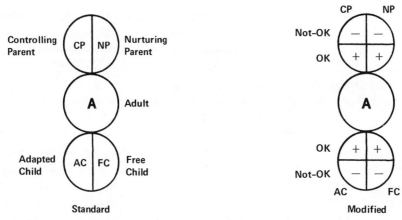

FIGURE 2-3. SECOND-ORDER FUNCTIONAL DIAGRAMS.

Child Ego State

Structural Analysis

CHILD IN THE CHILD (C_1)

The newborn infant bursts upon the world with months of development behind her as a fetus. She is born not only with a unique set of urges and feelings, but also with the usual needs for such things as food, warmth, and strokes. Bodily functions and reactions are paramount to the infant, and the related behavior patterns and feelings are appropriately called the first Child, or C_1. They may also be called the *Somatic Child*. This part is derived from the needs, wants, and feelings of the body and remains present throughout life, serving as our primary motivator for behavior. As the nervous and hormonal systems of the body mature, different impulses and feelings become available. This process continues at least through puberty and perhaps beyond. Certainly females undergo considerable changes during the course of pregnancy, childbirth, and nursing, and both sexes sometimes experience involutional changes accompanying old age. During the first part of life our bodies unfold their potential, while the last part of life generally involves a loss of some of that potential.

The Somatic Child also contains memories of our past experiences. These memories are often called *tapes* or *recordings*, since our brains store events in units which may be "played back" at any

11

time. A typical C_1 memory is a cozy feeling of warmth and comfort while being breast-fed. A C_1 tape from a later age might be an intense fear experienced when yelled at by dad for masturbating.

ADULT IN THE CHILD (A_1)

Although we express feelings, needs, and wants from the moment of birth, it is not clear that thinking is a function of the newborn. Some investigators believe that newborn infants react only with conditioned reflexes and do not show signs of actual awareness and conscious thought until about the third month. However, there is mounting evidence that thinking may begin as early as birth. Regardless of precisely when it begins, each of us quickly develops an intuitive, curious, and creative part that is very interested in himself and the world. This first Adult (A_1), or thinking part, is called the *Little Professor* because this style of thinking allows the preverbal infant to "know" how mother feels and gives him a method for figuring out what to do to get along. In addition, curiosity and creativity are like toys, and children of all ages delight in their ability to think. We easily become engrossed in such things as rattles, balloons, pinball machines, and especially our own bodies. Later we may become intrigued with such ideas as "How does the clock work?" "Where do babies come from?" and "How much ice cream can I eat?" We also use our Little Professors a great deal to figure out such other important things as "Why does mommy get mad at me?" and "What can I do about it?" Children are very concerned with big people's reactions, and the Little Professor plays the primary role in our process of making decisions about how we can best get along in the world.

It is not clear exactly how long the Little Professor's capacities continue to develop. Curiosity increases throughout the early years of childhood, and other A_1 functions probably do also. It is certain, however, that the Little Professor is available to us throughout life. If it is accepted and encouraged during childhood, it will flourish, enabling us as grownups to continue being boldly curious and excitingly creative. Unfortunately, there abound many prejudices against the whole series of processes called intuition. Our parents may not approve of our curiosity or our intuitive awareness of what is going on. For most people, a required part of the "social graces" is learning to ignore what their intuition says about other persons. Comments about "women's intuition" often imply a putdown, and men are not supposed to be intuitive at all, so most of us learn to discount our Little Professors in favor of more "acceptable" rational thinking. This is unfortunate, since the talents of the Little Professor are especially advantageous to fully appreciate what is happening in someone else. This is one of the best possible reasons for therapists to have personal therapy. A freed-up Little Professor makes for a better therapist, as well as for a more interesting and exciting life.

Since the Little Professor thinks intuitively, using subjective rather than logical ways of comprehending other people, a person in this ego state may not experience himself as thinking about something. Instead, his experience may be one of "feeling" about something, as in answer (*a*) below.

> Question: "What do you *think* about your boss?"
> Answer (*a*): "I *feel* he doesn't like me."
> Answer (*b*): "I *think* he's mean. He yells a lot."

Many such "I feel" statements are indications of reports from the Little Professor, rather than an avoidance of thinking. Answer (*b*) is ordinarily a report based on a different kind of thinking, which will be described in the section on the Adult ego state.

PARENT IN THE CHILD (P_1)

The Somatic Child becomes upset when parents react negatively to his spontaneous expressions. In response to these upset feelings the Little Professor attempts to "psych out" what his parents expect of him. He tries out his conclusions and discovers which behaviors and feelings will gain their approval. Those behaviors which work may become integrated into a course of action which eventually becomes routinized, thoroughly reinforced, and finally automatic. This collection of behaviors and feelings is called the *Parent in the Child* because it has many characteristics of a parent. It has definite opinions, a frame of reference for understanding and reacting to the world, and functions to control the other parts of a person's Child, notably the unacceptable eruptions of his own C_1 and A_1. This part of the Child has also been called the *Electrode,* a name which emphasizes its automatic responsiveness to certain environmental stimuli. The Electrode may be bossy or cautious (wanting to keep A_1 and C_1 out of trouble), grandiose (wanting to impress people), or full of energy (accomplishing many things to satisfy "big people"). This ego state expresses itself both internally by telling C_1 and A_1 what to do, and externally by behaving as it believes others want it to. It may occasionally consult with A_1 regarding modifications or elaborations of the set patterns, but more often, once set in motion P_1 will only reluctantly pay attention to C_1, A_1, or any other ego state or person who might suggest a change. This may result in very self-destructive behaviors, including suicide, homicide, or insanity. For example, if a person's Electrode (P_1) believes that it must please others in order to survive, he may commit suicide when he believes that he has failed. This may occur despite the fact that his Somatic Child (C_1) still wants to live and his Little Professor (A_1) still has the ability to work out other solutions—especially with help.

Although Electrode behavior is essentially automatic, it is the child's behavior and not that of the parents. These behaviors are based on the child's decisions about how to get along, made in response to expectations of parent figures. Once a person recognizes that the Electrode is part of her Child and so contains valuable energy, she can devise new solutions which incorporate that energy, instead of bottling it up in behaviors which no longer work.

> Cora came for help because she was having difficulty relating with her employer. During therapy she discovered that as a child she had decided to stay away from authorities because her parents had been very hurtful to her. Cora reacted to this information by pushing herself to relate more openly with her boss. She soon became aware that she was becoming increasingly anxious and was performing even more poorly at work. In treatment, Cora learned that her Electrode was reacting with fear to her new behavior and wanted her to stop it. She allayed these anxieties by deciding that she would let the part of her that was wary of authority figures (P_1) observe her boss very closely for any signs of similarity to the feared figures from her past. While doing this she proceeded very carefully in opening up, and pulled back at each sign of difficulty to reevaluate the data with her Adult and Little Professor. Following this, her work improved and she was much less anxious, since her Electrode was no longer feeling ignored. Instead she was using her accumulated information to help her differentiate between scary and nonscary authorities.

The Electrode is less likely to behave autocratically when its concerns are not discounted. Once it is accepted as a legitimate part of the personality, its power and its special sensitivities can be used to achieve a goal that pleases all parts of the Child. The more this occurs, the less automatically it will respond. Eventually, the once-automatic behaviors of the Electrode may become mostly reintegrated into the here-and-now capacities of the Little Professor and the Somatic Child.

Functional Analysis

The Child functions in two basic ways—*Free* (FC), also called Natural Child (NC), and *Adapted* (AC). The Free Child expresses herself spontaneously without concern for the reactions of the parents of the world. The Adapted Child, on the other hand, behaves as if a parent were watching or listening, and so is much more restrained than the Free Child. The Adapted Child may be compliant, industrious, rebellious, or act in any other way that pays off with parent figures. The three typical styles of Adapted Child behavior, called Helpful, Hurtful, and Helpless, represent the discounted positions found in rackets and games which are defined more fully in Chapter 7 [29].

Both the Free Child and the Adapted Child may behave either in the here-and-now or by using patterned responses. Each may react creatively or with an old tape; the important distinction is whether or not the behavior is an adaptation to others.

Rebellious is a term commonly used to describe the behavior of someone else. Even though the word implies that something is being fought against, most so-called rebelliousness is actually motivated from the Adapted Child as a means of going along with other peoples' expectations. Ostensibly we may be doing the opposite of what we are told to do, but covertly we are cooperating. Parents often program children to rebel by transmitting two messages on different levels of communication at the same time. For example, each time Alan was obstreperous his father would yell at him while smiling as if he liked what Alan was doing. Alan noticed the smile and concluded that his father approved of his behavior, and so he continued to behave "rebelliously" to maintain his father's secret blessing.

Sometimes the approval for rebelliousness is quite overt. If Mother or Father want a child who will not be pushed around, they may reinforce his stubbornness, arguing, and fighting by praising it or noticing it. This often occurs when parents ignore their child when he is not acting out and pay attention to him only when he is upset or angry. Soon the child learns to be rebellious in order to get attention. A case in point is Bob, a sixteen-year-old who repeatedly ran away from home even though his mother verbalized dissatisfaction with his behavior. However, mother, who ordinarily ignored Bob, also had told him that he was like his father (who had left her), and after each runaway she would eagerly ask him to tell her in detail all the things he had done while he was gone. She was surprised to learn that her son's rebelliousness "pleased" some parts of her Child, which also wanted to rebel.

When a Free Child is "doing her own thing" and a parent disapproves, the parent may label the Free Child as rebellious. In these circumstances the child is not rebelling at all, and the rebelliousness label says more about the parent's opinions than about the child's behavior. However, by labeling the behavior rebellious the parents influence their child to feel guilty and perhaps even to stop it. If they persist they are very likely to train their child to be quite compliant, since he will believe he is rebellious (bad) when he reacts spontaneously. One way to train children to act a certain way is to label them as being opposite to that trait.

To produce a Victim, label the person a Persecutor.

To produce meekness, label the person stubborn.

To produce toughness, label the person weak.

However, if there is any ambivalence on the part of the parents, they will probably stimulate their child to actually develop the labeled trait. In other words, if at least a small part of the parents is pleased by the attribution they are placing upon their child, then they are likely to get it—just like what happened with Alan and his father. Commonly, a child who receives these mixed messages will respond to both, developing one ego state which appears to rebel and another which complies.

Adult Ego State

Structural Analysis

People have two major ways of organizing and dealing with the information from their thinking and five senses (visual, auditory, kinesthethic, olfactory, gustatory). One is intuitive and creative, and the other is rational and linear. Since the early days of TA the Little Professor and the Adult have been respectively designated as corresponding to those parts—in shorthand, A_1 and A_2, or the *first Adult* and the *second Adult.*

Early components of rational Adult thinking become operational late in the first year or so of life, along with the infant's increasing verbal abilities. These slowly develop until puberty or shortly thereafter, when logical and abstract thinking become fully available. The Adult gathers, stores, and uses information from many sources—internally from the other ego states as well as from the external world. Its recordings are essentially factual—for example, "2 + 2 = 4" or "Mother is angry when she looks a certain way." The Adult uses this information to make assessments and to estimate probabilities. These differ from opinions, which are stored as recordings in the Parent—for example, "Men are nasty" or "Girls are always nice." The Adult is often called the *Computer* because it functions like a digital computer, computing data and making assessments logically and essentially without feeling. Like a computer, the Adult must be programmed with accurate information in order to function effectively. If the Adult has inaccurate or insufficient data, it will not make accurate evaluations. A fully functioning adult (as opposed to Adult) uses both intuitive and logical thinking in ways which combine and enhance the benefits of both types. The creativity of A_1, honed by the logic of A_2, is behind every great idea and advance of civilization.

In the last few years, considerable research has been reported which distinguishes the functions of the right and left cerebral hemispheres of the brain [2, 22]. This research clarifies the physiological basis for the concepts of A_1 and A_2. One hemisphere, usually referred to as *dominant,* specializes in language integration and rational thought, while the other hemisphere, usually referred to as *nondominant,* specializes in intuitive, sensual, and nonlinear thinking.

Actually, each hemisphere is dominant in different areas, and each
has some capacity to take over both functions if the other is dam-
aged. A more complete list of these functions follows:

DOMINANT HEMISPHERE (A_2)	NONDOMINANT HEMISPHERE (A_1)
Full language	Simple language
Tempo	Melody, tonal
Grammar, syntax	Synthetic, metaphorical
Logical	Intuitive, creative, spontaneous
Abstract	Literal
Analytical	Mental imagery, spatial relationships
	Kinesthetic

The Little Professor, with its capacity for metaphor and intuition,
is closely connected with visual, tonal, and kinesthetic information,
and so in large part derives its information from inputs that we may
not think about consciously. The Adult, using logical and analytical
modes, tends to function more in our conscious awareness.

Some TA writers do a second-order analysis of the Adult
[8, 30]. They believe that the Adult consciously integrates aspects
of the Parent and Child, forming a Parent in the Adult, and a Child
in the Adult. We choose not to do this, since we believe that the
Child remains in ultimate control of energy outlays, and that the
Adult does not take over any of the functions of the other ego
states.

Functional Analysis

The Adult functions as a probability-estimating computer. It
appears not to be a fully autonomous ego state, but rather functions
mostly at the request of one of the other ego states. The Child needs
information to make better decisions and to maximize its creativity
and fun, and the Parent uses data to "prove" that its pronounce-
ments are correct. Unlike a computer, the Adult is always turned on
and available, albeit sometimes ignored. It is based in our neuro-
physiology and so has an independent fund of energy for scanning
the world and processing data. However, it is not self-cathecting (or,
self-energizing), but rather is used to meet the needs of the Child
and/or Parent.

Some schools of TA assume that the Adult is fully autonomous and believe that the Adult can take *social control* of the personality by making decisions about behavior and carrying them out even when the Child or Parent is in opposition. Our clinical experience, as well as that of others, indicates that when the Child is in opposition, the Adult has limited power [25, 40]. The conscious part of the personality—which is more likely the Adult—may attempt certain behaviors, but the unconscious part—which is more likely the Child—may subvert them. For example:

A person tries from his Adult to be friendly (by following a series of behaviors he knows to be friendly) while looking bored.

A mother tries to be nurturing to her children (by following a series of behaviors she knows to be nurturing) while holding her body rigidly and sounding slightly irritated.

The Adult cannot maintain social control in any situation without a certain amount of cooperation from the Child. A failure of social control is usually more an indication that the Child is becoming increasingly upset than that the Adult is not sufficiently programmed or informed.

Parent Ego State

Structural Analysis

The Parent ego state is a historical record of the important things that the parent figures did with, to, and around a person. While the child is *reacting* in her Child ego state to what mommy is doing, she is simultaneously *recording* in her Parent her version of what mommy is doing. These recordings include such events as mommy feeding her, yelling at her brother, ignoring her father, and so on. Figure 2-4 illustrates what happens to a typical message from a parent.

The Parent consists of a collection of tapes from significant others who had some kind of power relationship with the person. Mother and father are usually the most important, followed by older

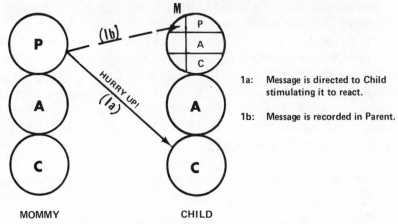

1a: Message is directed to Child stimulating it to react.

1b: Message is recorded in Parent.

MOMMY   CHILD

FIGURE 2-4. SITES FOR REACTING TO AND RECORDING A MESSAGE.

siblings, grandparents, substitute caretakers, others living in the home, peers, teachers, religious leaders, and so on. Cultural and ethnic messages are also taken in from these sources, and these, too, become part of the Parent ego state.

New information can be assimilated into the Parent at any age. The Child ego state decides what goes into the Parent using three criteria:

1. Vulnerability of the self
2. Power of the parent figure
3. Believability of the parent figure

The young child records almost everything in her Parent; she is so small and vulnerable that the relative power of her parents is enormous. The older child records more selectively, and the adult may only record from a trusted friend, spouse, or potent, believable authority such as a therapist, boss, or political or religious leader.

Parent tapes, like C_1 memories, are recorded experiences of past events which, once formed, become part of the person's physiology. Technically, these experiences are stored both in the chemistry of the organs and the muscle tonus of the body. No amount of new experiences can erase these recordings, since they will always be a part of the person's history. For example, if a person was abused as a child, years of positive, nurturing experiences in adulthood will not change the reality of her past abuse. However, once the new experiences are also part of the person's Parent, her Child may select which of these tapes she will replay. Either of these Parent recordings may be used by the Child as reminders for herself as well as guidelines for others. Figure 2-5 shows how messages are received and recorded in the recipient, internally transmitted, and then passed on to the next generation.

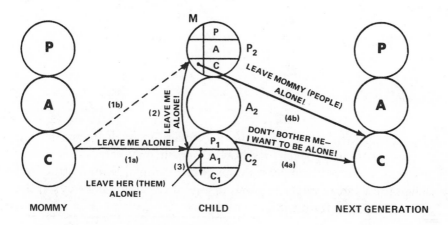

1a: Message sent to Child; Child responds.
1b: Message is simultaneously recorded in the Parent.
2:    Later internal transmission of message.
3:    Internal transmission of message from P_1 to C_1 to keep C_1 under control and out of trouble.
4a⎫ Twenty years later she may pass on a similar message to her children
4b⎭ from either her Parent (P_2) or her Child (P_1).

FIGURE 2-5. TRANSMISSION OF PARENT MESSAGES.

Functional Analysis

One of the primary things that parents do is to define for their children how to perceive and deal with the world. As a result, the Parent ego state is replete with opinions, judgments, values, and attitudes. These are of two major types: *Nurturing* (NP) and *Controlling* (CP); the latter is sometimes called *Prejudicial Parent* or *Critical Parent.*

The Nurturing Parent is caring, concerned, forgiving, reassuring, permissive, warmly protective, worried.

The Controlling Parent is opinionated, powerful, strongly protective, principled, punitive, demanding.

The Parent also functions both externally and internally [19]. The *Active Parent* expresses itself directly, as when the person acts toward someone else just as one of his parent figures acted. The *Influencing Parent* expresses itself inwardly, sending messages to influence his own Adult or Child ego state.

A person is using his Parent ego state only if he is playing back a tape of a parent figure. It is possible for a person to parent someone from any of his ego states, or to behave in either nurturing or controlling ways from his Adult, Adapted Child, or Free Child.

Examples

The complexity of a second-order analysis as demonstrated in Figures 2-2 and 2-3 clarifies how a person may respond in many different ways to a single stimulus. For example, from a structural viewpoint a father might respond in any of the following ways in the process of caring for his infant child.

From His Parent:

Parent in Mother: "Children are to be loved."

Adult in Mother: Information on feeding children which he accepted on face value from his mother.

Child in Mother: "Babies are scary."

Parent in Father: "Work hard for children."

Adult in Father: "Hold babies carefully."

Child in Father: "Babies are fun."

From His Adult:

Sequence of tracking potential problems in the infant—first check the diaper, make sure baby is warm, perhaps hungry, and so on.

From His Child:

Parent in Child: "I must take care of the baby."

Adult in Child: "Here, look at the pretty toy, then you won't cry."

Child in Child: "I love you."

From a functional point of view, here are some additional examples:

A *positive Nurturing Parent* cares for another person in a loving way when the latter needs or wants it—"Sure, I'll get that for you."

A *negative Nurturing Parent* is either overpermissive or else overnurtures by doing things for others which are not requested and not needed—"Let me do that for you."

A *positive Controlling Parent* is strong and opinionated and stands up for her own and others' rights without putting anyone down in the process—"Stop! That's not right."

A *negative Controlling Parent* tries to take away the self-esteem of another person—"Why do you always do that?"

An *Adult* computes probabilities using operationally definable terms—"If we use this type of steel, there is a high probability the bridge will withstand a wind of 150 miles per hour."

A *positive Adapted Child* gets what he wants or at least avoids pain by complying to his idea of what "big people" expect of him—"Yes, sir," to a superior, and "Please" and "Thank you" when appropriate.

A *negative Adapted Child* behaves in a self-destructive way in order to get attention from others—he forgets to salute the general and then wonders why things always go badly for him.

A *positive Free Child* expresses directly what is on his mind, has fun, gets close, and does not hurt anyone in the process—"Hi, let's play."

A *negative Free Child* hurts others or himself while expressing himself or having fun—"Let's go faster"—even though it is dangerous. Very few examples of this occur. Moreover, most behaviors which at first appear to be negative Free Child are actually self-destructive Adapted Child actions.

Sometimes a person will indicate how she is functioning in all of her ego states with merely a brief statement, as in the following example.

A college student discussing her roommate says: "She's a foolish, irresponsible, silly girl [CP], who needs me to smooth the way for her, so I go out of my way to help her [NP]. Sometimes I wonder if that's a good idea [A], but I want to be a helpful person like mother taught me to be [AC] even though I feel like telling her to leave me alone [FC]."

Ego State Options

An individual always has options as to which ego state he will use to *record* what is occurring, and from which he will *do* something. He may record an event in all three ego states, or only in some of them. The possible sites and types of recordings include: C_1 feelings, A_1 hunches and conclusions, P_1 patterned behaviors, A_2 data and thoughts, and P_2 tapes of how authority figures are behaving. Later the person may act by playing out an old tape from any of these ego states, by initiating some new thinking from either or both A_1 and A_2, or by having a new urge or feeling from C_1. The particular choices he will make are influenced by:

1. What he needs
2. What he wants
3. His sense of safety
4. His perception of what is available
5. His previously made decisions (life script)

Ego State Advantages and Disadvantages

Each ego state has both advantages (positive qualities or the potential for causing pleasure) and disadvantages (negative qualities or the potential for causing pain or discomfort). *Child* advantages include energy, spontaneity, joy, and assertiveness. The Child is intuitive and inventive and deals well with metaphor, imagery, music, and other forms of creative expression. The Child feels and expresses pleasant and joyous feelings and experiences closeness, intimacy, and love. Unfortunately, the Child also experiences sadness and fear, and often feels small and weak, and the Child's overriding need for safety and strokes often leads to unfortunate adaptations and script decisions.

The *Adult* thinks and analyzes well and can understand complex ideas. Its basic activity, besides the sheer enjoyment of its own functioning, is to help the Child meet its needs and wants. When the Adult is programmed with inadequate or inaccurate information, it performs poorly, computes probabilities badly, and so may get the person into trouble. It is comparatively weak and cannot use the information it has to insist that something be done.

The *Parent* contains a storehouse of useful recordings about how to do things and how to take care of children and other people. Unlike the Adult, which has to think about what to do and compute probabilities, the Parent "knows" what to do and does it. Its primary function is to protect and support the Child. Unfortunately, the parent tapes may contain inadequate, misguided, antiquated, or otherwise harmful information which is passed on to the Child in the form of destructive messages.

Comparison of Parent, Adult, and Child With Superego, Ego, and Id

Many theorists have attempted to compare the ego states of TA with the psychoanalytic concepts of id, ego, and superego. There are some similarities, and there are also some significant differences.

Id

Parts of the Child are reminiscent of Freud's concept of the id. Berne once made such a comparison, noting that "id activity resembles 'internal programming' " [8]. Both the Somatic Child (C_1) and the Little Professor (A_1) are based in our physiology and often function outside of our conscious awareness. However, the Child, unlike the id, is an organized ego state with both identifiable wants and needs and a specific history. Also, the Child and Parent are often not in opposition, while id and superego are basically opposed to each other.

Ego

Both the ego and the Adult test reality and mediate between the other parts. Both the Adult's thinking and probability estimating and the Little Professor's thinking and creativity are equivalent to functions of the ego. There is no TA parallel to Freud's concept of a weak ego. Everyone has a good functional Adult—the only question is whether or not it is being used.

Superego

The superego, like the ego and id, is an inference regarding functioning, whereas ego states refer to specific people who did specific things at specific times. Parent tapes consist of specific behaviors performed by parent figures and specific reactions to those behaviors are stored in the Child. The Parent also differs from the superego in that it nurtures.

Ego State Diagnosis

There are four ways to diagnose ego states—behaviorally, socially, historically, and phenomenologically. When all four methods point to the same ego state, the diagnosis is as certain as possible.

Behavioral Diagnosis

An observer with an uncontaminated Adult, a sharp Little Professor, and a thorough awareness of the normal development of children will often find behavioral clues to be the most useful, especially until the client is able to report accurately about his internal experience. A person's words, tone and tempo of speech, expressions, postures, gestures, breathing, and muscular tonus provide clues for diagnosing his ego states. Additionally, the overall gestalt of these behaviors presents a particular attitude which also facilitates the diagnosis.

Parent words typically contain value judgments, Adult words are clear and definable, and Free Child words are direct and spontaneous. If a person is crying silently, she is usually in her Adapted Child, since the Free Child makes lots of noise when upset. Slogans for living and phrases which begin with "You" or "One" usually come from the Parent. Typical examples are "One must learn to get along with others," and "You can't always get what you want." Sometimes the Parent statement is hidden in the middle of a sentence. For instance, consider Anna's statement, "I want to go to the movie tonight, but you know you can't always go out and have a good time." Anna begins with an "I" statement from her Child, but then switches to her Controlling Parent with a "you" followed by a slogan. The posture of the Parent is often evidenced by a leaning forward of the trunk and head; the Adult tends to be erect without any tilting of the body; and a sideways tilt of the head may indicate that the Little Professor is psyching out a situation. Additional behavioral and attitudinal clues are offered in Table 2-1.

TABLE 2-1. Behavioral Clues to Ego State Diagnosis

	Controlling Parent	Nurturing Parent	Adult	Free Child	Adapted Child
WORDS	"bad" "should" "ought" "must" "always" "ridiculous"	"good" "nice" "I love you" "cute" "splendid" "tender"	"correct" "how" "what" "why" "practical" "quantity"	"wow!" "fun" "want" "won't" "ouch" "hi"	"can't" "wish" "try" "hope" "please" "thank you"
VOICE	Critical Condescending Disgusted Firm	Loving Comforting Concerned Sugary	Even Precise Monotone	Free Loud Energetic Happy	Whiney Defiant Placating Demanding
GESTURE or EXPRESSION	Pointing finger Frowning Angry	Open arms Accepting Smiling	Thoughtful Alert Open	Uninhibited Loose Spontaneous	Pouting Sad Innocent
POSTURE	Shoulders up Hands on hips	Leaning forward Head in front of body	Erect	Loose Relaxed Agile	Collapsed Closed Tight
ATTITUDE	Judgmental Moralistic Authoritarian	Understanding Caring Giving	Interested Observant Evaluative	Curious Fun-loving Changeable	Demanding Compliant Ashamed

Keep in mind that behavioral clues are merely *indicators* that a particular ego state is cathected, not absolute *guarantees*. For example, the word *should* can be stated from any ego state, even though it is most often from Parent.

Parent: "You should do it!"

Adult: "To get to Hawaii quickly, you should fly."

Child: "I should do it or I'll get in trouble."

The more indicators you have which point to the same conclusion, and the more this is supported by the other methods of diagnosis, the more likely your diagnosis is correct.

Social Diagnosis

A social diagnosis is made by observing the kinds of transactions a person is having with other people. If he is eliciting responses from someone's caretaking Parent, he is probably coming on Child—either Adapted, saying "I'm helpless," or Free, saying "Help me." You may also use your own responses to another person to help identify his ego states, and the more your Little Professor is free of distortions from the past, the more accurately you can do this. For example, if you want to have fun with someone, he is probably in his Free Child. If you are inclined to respond from your Adapted Child, he may be in his Parent. If you feel an urge to respond with a fact, he is likely in his Adult.

Historical Diagnosis

Investigating the client's past history also provides important information. If as a child he reacted to his parents with feelings similar to those which he is experiencing now, he is likely in his Child. If his father or mother gestured and talked the same way that he is gesturing and talking now, he is probably in his Parent.

Phenomenological Diagnosis

A diagnosis made by self-examination is sometimes the most accurate. However, since the Adapted Child is often afraid to allow the person's Adult to know what is going on, it can also be the most inaccurate. To enhance the likelihood of a correct diagnosis, it is frequently helpful to exaggerate an experience by using various techniques, such as yelling, double chairing (dialogues with fantasied other people or parts of the self), encounter, and other such methods which bring the various ego states more fully into awareness.

Fran was tapping her fingers and feeling uncomfortable. Following a suggestion to do whatever her fingers wanted to do, she gradually began tapping harder and harder and finally pounded with her fist, yelling, "I won't stand for it!" It suddenly became evident to Fran that she was replaying a behavior of her father's which she had witnessed many times.

Don had a headache. Following a suggestion to "Be your headache and behave however you want to!" Don replied, "I'm

scared." After repeating this loudly several times, he experienced an old scene in which his mother was frightening him,
resulting in his deciding to hold back his feelings and hold on
tight. Don's headache was an Adapted Child pattern originally
established in response to a scene which frightened his Free
Child.

A phenomenological diagnosis is more likely to be accurate when it
is made during a deeply experienced behavior. Heightening the experience simultaneously makes the behavioral clues more obvious
and elicits very strong social responses from other persons. Quite
often during these experiences, historical data are also recalled which
validate the behavioral, social, and phenomenological impressions.

All four methods of diagnosing ego states may be used in
clinical settings where the therapist has a contract to help the client
to change. However, in nonclinical settings—at work, with friends,
and so on—the historical and phenomenological methods may be
unavailable. Nevertheless, behavioral and social cues are sufficient
for many situations, so keep in mind that any incomplete diagnosis
may be in error, and proceed with due caution. The following
examples illustrate the use of behavioral and social methods for
diagnosis and suggest some responses.

An employer notices that an employee is approaching her with
considerable *diffidence.* The employee uses a *careful* tone of
voice to say, "I *tried* real hard to get the job done, but I just
couldn't." The employee's initial behaviors suggest that he is in
an Adapted Child ego state. To gather more data, the boss
checks out her own experience, confirming a desire to respond
from Parent (social diagnosis). Once she realizes this, she may
then consider changing her automatic pattern of behaving in
order to invite a different response from her employee. In any
event, she can proceed to deal with her employee, who has
apparently cathected Adapted Child.

A wife asks her husband, "Where is my wallet?" (Adult), and
he notices that she has a slight smile on her face. The two
behaviors seem incongruent and indicate that two messages
are being sent, probably from two different ego states (behavioral diagnosis). He is also aware that he is confused about

what to do, which is another clue pointing to a two-part message (social diagnosis). He responds, "I don't know," whereupon she criticizes him for losing her wallet. He is now aware that the smile represented her negative Controlling Parent looking for an excuse to pounce. He recalls that her mother often had that smile in discussions with her own husband when she was putting him down (historical diagnosis). With this information, he has many options to consider, including: (1) to do something different about his inept Adapted Child behaviors (like losing his wife's wallet) which provide opportunities for his wife to criticize him from her Controlling Parent; or (2) to respond directly to his wife's smile before the tirade begins: "Oh, brother, I screwed up again, that's terrible of me! I'm sorry!" This may take the wind out of the Controlling Parent's sails, since there is no opposition. Then they can work out a different solution.

Egograms

A person learns to respond from certain ego states at certain times in order to get what she wants. Different people tend to spend varying amounts of time and energy in different ego states, and these tendencies can be illustrated by *egograms* [17]. An egogram is a visual representation of how an individual's psychic energy is distributed throughout her functional ego states. It is drawn as a bar graph with five separate bars, one representing each ego state, as illustrated in Figure 2-6.

The egogram is a relationship diagram, depicting the amount of energy a person uses externally, or actively, as she relates to others. This is contrasted with a very different diagram called an *internal egogram,* which is drawn by the individual herself to disclose her internal experience. For example, Ira experienced a heavy internal Controlling Parent message to "Shut up and be still!" and responded from his Adapted Child by sitting quietly. His internal egogram, drawn by himself, showed a very high Controlling Parent, whereas his transactional egogram, drawn by others, showed a low Controlling Parent and a high Adapted Child.

The egogram represents the person's entire personality, not

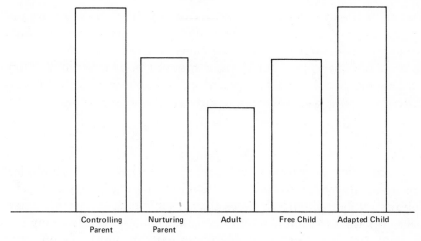

| Controlling Parent | Nurturing Parent | Adult | Free Child | Adapted Child |

FIGURE 2–6. EGOGRAM.

just those ego states which are cathected in a particular situation. It is drawn as a way of providing feedback to someone regarding how others experience her, and is most accurate when those drawing it use their intuitive Little Professors. When a number of people each draw an egogram of a person, there is consistently a great deal of agreement. Nonetheless, we suggest that a number of people each draws an egogram of a particular person and that these be combined into one composite egogram. This helps to balance out personal projections and results in a more accurate representation. Fritz Perls once noted that "if one person calls you an elephant, she may be projecting. However, if a whole group of people call you an elephant, then you had better buy a bag of peanuts."

It is often useful for a person to draw her own idea of how her egogram will look to others and compare this with the composite egogram which they provide for her. If the two diagrams differ, she may learn how she is setting up games and rackets outside of her awareness. For example, if Geri's own diagram shows a low Nurturing Parent and a high Adult, and others provide her with an egogram which shows a high Nurturing Parent and a low Adult, then she is perceived by others as "coming on" from her Nurturing Parent when she thinks she is in her Adult. Geri is probably Rescuing others without being aware of it: she is probably doing more for others than is asked for or is useful.

Egograms are based on the *constancy hypothesis*, which states that the amount of psychic energy within a person remains constant. For example, if a person removes some of the energy from her Controlling Parent, she will have more energy available for her other ego states. Conversely, in order to place more of her energy in her Controlling Parent, she must take energy away from some other ego state(s). This is one way to measure whether any changes have occurred during psychotherapy. Changes in personality will be demonstrated in the egogram as a shift in energy balance among the ego states.

The general principle in using the egogram is to emphasize raising the lower ego states rather than lowering the higher ones. This follows the behavioral principles that (1) it is easier to establish new behaviors than to eliminate old ones; and (2) it is easier to eliminate an unwanted behavior by establishing a new, incompatible one. The egogram in Figure 2-6 represents a client whose Controlling Parent and Adapted Child are highest, and Adult lowest. To change this egogram, begin by raising or increasing the use of the Adult. Shifting psychic energy to the Adult allows it to take over from the Controlling Parent, relieve the Adapted Child, and make it safer for the Free Child.

Frame of Reference

The decisions of our Child affect all of our ego states. They structure the responses from our Child, determine the content of our Parent, and influence our Adult functioning. This results in an individualized overall approach to the world which becomes our *frame of reference* [40]. Differences in frames of reference are a major reason why twenty witnesses to an accident can give twenty different reports. Each viewpoint is determined by the individual's frame of reference, which functions as a filter forged from the decisions of her Child. For example, a young boy senses (A_1) his father's disgust when he expresses fear (C_1), and decides never to act weak (P_1). He forms opinions that "Big boys don't cry" (P_2), and selectively discounts information (A_2) which contradicts his beliefs. Once he has made a script decision, he will form a consistent frame of reference to defend it. All of his ego states will tend to react to both internal and external events with a particular bias, as in the following examples:

> Henrietta notices a storm coming over the horizon and con-
> cludes that bad times are coming.
>
> A letter with a return address from a lawyer arrives in the mail,
> and Janice believes that the world has finally discovered that
> she is evil.
>
> Lester observes a group of people and decides that the tallest
> person is the leader. Other people, depending on their frame of
> reference, might think that the leader is the man, or the oldest
> person, or the best-looking, or whatever.

Ego State Cathexis

At least one ego state is turned on—or cathected—at any given
moment in time. If more than one ego state are cathected simultaneously, only one may be obvious. Most often this will be the one
uttered verbally, while another, less obvious one is expressed nonverbally. Any behavioral incongruity ordinarily indicates the cathexis
of more than one ego state. The only exception would be the occasional incongruity reflecting discordant parts of the same ego
state. Here are a few examples:

> Mother says, "Come here for a hug, sweetheart" (NP), while
> frowning and holding her body rigidly (AC).
>
> "Here are the facts" (A) while standing with legs spread apart
> and finger pointed at the other person (CP).
>
> "Here are the facts" (A) while talking with much enthusiasm
> and gesturing (FC).
>
> "I really like you!" expressed enthusiastically (FC), while one
> side of the body is turned slightly away from the other person
> (AC).
>
> "I'll do whatever you tell me!" (compliant AC) said with a
> slight sneer (rebellious AC).

When the most readily apparent ego state is not the Child, then the
Child is cathected in the background, and will be manifested by

subtly expressed muscular complexes. In the process of carrying out the script (life plan decided upon at an early age), or even when out of script, the Child may not let itself show for various reasons:

1. It may be more efficient for the Adult or Parent to be predominantly "out front," for example, gathering and disseminating information, or parenting someone.

2. The Child may stay in the background in an uncertain situation until it is clearly safe.

3. When something scary happens (stimulus), the Child may quickly recede into the background, directing the Adult or Parent to handle the situation (response).

   Examples: (a) S: "There is a tornado warning."
                      R: "When and where was it seen?" (Adult)
                 (b) S: "I'm mad at you and I want to hit you!"
                      R: "You will not! You sit down and we will talk about this!" (Parent)

4. The person may have made a script decision that it is too dangerous to show her Child, or some parts of her Child. Such a person may never play, show sadness or anger, or even ask for help.

In these instances, even though the Child appears to be excluded, with only the Adult and Parent of the person readily observable, the Child is keeping a vigilant watch. The Child will always be manifested in some way in the person's body—if you do not see it at first, look more closely! For example:

> Karl is usually in his Parent, making judgmental and opinionated comments, and occasionally in his Adult, making factual statements. Observing carefully, we note that his muscles are very tight and his breathing shallow, characteristics of an Adapted Child ego state.

> Martha is usually in her Nurturing Parent, caring for other people. She is also overweight and aware of a nagging sense of aimlessness and dissatisfaction (Adapted Child), even when taking care of others.

For full awareness of a person's ego states, check out all the messages of his words and body. Each represents an aspect of an ego state, and at least one will be from his Child.

Contaminations

An emotionally healthy individual is willing and able to cathect the ego state of her choice. She chooses that ego state which appears to her to be most useful in a given situation—such as her Parent for nurturing or protecting someone, her Adult for gathering data or solving a problem, and her Child for having fun or getting close. In addition to containing information about the external environment, her Adult also contains information about her own Parent beliefs and Child experiences. She is able to separate these Parent and Child experiences from her Adult appraisal of reality so that Parent prejudices and Child fears do not masquerade as Adult information.

One form of ego state pathology occurs when a person's ego state boundaries break down and her Adult becomes *contaminated* by her Parent and/or Child. A Parent contamination occurs when the person mistakes Parent information, prejudices, and slogans for facts:

"Women don't think; they're flighty."

"Blacks [Chicanos, Poles, Whites, Catholics, etc.] are inferior."

A voice is heard saying, "You are evil," and A_2 reports, "I am evil."

A Child contamination occurs when old experiences are not correctly identified as such, but rather are used to inaccurately assess here-and-now reality. This results in phobias, superstitions, or delusions being presented as truth:

"Spiders are scary."

"I am God [Napoleon, George Washington, etc.]."

"I would never walk under a ladder—it causes bad luck."

When the Adult is contaminated by Parent beliefs and Child experiences at the same time, it is called a *double contamination*. This is probably the most common form of contamination, since whenever the Parent has a particular prejudice, the Child is likely to respond with fear. The tendency is for both to simultaneously contaminate the Adult. In these circumstances, a person might hear words from her Parent (auditory hallucinations) and respond to them with old Child conclusions. Both the statement and the feelings are expressed in the here-and-now, disguised as Adult information:

"All men are evil!" (Parent) "I feel evil." (Child) "I am evil." (Adult)

"It's a fact that women don't think." (Parent) "Women are not safe to be around." (Child) "What women say is not trustworthy." (Adult)

Exclusions

Another type of ego state pathology, *exclusion*, occurs when one or two ego states dominate a person's behavior over a period of time. When a single ego state dominates a person's behavior, that ego state is called *constant or excluding*. A constant Parent, like some teachers and nurses, may be very preachy or authoritarian. The constant Adult, like some doctors and scientists, is someone who has excluded the feeling parts of her personality and seems to function like a breathing computer. The constant Child, like some actors and ski bums, may be someone who always wants to play or entertain others. Also, the psychotic individual may be in a confused, constant Child ego state. Figure 2-7 illustrates various examples of ego state pathology.

Some people essentially use only two ego states while excluding the third. When this occurs, the ego state which virtually is not used is said to be *excluded*. The Child ego state may exclude itself as a defensive maneuver in an effort to maintain functioning. This has

FIGURE 2-7. EGO STATE PATHOLOGY.

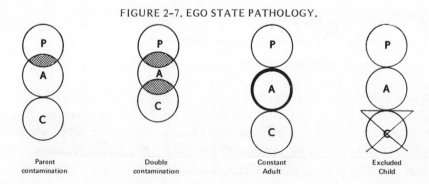

| Parent contamination | Double contamination | Constant Adult | Excluded Child |

been known to occur in persons who have been concentration camp victims, have undergone electroshock therapy, or who have had other repetitive experiences during which expression of the Child has led to great pain or discomfort. A less extreme example is Nora, who has very little fun, does not get close to anyone, and expresses very few feelings. A person with an excluded Parent ego state may behave irresponsibly and without conscience, or she may control the desires of her Child ego state with a totally Adult objective appraisal of reality, in which case her decisions will have a logical but ponderous quality. A sociopath is sometimes a person who has excluded her Parent while operating with Child contaminations of the Adult. If a person has excluded her Adult ego state, she may switch back and forth between Parent and Child with thoughts and behaviors somewhat unrelated to objective reality. An extreme example of a person with an excluded Adult ego state is a manic-depressive. Such a person may spend months in a manic, highly agitated Child ego state before switching to an oppressive Parent ego state, all the while not significantly cathecting her Adult.

No exclusion is total. The degree to which an ego state is excluded varies from time to time. A person's overall pattern of ego state cathexis is largely determined by her script decisions, but her behavior at a given moment is greatly influenced by any special inputs in the immediate situation. For example, Oliver's basic decision was to exclude his Child, and the world knew him as a person who was consistently Parent and Adult. However, he met a kindly woman who took an interest in him, and for a brief while he had a pleasant relationship with her. His dormant Child came out and played for the several weeks she was interested, and after she left, he resumed his previous pattern.

Treatment Considerations

All the ego states are useful when doing therapy. The Parent provides protection, opinions, and permissions when needed, as well as encouragement, support, and caring. The Adult provides information, probabilities, and analysis. The Child provides a different kind of awareness and thinking, creativity, enthusiasm, and love (which also may include protection and permissions). The Child also provides a model for how to feel, enjoy, and resolve needs and wants. Each school of therapy and each therapist tends to emphasize one or another ego state, and each style has merit and will help some people. For optimal effectiveness, the therapist will have all of her ego states available and will use them flexibly, depending upon the needs of her clients.

A sharp awareness of ego states provides a solid foundation for good treatment. For the therapist to help her client's Child feel safe and self-confident, it is essential to know the differences between nurturing and overnurturing, between the opinions of the Controlling Parent and the facts or probabilities of the Adult, and between the excitement of the Free Child and the eager compliance of the Adapted Child. Whatever you are doing—helping someone to change, trying to improve a relationship, or attempting to increase an employee's efficiency—if it is not going well, there is a high probability that you have misdiagnosed either the other person's ego state or your own.

In general, a therapist works most efficiently with someone she likes. If her Free Child is not attracted to a client, it may be that the client is in his Adapted Child and has not let his likable Free Child be exposed. Or it may mean that she experiences the client as threatening and is afraid to have her Free Child present. On the other hand, when a therapist notices that her Parent likes a client, she should check to see if it is her client's Adapted or Free Child that she likes. Therapy often goes slowly or nowhere at all because of a covert Parent–Adapted Child get-together between therapist and client. At other times, the mutual liking is Adapted Child–Adapted Child, and that, too, goes nowhere. Remaining aware of your own ego states is crucial—another reason for therapy for therapists.

A good way to check out how each of your ego states is responding to another person is to explore your reactions to him, making sure that each of your five functional divisions responds. Fantasize each of these (CP, NP, A, FC, AC) in a separate chair and let them talk to each other. For example, Pam, a therapist in one of our training sessions, was having trouble with a client and "felt" that the client was "difficult." We asked her to check out her ego states, and discovered the following reactions:

CP: "This person tries hard but is slow. He should move faster."

NP: "He often does not take nurturing from me. He shouldn't be so scared."

> A: "He had a very difficult childhood and is afraid of people."
>
> FC: "He wants the same things I want, he's just scared. I understand him."
>
> AC: "He's really difficult to make contact with. Sometimes I don't think he likes me. I'm working real hard, and I might not succeed at helping him."

Following this analysis, Pam decided not to nurture unless asked, to stop struggling, and to reassure herself that she is OK whether or not she succeeds. By taking such good care of herself, Pam not only felt better, but also reduced the pressure on her client. Once the client felt accepted by the therapist, he allowed himself to open up and began to get better.

Some therapists distrust the intuitions of their Little Professors and do not use them, giving up a most valuable tool. The visual, tonal, and kinesthetic inputs that go to the nondominant hemisphere (the home of the Little Professor) supply crucial information about the largely nonverbal scripty behavior of others. In addition to this general capability, the Little Professor has special sensitivities to certain stimuli. Growing up with people who emphasize particular behaviors results in an exquisite responsiveness to those behaviors in others. This is a similar process to how a blind person learns to hear and feel more accurately—or like a tuning fork, which after being set for a particular frequency, responds quickly and easily to that same frequency anywhere in the environment.

> Yvette's mother would get very upset at every sign of Yvette's assertiveness and interpreted any such behavior as competitive. Yvette's Little Professor became very sensitive to anyone who was concerned about competition.
>
> Rita's mother felt very inadequate and wanted Rita to take care of her. Rita became very sensitive to the vibrations of anyone who wanted to glom on to her in an overly dependent attachment.

The ideas or reactions of the Little Professor are likely to be at least somewhat correct. The problem lies in determining the amount of distortion. An antenna set for a certain wavelength will accurately pick up the signal, but the volume control may be set so high that it exaggerates the actual amount sent. It is quite possible for the Little Professor to become aware of where the volume control is set and to use the inputs accordingly. Furthermore, she may check the data through the other, more logical hemisphere—the home of the Adult—to find corroboration and eliminate distortions.

When using Little Professor insights, it is important not to insist that you are right, which might be harmful to the therapeutic relationship. It is also important not to worry about making mistakes, as if you should be perfect and making a mistake is a big deal. A mistake does not prove anything bad about you, nor will it harm the client if done from a caring position.

Examples of Little Professor Insights

1. Trudy: "I'm sad."
   Therapist: "You look like a little kid who's lost her mommy."
2. Eugene: "I don't know what to do."
   Therapist: "That must be great! Now you won't do anything, and no one will blame you."
3. Sam: "Help me!"
   Therapist: "Who used to help you when you felt bad enough?"

3

Strokes

"Don't go away, my spinal cord needs you!"

Stimulus Hunger

A *stroke* is a unit of attention which provides stimulation to an individual. It has been frequently noted that infants who are deprived of physical stimulation become prone to various diseases and even death. Research indicates that stimulus deprivation caused by immersing people in tanks of water at body temperature for prolonged periods results in adverse mental and emotional reactions, including psychosis. Berne concluded that "A biological chain may be postulated leading from emotional and sensory deprivation through apathy to degenerative changes and death. In this sense, *stimulus hunger* has the same relationship to survival of the human organism as food-hunger" [4]. Further research indicates that it makes little difference whether the physical stimulation invokes pleasure or pain. These studies, plus clinical observations of infants, children, and adults, point to a general conclusion that a negative stroke is better than no stroke at all.

Stroking

The quest for strokes takes many forms, and each person's stroke appetite is a little bit different. However, in terms of quantity, each person's stroke need is probably about the same. Some people are born more active and demanding than others, but it does not take much more than ordinary parenting to satisfy them. It is likely that the great variety of stroke needs and styles present in the world results from differences in wealth, cultural mores, and methods of parenting. In this book, we will deal primarily with the effects of parenting upon stroking styles. Besides being important in themselves, parenting methods are also the most influential ways in which general economic and cultural messages are promulgated.

I'm OK–You're OK means that no one is inferior and everyone is entitled to the opportunity to be treated as an equal and to have his basic needs met, including the need for strokes. However, this does not often happen. Most people behave as if strokes are in short supply, like money. Consequently, other people are treated as rivals or enemies and the free exchange of strokes becomes limited.

Stroke Economy

To describe this pattern of controlled stroking, Steiner developed the concept of the *stroke economy* [44]. When there is a limited circulation of strokes, each person decides upon a particular system for handling the giving, taking, and processing of strokes in order to satisfy his ever-present need for stimulation, and this is his stroke economy. The stroke economy is an important aspect of a person's overall script and largely determines how he responds to and uses the various kinds of strokes discussed in the remainder of this chapter.

External and Internal Strokes

External Strokes

Strokes from another person are necessary for healthy functioning; they satisfy most of the need for stimulation. The original model and the source of the term *stroke* is a parent physically stroking a baby. Berne noted that the infant "learns to do with more subtle, even symbolic, forms of handling, until the merest nod of recognition may serve the purpose to some extent, although his original craving for physical contact may remain unabated. . . . The result is a partial transformation of the infantile stimulus hunger into something which may be termed *recognition-hunger* [4]. The quest for strokes becomes a pursuit for attention, which enables a person to feel alive and energized. On the other hand, a lack of strokes leads to mental, emotional, and physical deterioration, or colloquially, "If you are not sufficiently stroked, your spinal cord will shrivel up."

Examples of external strokes:

"Hello!"

Your friend smiling when she sees you.

A handshake or a caress.

Your lover wearing perfume you like.

Your friend cooking your favorite meal for you.

Strokes from pets are also enjoyable, but for the most part do not satisfactorily replace strokes from people.

Internal Strokes

Besides coming from the recognition of others, stimulation also comes from inanimate external sources such as nature, plus internal sources such as old memories, new fantasies or ideas, movement, and other forms of self-stimulation. Since people respond to these stimuli in much the same way that they respond to the strokes of social intercourse, we use the term *internal strokes* for these essentially solitary and internal ways of satisfying stimulus hunger. We make a distinction between internal and external, while the common word *stroke* highlights their similarities and interconnections. The chart in Table 3–1 outlines the different ways a person may experience stimulation in her Child through the use of her senses and thinking, without other people being present [56]. Only examples of positive strokes are illustrated, although negative ones are equally possible. These examples can be either real or fantasized.

A very important part of internal stroking is the collection of strokes we have stored in our memories. We all keep a museum of our favorite positive and negative strokes. Some people concentrate on the negative ones and visit them often, each time reexperiencing the bad feelings connected with the scene. Others specialize in positive strokes for their museum. These individuals have available a most valuable pick-me-up for use on those days when their supply of

TABLE 3-1. Internal Stroking Chart

	C_1	A_1	P_1
Auditory	Beautiful music, a waterfall	Different and interesting music	Familiar music
Visual	Pretty colors, a sunset	Moving colors, kaleidoscope, clouds	Familiar place, one's bedroom, therapist's office
Kinesthetic			
a. Touch	Softness, warmth, masturbation	Unusual textures and shapes	Special blanket or teddy bear, nail biting
b. Proprioceptive	Movement, running, dancing	Tumbling, gymnastics	Fetal position while sleeping
Olfactory	Perfume	An interesting odor	The comforting smell of a special blanket
Gustatory	Strawberry ice cream	An unusual or foreign food	Hamburger or other familiar ("safe") food
Cognitive	Fantasy about mother	Thinking about an interesting idea	Remembering what "should" be done

external strokes is low. David Kupfer called this collection of positive strokes a "credit bank" [20]. Maintaining a credit bank is not the same as saving gold stamps.* Stamps are used to justify a behavior, such as taking a vacation, while the stroke bank is used purely for its own pleasure. Although they can provide much pleasure, these saved-up strokes are still not quite the same as new ones from a friend. An overreliance on visiting the museum of old strokes will eventually result in a feeling of depletion—and a desire for new strokes. We all need a fairly steady diet of external strokes for optimal functioning.

Different Strokes for Different Folks

Positive, Negative, and Filtered Strokes

Strokes come in assorted flavors. Positive strokes are pleasurable, carry a "You're OK" message, and usually result in good feelings for the receiver. They tend to encourage growth and foster self-esteem.

*Explained in more detail in Chapter 8.

Steiner calls a positive stroke a *warm fuzzy** to describe how it feels [44].

Negative strokes are painful, sometimes carry a "You're not-OK" message, and may result in unpleasant feelings for the receiver. Some people call these strokes *cold pricklies.*† Sometimes a stroke which is basically positive will contain a piece of critical information. For example, Aaron in the process of supervising Erin says with a look and tone of interest and caring, "You're doing better, but how about speaking with a louder voice and in a more assertive manner?" Each person in a transaction is free to exercise options regarding which strokes she will give and receive, so the ultimate responsibility for how a person feels lies within herself. When she receives a negative stroke with a not-OK message, she may accept it and feel bad, or she may refuse to accept it and choose instead to feel OK. Figure 3-1 is an example. Steiner calls artificial positive strokes *plastic fuzzies** [44]. These are strokes the participants do not mean or believe, and so have little sustaining power—like marshmallows or gumdrops.

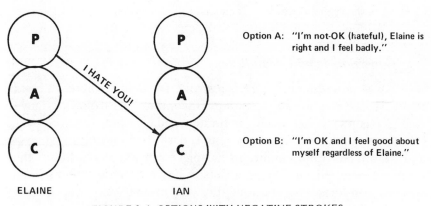

Option A: "I'm not-OK (hateful), Elaine is right and I feel badly."

Option B: "I'm OK and I feel good about myself regardless of Elaine."

ELAINE   IAN

FIGURE 3-1. OPTIONS WITH NEGATIVE STROKES.

Filtered strokes are strokes which are distorted or contain non-relevant information, and so are actually discounted strokes:

*Personal note (S.W.): This phrase is widely used; however, for me fuzz is a turn-off. I do not like how fuzz feels, nor do I like how all the z's sound. I personally would much rather have a *warm furry!*

†This term is sufficiently awful; I have no urge to modify it. (S.W.)

*Now here, *fuzz* is appropriate. (S.W.)

"I love your dress," while pinching in his nose and mouth and looking up disdainfully.

"Of course I respect women," said with a sneer.

"You're just like all the others!" (The "others" are irrelevant.)

Bruce and Erskine mention two categories with a total of four types of filtered strokes, and refer to all of them as *counterfeit strokes* [14].

Manufactured Strokes (Taking factual information and turning it into a feeling):

1. Positive: "Oh, you have a **new** shirt." "Thanks, I'm glad you like it."
2. Negative: "You have a new watch." "Yeah, now stop criticizing me for being late."

Reversed Strokes (Changing a stroke from negative to positive, or vice versa):

3. Polished: "Leave me alone!" "I can tell that you like me and want me to stay."
4. Blemished: "You're cute!" "You really think I'm dumb!"

Conditional and Unconditional Strokes

An *unconditional stroke* is a stroke for being, whereas a *conditional stroke* is a stroke for *doing*. Unconditional strokes pertain to characteristics which occur naturally and do not require special effort, such as being alive, male, tall, dark, handsome, brown-eyed, and so on. Since no conditions are placed on these attributes, they cannot be earned, and since a person has little choice about them, strokes for these natural qualities are usually experienced very strongly. Positive unconditional strokes are very desirable and do not lead to any constrictive script decisions. Negative unconditional strokes have no constructive use whatsoever, and often lead to a very destructive script.

"I love you" (just for being you) is the epitome of a positive unconditional stroke. Unfortunately, strokes which are meant to be positive and unconditional are not always experienced as unconditional or even as positive. "I love you" may be experienced in some instances as conditional, especially by someone who is afraid to trust. Another example is a beautiful woman who tires of being told she is beautiful, begins to think of it as an obligation, and eventually worries about what her life will be like when she is old and grey. Many people would like to receive unconditional strokes other than the ones they are used to, since the ones they are used to have been reinforced so much that the Adapted Child has taken charge of the attribute and now works at enhancing it. Thus, they have turned them into conditional strokes. For example:

- □ Women: Strokes for being pretty or nurturing.
- □ Men: Strokes for being strong or smart.
- □ Children: Strokes for being lively and adorable.

Instead they might prefer:

- □ Women: Strokes for being intelligent or witty.
- □ Men: Strokes for being gentle or warm.
- □ Children: Strokes for being OK even if they are not performing.

Most people get the majority of their strokes for what they do. Conditional strokes, both positive and negative, are often used to influence the behavior of other persons and to provide a valuable source of feedback. Used appropriately and consistently, conditional strokes provide a powerful tool with which persons are taught healthy, adaptive responses. For example, a mother gives her child a positive conditional stroke by praising her when she uses the toilet, and she gives her negative conditional strokes by scolding her when she has bowel movements on the floor. Here are some other examples:

Positive Unconditional: "I like to be with you!" or "You have beautiful green eyes."

Positive Conditional: "You look nice today." or "Thanks for your help."

Negative Conditional: "I don't like your tone of voice." or "You look awful in that color."

Negative Unconditional: "I hate you!" or "I don't like short people! Why are you so short?"

Each person develops a style of giving and receiving strokes based on her life position. Persons who feel OK about themselves and others tend to seek out exchanges of positive strokes. Persons who

feel not-OK about themselves and/or others tend to seek out negative strokes, which they use to maintain or increase their not-OK
feelings. When positive unconditional strokes are not given to or accepted by an individual, she will seek out other kinds of stroke
exchanges, rather than do without any strokes at all. Since strokes
are necessary for survival, a person will do whatever she thinks she
must in order to receive the strokes she needs. Steiner lists five restrictive rules regarding stroking which many children are taught,
and suggests that following one or more of these rules results in what
he calls a loveless script [44] .

1. Don't give strokes if you have them to give.
2. Don't ask for strokes when you need or want them.
3. Don't accept strokes even if you want them.
4. Don't reject strokes when you do not want them, even if you do not like
   them.
5. Don't give yourself strokes.

Unfortunately, most people follow some or all of these rules and so
remain at least a little stroke-deprived. They either reject or do not
bother to seek unconditional positive strokes, and settle for more
positive conditional strokes and negative strokes than they really
want.

Stroke Value

Stroke Power

Each stroke can be thought of as having a certain amount of
stimulation power, ranging from one up to 100 for positive strokes,
and perhaps to 1000 for negative strokes. The disparity between
negative and positive strokes exists because negative strokes are
potentially more powerful than positive ones. People can yell and
pound out their anger very loudly and powerfully, while love cannot
be expressed so potently. Unfortunately, many people do not even
express their love as strongly as they could. Even if they did, the
power of that expression could not equal that of a destructive
negative message—no amount of love can equal the power of a death
blow.

Not only can negative strokes be delivered more powerfully, but humans are physiologically structured so that negative strokes will have a stronger impact. Our instinct for survival requires that we respond to negative inputs with more immediacy and energy than we need for positive inputs. Furthermore, our bodies can only take a limited amount of negative input. A terrorized infant (or even an older person) will blank out when his circuits are overloaded, and he will only remember amorphous dread and tension in his mind, gut, and muscles. People *want* the positive strokes, but *must* pay attention to the negative ones.

A stroke with a given verbal content may vary considerably in power depending on how it is said or done. A stroke given in a perfunctory manner will be less powerful than one given enthusiastically. Congruency also makes a great deal of difference. For an important permission to be credible, it must be delivered with all parts of the body congruent. In other words, all the ego states must agree. Here are some examples of strokes with various amounts of power:

1 positive stroke	— "Hi!"
10 positive strokes	— "Hi, Mike!"
50 positive strokes	— "You're doing great!"
100 positive strokes	— "I love you!" delivered with a warm smile and a soft touch.
1 negative stroke	— "Hi," in a disinterested tone of voice.
10 negative strokes	— "I don't like what you just did."
50 negative strokes	— "That's terrible! Don't do that!"
100 negative strokes	— An angry "Go away!"
200 negative strokes	— "You're just like your father!" Slap!
1000 negative strokes	— A beating with unintelligible anger.

Stroke Source

The value of strokes is also significantly affected by the source. A stroke from a casual acquaintance usually will not have as much impact as one from someone important to you, such as an employer, respected peer, or lover. And regardless of who gives the stroke, the ego state used may also make a large difference in its value, as illustrated in Figure 3-2.

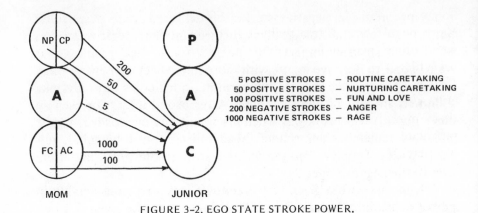

5 POSITIVE STROKES	— ROUTINE CARETAKING
50 POSITIVE STROKES	— NURTURING CARETAKING
100 POSITIVE STROKES	— FUN AND LOVE
200 NEGATIVE STROKES	— ANGER
1000 NEGATIVE STROKES	— RAGE

FIGURE 3-2. EGO STATE STROKE POWER.

Stroke Filter

In the process of deciding upon a life script, our Little Professor creates a *stroke filter* [56]. Each person's stroke filter is unique and functions in such a way as to let in certain types of strokes and information while filtering out others. This filtering process is affected by a person's individual proclivities, learning patterns, personal interests, and belief systems. The stroke filter can be used to maintain a person's script decisions by letting in information which confirms them while filtering out information which is contradictory. When this occurs, the filter is functioning as a discounting mechanism to maintain the person's frame of reference. Since every stroke carries a piece of information—for example, "You are nice!" or "You are evil!"—as well as a unit of attention, each stroke has the potential to foster or modify the person's script. The script is decided on for safety's sake as a way of pleasing mom and dad, and the individual uses her stroke filter to maintain this safety while getting strokes. If a stroke fits neatly into the frame of reference, then it will be taken in at the value with which it was given. If a stroke only partially fits, the stroke filter may reject it, or perhaps modify it so that it will fit in. Sometimes the stroke must be greatly distorted in order to force it into the frame of reference determined by the script. For example:

Olivia says to Rex, "You are handsome!"

Rex, after processing that through his filter, says to himself, "She really thinks that I'm ugly."

Some people's filters are very tight and let through very little. Many people have filters that let through mostly negative strokes, while others may allow for positive conditional strokes. Still others have filters with a few large holes that let through information and strokes which disagree somewhat with their frame of reference. Others have porous filters that let through almost everything, giving them much flexibility regarding types and sources of strokes and plenty of opportunity to gather information to change their frames of reference and scripts if they wish.

Every transaction goes through the stroke filter, where the stroke may be accepted, modified, or rejected. Even though people want external strokes, they may not take them at face value. For most people, this internal filtering process affects the final score much more than the actual count of external strokes sent their way.

Stroke Mix

The healthy individual seeks out and accepts both internal and external strokes. External strokes are generally preferable, as demonstrated by the very strong urge which most people have to get strokes from others. That urge, though, is partially programmed. Parents teach their children that they "should" try to get strokes from certain people, usually parents and other authorities, and the child's self-stroking, such as masturbating and creative fantasizing, is often devalued.

We know from observing infants that internal strokes are a normal part of being human. However, the urge for internal strokes is partially programmed, too. Parents who say, "Leave me alone!" or in other ways put down their children's behavior channel their children into self-stroking by making it unsafe for them to continue their search for external recognition.

A certain minimum number of external strokes is necessary for healthy functioning. However, it is the child's need for safety and her consequent script decisions which determine the particular mix of internal and external strokes she will pursue. To illustrate the wide range of stroke appetites, Berne compares a movie star who is adored by thousands yet seems always to need more strokes with the scientist who is seemingly satisfied with only one small recognition a year. Although their stroke *appetites* are very different, it is likely that these persons' stroke *needs* are similar. The movie star probably has a stroke filter which lets in very few strokes, and keeps out or severely modifies the others. The scientist, on the other hand, probably replays many times the yearly stroke from his "respected master," as well as a lot of old tapes in which his parents and others stroke him for his industry and exhort him to keep on trying.

Changing the Stroke Mix

When a client gives up a game, racket, or any portion of his script, he is giving up an important source of strokes. Since negative strokes are better than no strokes at all, the usual recommendation is that he replace the old strokes with at least an equivalent amount of new positive strokes. Many clients do this satisfactorily, but some have considerable difficulty in finding something positive which fills the void left by giving up the old system. These latter people have a very active negative Controlling Parent and/or negative Adapted Child which closely monitor the Free Child's behavior, thoughts, and feelings.

One client, Jack, had Parent tapes which put him down for almost everything he did, such as "That's bad!" "Do it better!" and "Don't do that!" This almost constant Parental barrage of criticism produced huge numbers of internal strokes. He learned to expect this kind of stroking during his childhood when, besides being fearful that his mother would abandon him, his stroke economy was quite severe and harsh. Even though mom's messages were negative, they served to reassure Jack that he existed and that mother was near. As he internalized these messages, he became accustomed to having a great deal going on in his head and rarely, if ever, experienced periods of peace and quiet. Jack's initial experience of inner tranquility occurred early in treatment, and he reacted with fear—he thought something was wrong and wondered if he existed. He would sometimes agitate by pinching, rubbing, or digging at himself to assure himself of his presence while looking around for mother's familiar angry voice. Finally, Jack decided to give up waiting for his mother to love him and told her so in a fantasized confrontation. As he finished telling her, he sounded strong and smiled freely. It appeared from this that he felt good with his new decision and when asked, he said he did. However, while saying he felt good, he was rubbing his arm with his fingers. When asked to focus on this, Jack became aware of feeling scared that maybe now he would be alone and that the self-stroking was pacifying him. The new decision was from Jack's Free Child, but his Adapted Child was not yet sufficiently reassured. A client such as Jack wants constant reassurance that he exists and that the stroker will not go away. Positive strokes, whether physical or verbal, will help fill the void only temporarily, since positive stroking is not nearly as intense as negative stroking. No ordinary system of positive strokes, external or internal, can possibly compete with the amount of negative internal strokes per minute which someone like Jack is used to. Therefore, if Jack is going to change, he must give up some internal strokes and not try to fill all the quiet with new strokes.

Parenting a healthy child does not include nearly as much stroking intensity as raising a scared child. Healthy kids are not so often watched over, interfered with, or told what to do, and when they are stroked it is usually done with less intensity. The scared child receives an unnatural and unnecessary number of strokes, but eventually learns to expect them and to believe that they are vital. By avidly searching for strokes, he behaves as if he must constantly prove he exists or belongs. Instead he needs to learn that positive strokes are available, and that it is unnecessary to escalate internal or external interactions to get a large quantity of strokes quickly. Once he believes that he exists and belongs and gives up trying to prove it, he can relax and experience some internal peace and serenity. As a matter of fact, with the new "quiet" in himself, his Free Child has the opportunity to really express what he wants and enjoys and to unleash his creativity. Although his world may not seem to be as exciting or intense as when he was responding to all the negative strokes, the fewer strokes allow for far more pleasant experiences.

As a client changes her script, she also changes her stroke filter; conversely, by changing her stroke filter she changes her script. As a result, she may need fewer strokes from outside sources, since she is now accepting the ones that come her way. On the other hand, she may seek out more external strokes because she is paying less attention to her old tapes and not settling for recycled or fantasized strokes [59].

Stroking Profile

The *stroking profile* is a device for measuring what an individual does with strokes in four different categories [38]. It is illustrated in Figure 3-3, followed by instructions for its use.

FIGURE 3-3. STROKING PROFILE. *(Copyright 1973 by Jim McKenna, M.S.W., St. Louis, MO.)*

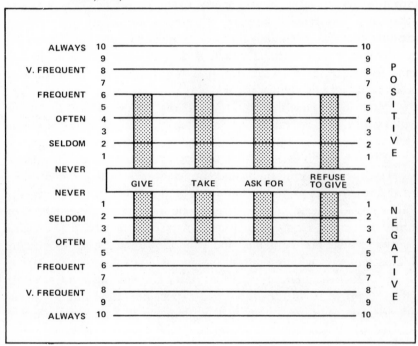

Instructions:

1. Rate yourself in each of these categories (GIVE, TAKE, ASK FOR, REFUSE TO GIVE) as to how frequently you give, accept, ask for, and refuse to give positive recognition to and from others.

2. Do the same on the negative scale. (The negative and positive scales tend to have an inverse relationship.)

3. In rating yourself, consider *all* the strokes you give, take, etc. For example, include soft strokes like "Hi! How are you?" as well as heavy strokes like embraces and "I love you."

4. In the REFUSE TO GIVE category, ask yourself how often you say "No" to what people ask or expect of you. On the negative scale, if you never refuse to point out someone's faults or errors, you would rate yourself as "0"—never refuse to give a negative stroke.

5. Think of all transactions as strokes. "I want you to go to the dance with me Saturday" is *Asking For* recognition, and answering "No, I'd rather go to a show" is *Refusing To Give*.

Clients often make contracts for change using the information derived from the stroking profile. Generally, since people do not like to give up strokes until a replacement is assured, it is easier to raise a low rating than to lower a high one. When the low rating goes up, the high one will usually come down. The profile also provides clues about a person's script, since an individual's stroking pattern both reinforces his script and provides a way to carry it out. The profile in Figure 3-3 is a typical one for a well-functioning person with no severe negative messages (injunctions) and many permissions. Other profiles representative of individuals with decisions made in response to particular injunctions are shown in Figure 3-4.

The four categories of stroking used in the stroking profile are very important, even apart from their use in the profile itself. Each has considerable implications for living.

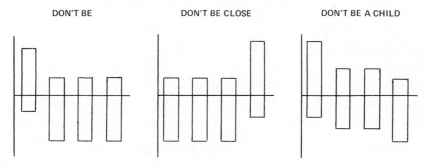

FIGURE 3-4. SCRIPT PROFILES.

Give

Giving strokes is OK. You will rarely spoil anyone by giving him too many positive strokes. For their first eighteen months or so, you can freely give positive strokes to your children, and they will soak them up and become happy, optimistic, and have a loose, healthy body—all of which will help to pleasantly sustain them for the rest of their lives. Positive strokes are also welcomed and needed by older children—just omit overnurturing, which slows down their growth. Positive strokes given to friends, lovers, employees, and others will also result in good feelings and warm, pleasant interactions. If you are open to them, you will tend to get back an amount equal to what you give. Many people want to give strokes only after others have given to them. Giving first works better.

Take

Taking strokes is OK, too. You deserve them! Don't let fussiness get in the way. Notice how babies and young children do not care if the stroke is gilt-edged or superlative. They flourish with anything positive, and are not concerned about being better than someone else or being the best. They often do not even bother with a thank you, they just slowly absorb the stroke and feel good. When they do say thank you, it is a sign of stroke acceptance, not to please someone else. Well-trained adults, who do not know it is OK to take positive strokes, may quickly say thank you and shrug off the stroke, or tighten up and wonder what they must do to repay the favor. A freely given stroke does not obligate a response. If it feels good, take it, enjoy it, and do not look for attached strings!

Ask For

It is also OK to ask for strokes, and the ones you get by asking can count just as much as spontaneously given ones. Do not expect people to read your mind for what you want. A baby cries to get the kind of attention he wants and enjoys it when he gets it. Such a system of directly asking for what you want maximizes your chances of getting it, and is good for every age.

Refuse to Give

You do not have to give what someone else wants. If you give when you really do not want to, you will not enjoy doing it, and the other person will not get much of a good feeling from it either. Unfortunately, those people who give whether they want to or not assume that other people are behaving the same way, and so discount most of the strokes they are offered. Give only what you want to give and help establish an honest stroke economy.

Treatment Considerations

The Therapist

Therapy is a big stroke. The therapist, whatever her theoretical framework, is paying attention to the client and therefore stroking him. Many clients feel better just because of the stroking they receive, and leave without insight, overt redecisions, or anything else therapists may believe is necessary. On the other hand, if clients do not get the strokes they need or want, they may leave therapy without changing at all. Some therapists are effective with most of their clients and others are not. The therapist's stroking style has a lot to do with the degree of her success. Therapy is most effective when the therapist is aware of each client's particular stroke needs and expectations, as well as her own stroking style and preferences. If the therapist's stroking style matches what the client needs, the client is more apt to respond to her and to change. On the other hand, if the therapist's stroking style matches too closely what the client is accustomed to, the client may not change.

Stroking from an I'm OK—You're OK position is crucial. A therapist who *takes care of herself* feels OK and has the energy to deal with whatever problems may arise during treatment. When her own stroke needs are satisfied, she will not only do better therapy, but will also model that positive strokes are not in short supply, and that it is possible to get enough of them.

Touching

The issue of touching clients provokes varied reactions—especially among therapists. Psychoanalysts have voiced concern that touching will interfere with transference (the projection of feelings, thoughts, and wishes from the past onto the therapist) and foster dependency, and Berne was troubled by the possibility of sexual misbehavior on the part of the therapist. However, in spite of these arguments, we believe that touching is both natural and very helpful. We have several reasons for this belief. First, touching provides considerable sensory (kinesthetic) information to both the therapist and the client regarding one another's feelings. Next, and perhaps most important, touching is normal. Not to touch is really abnormal and likely to cause transference distortions. If the therapist never touches a client, the client may see his helper as a cold, withholding parent. This may be a difficult transference issue to resolve, especially since there might be much reality to it. Touching is especially important for a client who had a parent who either touched her harshly or did not touch her at all.

Touching a client certainly may stir up countertransference problems (inappropriate feelings and thoughts), especially if the therapist has problems touching people. If the therapist was uncomfortable touching or being touched by her father or mother, she will likely have problems touching her clients. Other problems may occur if the therapist is uncomfortable when touching a client because of sexual desires or fears. Not to touch may avoid these problems, but it will also be artificial and limit her ability to help her clients work through many important issues, such as:

- □ *Being close to others.*
- □ *Liking their own bodies.* Children like their bodies and how they function because their parents like their children's bodies (as well as their own) and were not disgusted by them.
- □ *Feeling secure and trusting.*
- □ *Existing.* Babies learn that they exist and the limits of their bodies from the physical strokes they receive in the first year or so of life.

In some ways, the therapist is in a parent position in her relationship with the client. Even if the therapist intends otherwise, the client will make it so, since his problems stem from decisions made during childhood, and it is his scared and unhappy Child who comes for help. Thus in some respects, therapists should do what good parents do. Good parents get their own needs met from people other than their children. This includes sex, nurturing, closeness, love, and approval. When parents are with their children, they are not there to get, but to give what is needed—caring and strokes, acceptance and approval, help for growth, and information. A good parent does not have a sexual relationship with her children, but will appreciate their sexual growth. Finally, a good parent promotes the child's growth and eventual independence. A good therapist will do these same things. Specifically, in regard to touching, she will take care of her own needs outside of the therapy situation and will be able to safely touch, hold, play with, and stroke her clients and deal with their reactions, even when those reactions are quite intense.

The more active, involved, and nonpassive the therapist, the more intensely the client is likely to respond. Touching especially tends to evoke conflicts and response patterns from the first two or three years of life. This actually is an advantage, since it allows these issues to be worked on, but it may also cause strong transference reactions. This applies not only to touching, but also to many of the other overt and authentic behaviors of the therapist.

If these behaviors remind the client of a real or fantasized figure from his past, his transference reaction may occur more quickly and intensely than if the therapist had been more of a "blank screen." When dealing with the intense reactions which may result from the use of such stimulating methods, the therapist must make sure that she is not involved in a countertransference problem where she, herself, is discounting and distorting. If the therapist is willing to do this, the advantages of touching greatly outweigh the disadvantages. Our guideline for touching a client is that it is OK and a good idea if it will facilitate the accomplishment of the contract without creating another problem that the client does not want to solve.

Touching between clients in a group has the same advantages, and so usually may be promoted. Because of the number and variety of people present, group therapy offers many opportunities for learning and practicing new stroking patterns during the session. Be wary, though, of the Rescuing or overnurturing client who gives when it is not needed or when she would rather be given to. Some examples of useful touching include:

> Beth, who was working on getting close to people, went around the group sharing a particular stroke with each person—a desire for further contact, a touch, a hug, staying together for awhile, and so on.
>
> Jason, who ordinarily appeared strong and unneedful while avoiding feelings of loneliness, began crying as he more fully experienced his feelings. The therapist asked if he would like to be held, implying that it would by OK by leaning forward and speaking with a nurturing voice. Jason nodded yes and was soon crying loudly while holding on tightly to the therapist. Afterwards, Jason decided that it is OK for him to have feelings and not be alone.
>
> June was an overly nice person who wanted to be more assertive and feel strength in her body. An exercise was structured for her to break out of a circle of group members standing around her (always remove shoes, glasses, earrings, and any other hard objects first). After great and prolonged effort, she finally succeeded. Exuberant, June decided to continue using her power.
>
> During a group session, many members freely exchanged

friendly touches and hugs, raising the general level of safety, trust, and risk taking.

The therapist places her hand on the client's chest to determine his level of tension and to assist him in breathing more deeply and slowly.

Stroking Strategies

Samuels noted that people tend to give the kind of strokes they want to receive [39]. That is, people tend to take care of other people the way they themselves would like to be taken care of. Unfortunately, they may wait for other people to read their minds, and so often end up disappointed.

> Jill wants to be held and physically stroked. Instead, she strokes and holds her husband. He wants to be held also, but believes that she wants sex and proceeds in that manner, even though he feels pressured by her frequent "advances." Thinking that is what he wants, Jill cooperates since it gives her some of the touching which she craves. Neither gets what they really want.

It is OK for people to ask specifically for what they want. They may start by having a fantasy about it, and then arrange to get it. Unfortunately, many people ask for what they think they must settle for (a discounted choice); be alert to make sure it will feel good to the Free Child. Some people want:

☐ To touch something (softly? firmly? gently?)

☐ To be touched (where? when? how?)

☐ To taste something (what? prepared by whom?)

☐ To hear something ("I love you," "You're important")

☐ To see something (a smile, a dozen roses)

☐ To smell something (perfume, flowers)

4

Transactional Analysis

"I know you believe you understood what you thought I said, but I am not sure you realize that what you heard is not what I meant."

Common Transactions and
Rules of Communication

A transaction is an exchange of strokes between two persons, consisting of a stimulus and a response between specific ego states. Transactions can be simple, involving only two ego states, or complex, involving three or four ego states. A conversation consists of a series of transactions linked together. Whenever an individual initiates a transaction or responds to a stimulus from another person, she has a number of options regarding those of her own ego states she will use and the ego states in the other person to which she will direct her communication. The healthier the individual, the more autonomous she is in her choice of options. There are three kinds of transactions—complementary, crossed, and ulterior; and for each there is a corresponding rule of communication [5]. The eventual outcome of any series of transactions will be determined by these rules of communication.

Complementary Transactions

A *complementary* (also called *parallel*) *transaction* is one in which the stimulus and response vectors (communication paths) are parallel, so that only two ego states are involved, one from each person. More specifically, a complementary transaction must meet two criteria: (1) the response comes from the same ego state that the stimulus was directed to, and (2) the response is directed back to the same ego state that initiated the stimulus. Note the examples in Figure 4-1. Complementary transactions can occur between any two

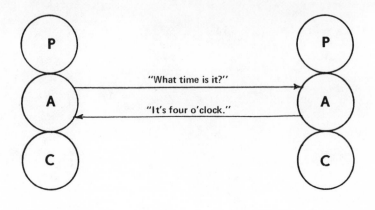

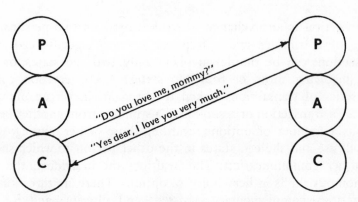

FIGURE 4-1. COMPLEMENTARY TRANSACTIONS.

ego states. The first rule of communication is: *So long as the transactions remain complementary, communication may continue indefinitely.*

Crossed Transactions

A *crossed transaction* occurs when the communication lines are not parallel and do not meet the above criteria. The second rule of communication is: *Whenever the transaction is crossed, a breakdown* (sometimes only a brief, temporary one) *in communication results and something different is likely to follow.* Notice the examples in Figure 4-2. Conversely, any break in the interaction, no matter how

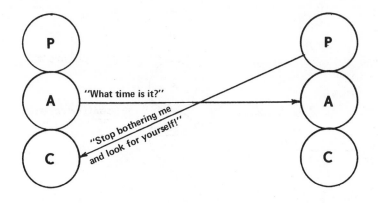

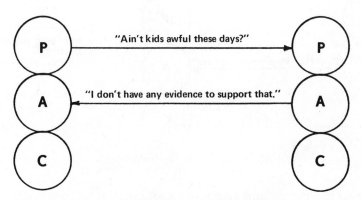

FIGURE 4-2. CROSSED TRANSACTIONS.

small, may be an indication of a crossed transaction. Many times a person is afraid to overtly cross a transaction and so will try to slip it by as unobtrusively as possible, as demonstrated by the examples in Figure 4-3. In the first example, "Of course I do" appears to be a Free Child-to-Free Child response, but the swallow (break in conversation) indicates a crossed transaction from Adapted Child. In the second example, what appears at first glance to be an Adult response is actually a crossed transaction from Child to Parent, as demonstrated by the recipient's hesitation and darting eyes.

Sometimes a crossed transaction (and communication breakdown) occurs even though it appears that the two conditions for a complementary transaction are met. To illustrate this it is necessary

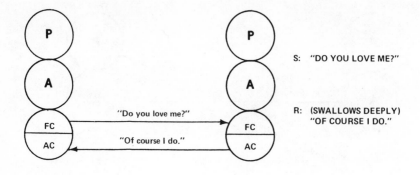

S: "DO YOU LOVE ME?"

R: (SWALLOWS DEEPLY)
"OF COURSE I DO."

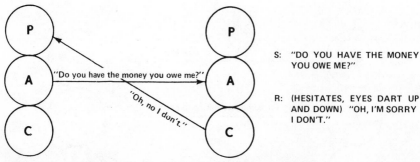

S: "DO YOU HAVE THE MONEY
YOU OWE ME?"

R: (HESITATES, EYES DART UP
AND DOWN) "OH, I'M SORRY
I DON'T."

FIGURE 4-3. CROSSED TRANSACTIONS.
(S = STIMULUS; R = RESPONSE)

to divide the Parent and Child ego states into their functional parts, as shown in Figure 4-4. This demonstrates that they are functioning as if they were two separate ego states, and thus fulfill the requirements for a crossed transaction.

In ordinary social conversation, complementary transactions are very useful, since they follow the first rule of communication and allow the conversation to continue indefinitely. However, in therapy and at other times when it is desirous for someone to change her mind or to think differently, it is necessary to effectively cross transactions. For example, when a client comes on like a "poor soul" who cannot figure out what she needs to do, she probably is in her Adapted Child inviting a Nurturing Parent response. The therapist may choose to respond from a different ego state in order to break off that flow of transactions (second rule of communication), hoping to motivate the client to switch ego states. As ex-

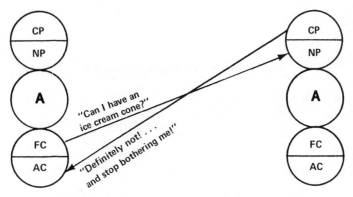

FIGURE 4–4. CROSSED TRANSACTION (BY EGO STATE
FUNCTION).

amples, a therapist could respond to the client from any of the
following states:

Free Child: "Wow, you really are in bad shape! What are you going
to do?"

Adult: "You are capable of figuring out what you need to do."

Positive Controlling Parent: "Stop discounting yourself and figure out
what to do!"

Once the client is in her Adult or Free Child, the therapist can use
complementary transactions to reinforce the Adult or Free Child
behavior.

Ulterior Transactions

An *ulterior transaction* is a transaction which contains a social
message as well as a psychological (secret) message. Ulterior transactions can be *angular* or *duplex*. An *angular transaction* involves
three ego states and occurs when messages are sent simultaneously
from one ego state of the initiator to two ego states of the respondent. When diagrammed, the social message is depicted with a solid
line, and the psychological message with a dotted line. Consider the
transactions in Figure 4-5.

In the first example the salesperson provides Adult information
to the prospective buyer. This Adult-to-Adult stimulus is overt and is
called the *social message*. However, she simultaneously sends a

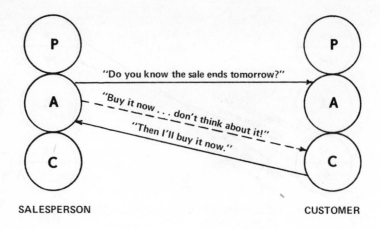

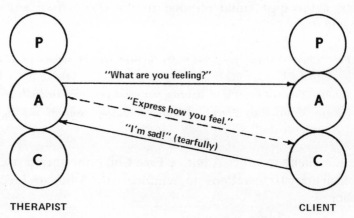

FIGURE 4-5. ANGULAR TRANSACTIONS.

psychological message to the customer in an attempt to hook the latter's impulsive Child and quickly close the deal. Both messages initiate from the salesperson's Adult, since she is aware of both messages and her intentions. Although the respondent may reply from any of her ego states, in this example the salesperson is successful in hooking the customer's Child and the angular transaction is completed. In the second example the therapist is ostensibly requesting information from the client regarding the client's feelings. The psychological invitation to express feelings is also communicated, and the client accepts the information, cathects Child, and responds with much feeling.

A duplex transaction involves four ego states, two in each person. During the course of a duplex transaction, two sets of complementary transactions are occurring simultaneously, one on the social level and another on the psychological level. Some examples are shown in Figure 4-6.

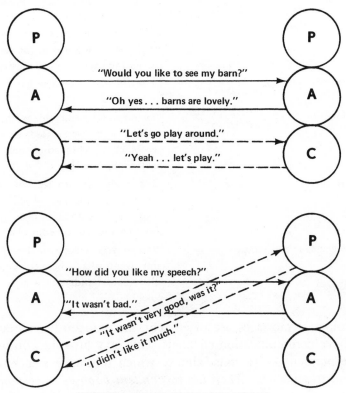

FIGURE 4-6. DUPLEX TRANSACTIONS.

The third rule of communication states: *The outcome of the transactions will be determined on the psychological level rather than on the social level.* Often the only persons aware of the ulterior transactions are the participants themselves, and even they may not be fully aware of them. Ulterior transactions are not inherently dishonest, but often the psychological message is used to invite people into games and their ensuing payoffs. The psychological message is usually nonverbal and is communicated via facial expressions, gestures, postures, and changes in voice tone and/or tempo. It may also be communicated via syntax, word selection, slips of the tongue, and so on. Some examples are listed in the following table:

Vehicle of Psychological Message	Example
Word selection:	"Where did you *hide* the newspaper?" (Said with calm voice, expressionless face, looking toward respondent). Here the nonverbal cues are ostensibly Adult, while the use of the word *hide* carries the psychological message.
Facial expression:	"I really like your new hat." (Frowning)
Posture:	"I want to hear your side of the story." (Sitting with legs crossed, arms folded across chest, chin stuck out, leaning back slightly in chair)
Gestures:	"It's really nice to see you." (Quick handshake, rapid pat on back, leaning away and glancing over person's shoulder toward someone else)
Voice tone and tempo:	"I love you. Of course I love you. I only want what's best for you, that's all!" (Said rapidly, in a high tone of voice)

Psychological messages are often sent simultaneously via several of the above communication channels. This may provoke confusion in the respondent, who must choose which of the messages she will respond to and how. *When the respondent chooses to respond only to the social message and does not respond to the psychological message, the result is a crossed transaction.* Since the intended communication is crossed, a momentary breakdown in communication results. Consider the example in Figure 4-7. Here Joe is sending an ulterior (psychological) message to Jane, attempting to hook a Child response. Since Joe's true intentions are communicated on the psychological level, he experiences a breakdown in communication when Jane remains in her Adult and responds only to his social message. This type of crossed transaction is particularly effective when Jane's intention is to avoid Joe's hook, stay OK, and invite a straight response from Joe, rather than to actively confront Joe's ulterior motives or force a resolution.

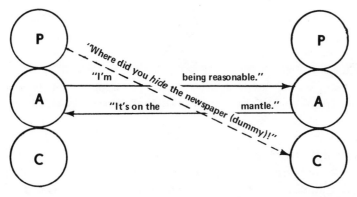

FIGURE 4-7. CROSSED TRANSACTION (WITH ULTERIOR STIMULI).

Options

Whenever two persons are communicating, each is free to choose from which ego state she will respond and to which ego state in the other person she will direct her transactions. This is called exercising *options* [36]. Each person is responsible for choosing her ego state at any given moment, and she bases her choice on the kind of stroke she wishes to give or receive and what she thinks is possible. *Autonomy* refers to the exercising of options which maintain OKness in self and invite OKness in others. This occurs whenever a person assumes an I'm OK—You're OK position and relates to others with a get-on-with-it attitude. When two persons are relating in this manner, they will indeed get on with whatever it is they intend to do—exchange information, make love, build a boat, or whatever.

Since each person is ultimately responsible for her own attitudes, feelings, and choice of ego states, it is not possible for one person to make another person feel good or bad. This refers to emotions, not physical sensations; of course, it is possible to make another person feel bad by physically striking that person, or to feel good by gently massaging her back. Even so, it is not possible to hook an ego state of another person unless the latter chooses to allow that to happen. Once a person has accepted the responsibility for staying OK regardless of what other people say and do, she is exercising her autonomy and taking charge of her destiny. This is an idealistic goal which one may work toward. More realistically, there are variable probabilities as to how likely it is that someone will hook someone else—for good or ill. This depends on circumstances, who is involved, and how transactions are done. Infants are most easily hooked; adults who feel good about themselves least easily hooked. Although we cannot cause another person to feel a particular way, we can and do *invite* others to feel certain ways and to respond from certain ego states. In fact, people respond to these invitations from others a large percentage of the time. OKness invites OKness, and not-OKness invites not-OKness. If Louise transacts with Max from an I'm OK—You're OK position, Max will most likely respond from an I'm OK—You're OK position. However, if Alfie transacts with Zelda from one of the not-OK positions, Zelda will most likely respond from a not—OK position. In order for therapy to be effective it is imperative that therapists take responsibility for staying OK and transacting with clients in ways that invite OKness. This is also true for parents, teachers, and any others who wish to be effective communicators.

A common way in which people allow themselves to experience bad feelings is by responding to someone's negative Controlling Parent with Adapted Child feelings. For example, the following statement said in a harsh tone by a person with a furrowed brow and finger pointing toward you in an accusing way may elicit a bad feeling on your part: "Stop what you're doing, you're doing it all wrong! You never do anything right!" However, even such a strong invitation into Adapted Child behavior can be avoided by an autonomous person. Since any response that is not complementary will in turn invite (but not coerce) the first person out of her Controlling Parent and into a different ego state, these can all be considered *Parent shrinkers* [37]. Consider the following options with the same stimulus:

> *Stimulus:* "Stop what you're doing, you're doing it all wrong! You never do anything right!
>
> *Optional Responses:*
> Adult with Little Professor: "I acknowledge your intention to invite me into some ill-chosen response, but considering the relative lack of merit in your rather vociferous remark, I respectfully decline."
> Adult: "Yes, you may be right about that. What do you suggest that I do?"
> Free Child: "Have you heard the one about . . ."
> Nurturing Parent: "Oh, dear, are you feeling well? You look *so* tired."

These are only a few of literally thousands of possible Parent-shrinker responses. Their primary value lies in maintaining personal OKness and declining the invitation to Adapted Child. Secondarily, they invite the initiator out of her Controlling Parent.

Special Types of Transactions

Caroms

Occasionally a person will send a message to someone indirectly through a third person. This type of transaction is called a *carom* because the first person's intent is to carom, or bounce, the message off the second person so that it is received by the third, who is actually the intended recipient. The second person may or may not be aware of the first person's intentions, and may or may not respond. The carom transaction is completed if the third person responds to the indirectly communicated message.

Gallows Transaction

A *gallows laugh* is any laugh or smile which accompanies a discounting statement about either the self or someone else. The gallows laugh serves to reinforce the person's script decisions, "tightening the noose" around her neck as she proceeds along her way toward a script payoff. Most discounting laughter comes from Adapted Child, which is in effect saying to her Parent, "Isn't it funny [cute, silly, etc.] how I make myself and others not-OK?" It may also come from Parent as a direct reinforcement of her own or someone else's script behaviors. In addition to pleasing some part of the person's Parent, a gallows laugh is intended to elicit approval from others by inviting them into a gallows transaction [9]. A *gallows transaction* occurs when someone else laughs along with the person, which the latter interprets as approval and encouragement for her not-OK behavior. Here are some examples of gallows laughs, any of which becomes a gallows transaction if someone responds by laughing along:

From Adapted Child
Client to Therapist: "Well, I guess you've tried, but I suppose you can't help me . . . I'm a tough client, aren't I?"—with a chuckle.

Therapist to Supervisor: "I just can't seem to get anywhere with Molly, no matter how hard I try"—with a slight smile.

From Parent

Teacher to student: "Your paper is late again . . . What am I going to do with you?"—with a smile.

Parent to Counselor: "I just can't get my son to do his homework . . . he's a cut-up just like his father"—with a smile.

It is important for therapists and other helpers not to laugh at someone's misfortunes, discounts, or scripty behaviors. In a treatment situation, it is often useful to ask the client if she is aware of her gallows laugh (or smile), find out what it means to her, inform her as to how it reinforces her life script, and ask her not to laugh in that manner. Exaggerating the laugh may help clarify its meaning. Sometimes a double-chair technique can be used to help the client discover who in her past was pleased when she acted out in scripty ways.

Bull's-eyes

A *bull's-eye* is a direct Adult comment that effectively reaches all three ego states in another person at the same time [36]. Sometimes this type of transaction is the only kind that will successfully cross a transaction when a person is "stuck" in Parent or Child, since an Adult statement which speaks to the experience of a person's Parent, Adult, and Child tends to invite a new awareness. A bull's-eye transaction is completed when the Adult interpretation is responded to with a switch in ego states and an Adult response; hence, a completed bull's-eye transaction is Adult to Adult. Consider the examples in Figure 4–8. Bull's-eyes are especially useful in treatment and other problem-solving situations, since they let the respondent know that someone takes all of her ego states seriously. This also invites the person to seriously consider all of her own ego states and to take them into account as she solves a personal problem.

Treatment Considerations

Therapy proceeds best when the therapist uses all of her ego states to communicate with her client. At first, the client may limit her

EXAMPLE I

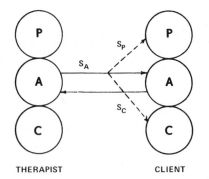

THERAPIST TO CONFUSED CLIENT: "PERHAPS YOU WOULDN'T BE CONFUSED (S_A) IF YOU STOPPED HASSLING YOURSELF (S_P) AND LET YOURSELF KNOW HOW YOU FEEL AND WHAT YOU WANT (S_C).

CLIENT: "THAT'S WHY I'M CONFUSED . . . I'VE BEEN HASSLING MYSELF INSTEAD OF STAYING IN TOUCH WITH MY FEELINGS!"

EXAMPLE II

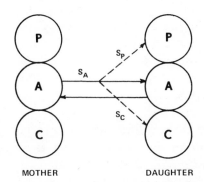

MOTHER TO SULKING DAUGHTER: "I KNOW YOU'RE ANGRY AT ME (S_C) AND YOU THINK I HAVE NO RIGHT TO INTERFERE IN YOUR BUSINESS (S_P), BUT WILL YOU DISCUSS THE PROBLEM WITH ME ANYWAY (S_A)?"

DAUGHTER: "I DON'T LIKE IT, BUT I'M WILLING TO TALK ABOUT IT."

FIGURE 4-8. BULL'S EYE TRANSACTIONS. (S_A = STIMULUS TO ADULT, ETC.)

choices, but eventually she, too, will be using all of her ego states to transact with the therapist. Each person continuously exercises options regarding which of her ego states she uses to send messages and to which ego state in the other person she directs her communication. The therapist has two particular responsibilities in this regard. First, she should have her Adult processing what is transpiring regardless of which ego state she is actually using. Second, she should be aware of her psychological-level communication and make sure that she is not sending messages which reinforce her client's script behaviors. We transact with clients from all of our ego states at various times and with varying amounts of intensity. However, even when we are transacting from Parent or Child, we use our Adult and Little Professor to monitor our responses carefully. We use our

Adult and Little Professor to decide how to intervene and which ego state is best for the intervention. Ideally, we can stop our work at any time and explain what we are doing, where we have been, and where we are going. Otherwise we are in danger of "laying our own trip" on our clients instead of transacting with them in ways that make sense for them.

In order to make sure that she is not sending off harmful messages on a psychological level (outside of her awareness), a therapist needs to "have her own house in order." The only real way she can be reasonably sure of this is to have been in personal therapy so that she understands herself and has worked through her own issues, and is open to feedback from clients, peers, and supervisors. Psychological messages are always occurring, with or without awareness, and can be used to invite others into rackets and games or to convey acceptance and caring. The important thing is to be aware of them, take responsibility for them, and change the ones which are not working. In addition to resulting from unresolved personal issues, harmful psychological messages may also be sent from a therapist who is distracted, absent-minded, or not centered in the here-and-now as she treats her clients. Taking care of her own needs and feelings will alleviate this.

It is also important to be aware of how the client transacts. Which ego state(s) does she use most often? Which are avoided? How does she respond to messages from different ego states? Does she cross transactions? What psychological messages does she send off? Does she use different ego states to transact with men, as opposed to women . . . to therapists, as opposed to group members? The answers to these and other questions can provide a great deal of useful information about how to open communication channels, and about what her various ego states are thinking, feeling, and doing.

Relationship Diagram

A *relationship diagram* can be drawn to illustrate which communication or stroking channels are used between two people [6]. When all of the stroking channels are open, the relationship diagram looks like Figure 4-9. Each line connecting two ego states indicates an open stroking channel. In this example, all channels are open; there-

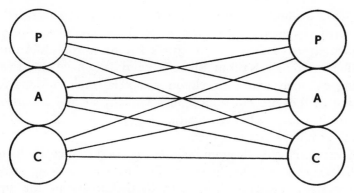

FIGURE 4-9. RELATIONSHIP DIAGRAM WITH ALL STROKING CHANNELS OPEN.

fore, strokes are exchanged between all three ego states of both persons, or along all nine possible channels. For a more detailed analysis, the ego states can be divided into their functional parts, yielding twenty-five stroking channels to be analyzed. If two people relate in such a way that they do not exchange strokes between some of their ego states, then those channels are closed, and the lines are omitted from the diagram. In the example in Figure 4-10, Jim and Sally do not like each other much, do not play together, and do not share feelings with each other. Therefore, the Child-to-Child channel is omitted in their relationship diagram. Additionally, Jim's Parent is not available to stroke Sally at all, since he refuses to take re-

FIGURE 4-10 RELATIONSHIP DIAGRAM WITH FOUR CLOSED CHANNELS.

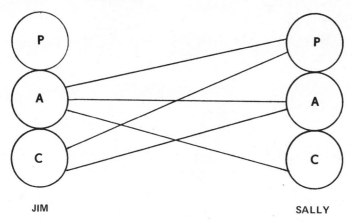

JIM   SALLY

sponsibility around her and lets her dominate him. Therefore, three other stroking channels are omitted in their relationship diagrams: Jim's Parent to Sally's Parent, Jim's Parent to Sally's Adult, and Jim's Parent to Sally's Child. Since Jim and Sally have only five open stroking channels and four closed channels, their options for exchanging strokes are cut almost in half. Sally's Child is particularly likely to be unhappy in their relationship, and this will probably lead to many problems between them.

The relationship diagram may be modified to increase its usefulness by varying the thickness of the lines or by using arrows of different sizes to signify variations in the power of the stroking channels which are open. Any of these diagrams are especially useful for analyzing a relationship between couples or family members who are experiencing communication problems. They can also be used as a premarital counseling tool to highlight the strong and weak points in a relationship. Finally, they may be used to highlight the stroking patterns between any two persons—therapist and client, therapist and supervisor, teacher and student, employer and employee, and so on. Once these patterns are identified, the persons involved may choose to change their ways of transacting, find someone else to fill unmet stroking needs, or remain as they are.

5

Time
Structuring

"Tempus fidgets"

Structure Hunger

We all have a need to structure our time in order to avoid the pain of boredom. This need is called *structure hunger* [9]. Structure hunger can be thought of as an extension of stimulus hunger, since the need for stimulation requires that we establish situations in which strokes can be exchanged. The particular ways in which a person structures her time depends upon whether or not she feels OK about herself and others, the kinds of strokes she is seeking to give and receive, and other learned patterns of behavior. There are six ways of structuring time, and at any given moment each of us is involved in one or more of these time structures. Each of these ways of structuring time has both advantages and disadvantages. They are listed below in ascending order, from the lowest emotional risk to the highest.

Withdrawal

A person *withdraws* by mentally removing herself from others. She may do this alone in her room, at a party, or while walking down a crowded street. Daydreams, fantasy, and meditation are all forms of withdrawal. When a person withdraws she is choosing to shut others out, relying on herself for stimulation and time structure. Withdrawal is usually safe, requires little emotional investment, and does not provide stroking from others. A certain amount of withdrawal is healthy, normal behavior; everyone does so at certain times in order to be with herself, collect her thoughts, and reflect upon her experiences, needs, and feelings. Some people avoid withdrawal because they are afraid to be alone with their experiences, and choose instead to structure their time in ways which distract them from their personal thoughts and feelings. On the other hand, some people spend a great deal of time in withdrawal because they are afraid to share themselves with others. A person who spends too much time withdrawing may become stroke-deprived, lonely, and depressed, and in severe cases withdrawal may lead to autistic thinking. A person who lacks contact with others sacrifices an external check on her fantasies; when not checked out with outside sources, these fantasies may be mistaken for reality.

Rituals

A *ritual* is a safe and predictable exchange of strokes in which persons behave toward one another in a fixed manner. When people are involved in a ritual it sounds and looks like they are reading their transactions verbatim from a script, and sometimes they are actually doing so. Much that transpires during a church ceremony, lodge meeting, or business conference is right out of a book, ranging from a book of prayers to *Robert's Rules of Order*. Rituals may be brief and simple, such as an exchange of "Hellos" or "Good mornings." Sometimes they are longer and involve more strokes:

> Stan: "Hi Mike!"
>
> Mike: "Hi Stan! How are you?"
>
> Stan: "Oh, I can't complain . . . and how is your family?"
>
> Mike: "Just fine . . . and yours?"
>
> Stan: "We're doing well . . . it's nice to see you again."
>
> Mike: "Same here . . . long time no see."
>
> Stan: "Yeah . . . say hi to Sue for me."
>
> Mike: "I sure will . . . you say hi to Pris for me. So long!"
>
> Stan: "See you later."

Rituals may also be quite long and complex and involve larger numbers of people, such as in religious ceremonies. Rituals are useful in that they are predictable exchanges which provide important maintenance strokes. Think of the many times during an average day when you exchange greetings and farewells with the people you encounter. Now consider how you would feel if your greetings were ignored and no one responded to you. Rituals also provide introductions into other forms of time structuring, since a person generally does not feel invited to begin a conversation with someone who refuses to say hello.

Some people spend most of their time transacting with others via rituals. People will experience such a person as well-mannered and pleasant, but will not really know anything about her and may think of her as shallow. Although rituals do provide some maintenance strokes, the yield is very low. A person who structures her time primarily in withdrawal and rituals is likely to experience stroke deprivation and loneliness.

Pastimes

When people transact with each other and their purpose is not to accomplish a goal but rather to "talk about" something, they are engaging in a *pastime*. A pastime is a semiritualized conversation in which people share opinions, thoughts, or feelings about relatively safe topics. A pastime is not as prescribed as a ritual, but there is a covert agreement between the persons involved that they will follow certain guidelines in the discussion. Whereas in a ritual it seems as if each person is reading from a script, in a pastime it is as though there is a general outline of the topic of conversation. Each person is free to fill in the spaces so long as she sticks to the major guidelines. Although these guidelines may be broad, they are often strictly enforced. If a person decides to change the topic or the flavor of the discussion, a breakdown of communication will occur and the conversation will stop. It may begin anew, but new subgroups will form according to the stroke needs and wants of each person. For example, if a group is organized around "Ain't It Awful About Kids Nowadays" and someone joins who wishes to play "Ain't It Wonderful," she will likely be thrown out or leave to join some other group. A similar phenomenon is likely to occur if a person attempts to change a group pastime into another form of time structuring. For example, a group of people chatting about corruption in politics is usually uninterested in actually taking steps there and then to solve the problem, and will probably become restless or angry and break up if someone decides to call an impromptu meeting to organize useful actions (activity).

Cocktail chatter, bull sessions, and rap groups are all variations of pastimes. Some common pastime topics are politics, ecology, sports, weather, inflation, fashions, worries, travel, sex, food, and drugs. The list is virtually endless and covers the entire spectrum of people's personal interests. These discussions are intended to exchange strokes, not solve problems. If the latter is the case, then what is occurring is not a pastime but an activity. Pastimes may supply a relatively large number of strokes, usually pleasant, without much risk of closeness. They also allow a person to collect information about another person's ideas and interests. As such, they can be used to "get a feel of" the person you are speaking to in order to decide whether or not to risk other types of time structuring. The topic selection can also be used to maintain and invite not-OK feelings and to support script decisions.

Activities

When a person's energy is directed to external sources, such as objects, tasks, and ideas, the person is engaged in an *activity*. Work, hobbies, and chores are common examples; hence, it is apparent that many people spend a great deal of their waking hours involved in activities. Activities produce strokes in many ways. When a job is well done, positive strokes are often obtained in the form of praise from friends, relatives, or co-workers. Negative strokes may be received if a person does a job poorly or chooses to work with people who find fault easily.

Strokes for activities come from direct rewards, like school grades, trophies, and paychecks, and some people use these rewards as their major source of strokes. Activities also provide a setting in which other forms of time structuring may be established. For example, two persons who spend a great deal of time working together on a project may detour from the job to engage in rituals, pastimes, rackets, games, or even intimacy. On a negative side, a *workaholic* is a person who engages in activities to the extent that she does not allow herself to truly experience her own feelings or to

share closeness or fun with others. This type of person i
who is either afraid to share strokes with others or who
she is only OK when she is producing something.

Rackets and Games

A psychological *game* is "an ongoing series of complementary transactions which lead to a well-defined predictable outcome" [4]. A
racket can be either an internal process or a series of complementary
transactions which a person uses to "justify" a not-OK position.
Rackets and games will be discussed extensively in a later section of
this book. For the moment it is sufficient to know that these ways of
structuring time tap the very basic parts of the personality and have
the capacity for producing very large quantities of intense strokes
that are mostly negative.

Intimacy

Intimacy is the most risky and the most rewarding of all ways of
structuring time. Intimacy involves the sharing of feelings, thoughts,
or experiences in a relationship of openness, honesty, and trust.
There is a straight, spontaneous exchange of strokes in the here-and-
now with no ulterior motives, no exploitation, and no other form of
time structuring occurring. The Free Child is always involved during
intimacy, and remains open to whatever happens. The intimate
experience may be physical or emotional, pleasant or unpleasant, real
or imagined. Although intimacy provides the highest stroke yield,
people often avoid it because they believe it to be risky and unpre-
dictable. A person who believes that she and others are OK will
risk being open and intimate in many more circumstances than will
the person who doubts her or others' OKness. Intimacy can occur on
a number of levels and usually involves very pleasant feelings. Below
are some examples of intimate experiences.

Two friends running down a grassy hill, hand in hand, laughing,
carefree, and oblivious to any pressures from the outside world.

A group of people in a therapy group witness a member's release of long-held pain and her new experience of naturalness and joy. The members spontaneously join her in the center of the room, where they engage in a group hug and share her experience.

You are lying on a beach enjoying the sound of the surf and feeling at one with yourself and the world. You look across the sand and notice a partner in the universe. She looks back, smiles at you, and you know that you are sharing a special moment with her.

Three brothers are very close. Two of the brothers receive word that the third has been killed in an accident. The brothers hold and comfort each other as each openly expresses his anger, pain, and sorrow.

The amount of time spent and strokes received in each way of structuring time will vary a great deal from person to person. One person may spend most of her time in withdrawal having frightening fantasies, another in ritualized exchanges or by pastiming superficially, and still another by working very hard. Some get most of their strokes in rackets and games, and a few get many strokes in intimate relationships.

A person's script (life plan) determines how she will spend her time and which ego state she most often uses. If she does not want to get close to others, she may spend a lot of time withdrawing or in rituals, and perhaps playing games which result in distance. Or, if she is afraid to feel, she may stay mostly in her Adult ego state and choose fantasies, rituals, pastimes, and activities in which she primarily uses her Adult. There is no single right or wrong way in which to structure your time. Examine your methods of time structuring to determine whether or not you are getting what you want. If not, it is never too late to change and to sample different ways.

Time Structuring and Ego States

The first four ways of structuring time—withdrawal, rituals, pastimes, and activities—can all be done from any of the ego states. For example, while withdrawing a person can have either a pleasant or scary Child fantasy, an interesting Adult fantasy as she plays with numbers in her head, or a Parent fantasy of "Ain't It Awful About Kids Nowadays." Rituals, pastimes, and activities not only can be used for their own value, but also are often used to select people for the more risky ways of structuring time—rackets and games, and intimacy. Rackets and games are always played outside of Adult awareness by either the Parent or the Child ego state. Intimacy always involves the Free Child. The chart in Table 5-1 gives some examples of how the various ways of time structuring can be used while functioning in various ego states.

Time structuring is a very flexible phenomenon, and most persons change time structures readily and often. It is also possible to be involved in more than one form of time structuring at a given time. For example, a woman may *withdraw* from her husband in order to avoid his complaining and busy herself by washing the dishes (*activity*). Another person might attend a religious service (*ritual*) in order to maintain a guilt *racket*.

A person may also switch ego states during the course of one or more time structures. For example, a baseball game (*activity*) calls for various ego state functions at various times. These changes in ego states and time structuring present an overall pattern of how and where a person chooses to direct her energies. One goal of TA therapy is to assist the client in exercising options regarding her choices of ego states and time structuring.

Treatment Considerations

Time Structuring During Treatment Sessions

Treatment is an ongoing relationship process between the client and the therapist and perhaps a group. Each of the ways of structuring time will occur as a part of the natural course of events. Each can also be controlled and directed as part of the treatment process.

WITHDRAWAL

At times the client may mentally remove herself from others during the treatment sessions. The therapist should be aware that this

TABLE 5-1. Time Structuring in Various Ego States

	Controlling Parent	Nurturing Parent	Adult	Free Child	Adapted Child
Withdrawal	Silent self-criticism	Silent self-comfort	Thinking about what cities are along the route from Chicago to Los Angeles	Singing to oneself	Frightening fantasies
Ritual	Taking the children to church	Tucking kids in bed each night	Watching the evening news	Nightly tickle match or pillow fight before retiring	Obligatory yearly church service
Pastime	"Ain't It Awful" (about kids, inflation, etc.)	"Ain't It Wonderful"	Exchanging nonessential information ("Did you read where . . .")	Telling and knowing jokes for fun	"If It Weren't For Her . . ."
Activity	Supervising others' work; disciplining employees	Making beds, bathing the children	Figuring a budget	Playing baseball	Doing chores
Rackets/Games	"Now I Got You, You Son of a Bitch," "Blemish," "Rapo," etc.	"I'm Only Trying to Help You," "Cavalier," "Happy to Help"	—	—	"Poor Me," "Kick Me," "Stupid," etc.
Intimacy	—	—	—	Sharing love, joy, or pleasure	—

is occurring and choose whether or not to intervene. On the other hand, the therapist may suggest that the client spend time alone with her thoughts and feelings, undistracted by others. This is especially useful when the client needs time to think through a problem or to get in touch with her feelings. It may also be useful if she has been in a racket or game with other members, and the therapist wants to cut off the strokes which she is receiving for her not-OK behavior.

RITUALS

Many ritual strokes are exchanged before, during, and after treatment sessions. Customary hellos, good-byes, and hugs may be important positive anchors for the client's Child and add greatly to her sense of security in the treatment session. On the other hand, some clients need practice at refusing to exchange ritualized strokes that they do not want to be involved in but nevertheless participate in from an adapted position.

PASTIMES

Pastimes are used infrequently as part of the therapeutic process, although they are sometimes used to change the pace between intensive pieces of work. They may also provide a way for members to get to know each other in the early stages of a group.

ACTIVITY

The process of therapy is essentially an activity, since its purpose is goal-oriented. The therapist's responsibility is to ensure that whatever occurs in treatment is aimed toward the client's desired outcome. Homework assignments are also activities whose purpose is to help the client meet her treatment goals.

RACKETS AND GAMES

When a client plays out her rackets and games in the treatment session they are analyzed, confronted, or dealt with in some way which helps her to own, understand, and avoid them. The therapist is responsible for not initiating her own games and rackets, and for not hooking into those of her clients.

INTIMACY

Clients and therapists usually reach some level of intimacy at certain times during the course of treatment. Sometimes this is a new experience for the client, in which case the therapist helps her to fully experience her feelings, to enjoy them, and to work through any fears she has about these new and intense emotions. Group members may share intimate experiences as well, and this should be encouraged and dealt with in the same way. Some clients (and therapists, unfortunately) confuse intimacy with rackets and games, which may lead to exploitation. This must be confronted and resolved if therapy is to be productive.

Working With a Client's Time Structuring

Analyzing a client's time structuring provides information about how she exchanges strokes, which in turn tells us how she maintains her script decisions. Helping the client understand and change how she structures her time provides new ways for her to give and get the kinds of strokes her Free Child wants and needs. As clients change their ways of structuring time and exchanging strokes, they may also need to work through the feelings connected with giving up their old patterns and relating in new ways.

WITHDRAWAL

Many clients spend a great deal of time in withdrawal, living primarily off internal strokes that support their scripts. These clients may need to proceed slowly at first, so that their Child learns that it is safe to change. For example, an extremely withdrawn client may begin by saying hello to ten people each day for a week; the next week she may increase this to hello followed by a person's name; and so on. She is most likely to succeed if she is stroked for success at each step. Other clients need to spend more time in withdrawal in order to get more in touch with themselves. These are persons who fill their lives with activity and/or idle chatter in order to avoid dealing with their own thoughts and feelings.

RITUALS

Some clients get most of their external strokes via rituals and wish to learn other ways to exchange strokes. Others discount these strokes and so deprive themselves of their benefits. It is OK to enjoy rituals! Hellos, goodbyes, and so forth with persons you care about can provide many safe, easy, and comfortable strokes. It is much more fun to exchange these pleasantries and enjoy them with people you know than to walk around all day in silence. A client who is stuck in rituals and wishes to move into more intensive stroke exchanges may need to progress slowly, similar to the client who is withdrawn.

PASTIMES

Some clients have not learned how to engage others in pastimes and so deprive themselves of a very rich source of pleasant strokes. People who have not learned how to pastime often have difficulty in establishing deeper relationships, since it is so customary in our society to spend time "getting to know someone" before attempting to get close. Such people commonly believe that they have nothing of value to share or that the interests and opinions of others are not worth listening to. They can use the group as a resource to practice new communication skills and often benefit a great deal from the informal exchanges which take place during breaks. On the other hand, clients who remain at the pastiming level because they are afraid to experience intimacy may bore those around them, and can benefit from learning to risk being close.

ACTIVITIES

Many people fill their lives with activities, responding to a Parent message to Work Hard. These clients may choose to alter this and spend more time living, being, and enjoying. Other clients may not have a Parent which strokes them for accomplishing, but instead tells them Don't Make It. They may choose to learn how to set and meet goals, perform tasks, and get strokes from themselves and others for doing things.

RACKETS AND GAMES

These time structures should not be encouraged in clients, since they are ways of maintaining not-OKness. Treatment is largely a process of helping clients become aware of and eliminate their rackets and games.

INTIMACY

Many clients wish to experience more intimacy in their lives. To accomplish this is not always easy. Clients can be taught some specific behaviors which enhance closeness—maintaining eye contact, "I-you" exchanges, sharing feelings, staying in the here-and-now, and so on. Also, the therapeutic situation can provide an environment conducive to trust, risk, and change. Generally, before clients can experience intimacy they must work through their personal fears and blocks about it and be willing to risk fully experiencing their Free Child feelings.

6

Symbiosis
and Discounting

"Do you remember when you were nine and I was eight, and together we were seventeen?"

Emotional disorders are learned behaviors based on childhood decisions, and represent the child's compromise between satisfying her own needs and getting along with parent figures. People always do whatever they can to maximize their pleasure and minimize their discomfort. Even a person who is being harmful or oppressive to someone else is not doing so primarily to be hurtful, but rather to relieve herself of fear, anger, or some painful experience. Each of us makes our decisions from the standpoint of "How can I best get along in the world?" Unfortunately, these decisions are not always appropriate, or are overgeneralized to inappropriate times, places, or people. For example, a child may learn that when she expresses her needs assertively her parents become angry and violent, and so decide not to express them to her parents in order to protect herself. Regrettably, she may also generalize her decision, that is, "It is not safe for me to express my needs, so I will remain quiet and just take what I can get when it's offered." Long after the threat of her parents' violence is gone, she maintains her decision to discount her needs and quietly adapts. Behavior patterns such as symbiosis, discounting, passive behaviors, redefining transactions, rackets, and games are part of the process of carrying out this decision.

Symbiosis

Emotional disturbances, including games and rackets, are learned behaviors which result from unresolved symbiotic relationships. *Symbiosis* occurs when "two or more individuals behave as though between them they form a whole person. This relationship is characterized by neither individual cathecting a full complement of ego states, and the mechanism used to maintain it is discounting" [40]. It is usually illustrated as in Figure 6-1.

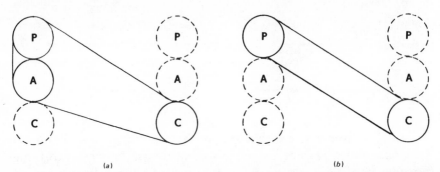

(a)   (b)

FIGURE 6-1. SYMBIOSIS DIAGRAMS. (DASHED LINES DENOTE EGO STATES NOT CATHECTED)

Actually, in most cases, especially those which involve rackets and games, we believe that neither person is using her Adult ego state; or at best only minimal Adult thinking is occurring while the rest is being discounted, allowing the racket or game to be continued outside of Adult awareness. Figure 6-1 (*a*) illustrates this.

Symbiosis may be established in a parent-child relationship whenever the child is not allowed to complete the developmental tasks relevant to her age. The most important symbiotic relationships are those which occur between a child and her primary caretaker. In our society the primary caretaker is usually the natural mother; it could also be a father, aunt, grandparent, older sibling, and so on.

Normal Dependency and Symbiosis

A very special relationship exists between the primary parent and the infant, which we choose to call *normal dependency* [54]. Unlike symbiosis, this relationship, which is at first very close, all the while aims at eventual autonomy for the maturing youngster, and neither parent nor child needs to discount an ego state during this process. Normal dependency continues between parents and children throughout childhood, and ends only when the child has matured sufficiently to take care of herself as a grown person. Normal dependency is illustrated in Figure 6-2, which shows a

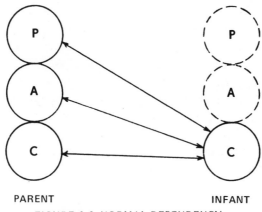

PARENT   INFANT
FIGURE 6–2. NORMAL DEPENDENCY.

mother relating to a child who has not yet developed much of a
Parent or Adult ego state.

The normally dependent infant does not discount her Child
ego state, since it is that part of her which is crying and asking for
help, or laughing and engaging others in play. In the first few months
of life the infant essentially does not have an Adult or Parent, and so
neither can be discounted. In a healthy family, when the infant's
first Adult (Little Professor) does appear, it is not discounted, but
rather its curiosity is fostered. In turn, each ego state of the developing child is responded to appropriately in growth-inducing ways.

Neither do any of mother's ego states need to be discounted
for good childrearing to occur. Her Parent ego state is important
and contains tapes about childrearing which may be effectively used
to nurture and protect the baby. Her Adult also contains important
information and knows how to solve problems for the baby. Last,
her Child ego state is used to express and model love, fun, and
caring. Strokes from the Child are received with much impact and
power, so mom's energy-containing, enthusiastic Child can be used to
give potent permissions to the infant. When the Child of the parent
is feeling good and is turned on by the infant, intimacy can occur
and great quantities of positive strokes may be exchanged. In this
warm situation, the infant feels the protection she needs to develop
her own special capabilities and to respond to the permissions which
she is given. On the other hand, if the parent discounts her own Child
ego state, she will eventually feel resentful and angry. It is exactly

under these circumstances that the parent is likely to discharge her anger in a powerful negative message (injunction) from her Child.

For the best parenting to occur, a parent should give priority to taking good care of herself and making sure that she receives the strokes she needs for her own well-being from sources other than the infant. Under these circumstances, the infant is least likely to be experienced as a burden. Then, when the infant cries for something, the mother need not discount her own Child in order to feel like taking care of the infant's need. For example, when the baby cries in the middle of the night, mother may awaken and have the following internal dialogue:

> Parent: "You should get up. The baby needs you!"
> Adult: "She's probably cold."
> Child: "I don't want to get up."
> Parent: "It will be OK. You can have some extra sleep in the morning."
> Adult: "If you get up now, she will be easier to take care of."
> Parent: "She's cute at night, too."
> Child: "OK, I'll go."

Externally:

> Parent: "Here I come!"

Here mother's child is not excluded or discounted, but instead is given information by her Adult and a promise of future caring by her Parent. If morning comes and the baby is crying again, mother might not get her extra rest. It would be wise for her husband to stay home from work for a while, to hire a temporary babysitter, or to find some other solution to take care of mother's Child. Often a mother will try to get through the day by discounting her exhausted Child and taking care of her infant from her Nurturing Parent. If she is in good health and if her stroke reservoir is good, this may work for a while. Sooner or later, though, if the stress continues, her Child will refuse to be discounted and she will start giving off negative messages and strokes. It is easy to understand how overworked mothers, such as wives of workaholics, and especially single parents, can be prone to giving out destructive injunctions because of lack of care and support for their own Child. On the other hand, when mother's Child is taken care of, she is in a much better position to care for her infant. This must be clearly differentiated from the message "parents' needs come first," which can result in serious psychopathology. In normal dependency, the child's needs are heard and met without the parents' discounting themselves and getting into the suffering, self-sacrificing positions from which the child is later manipulated.

It is true that probably all parents at times will discount either their own or the infant's needs, and so produce at least temporary symbiosis. When this occurs, it is because the parent is in her script, or ill, or fatigued, or, at the very least, misinformed. When mother has been adequately stroked and properly informed, normal dependency may occur safely for the infant, and each growth stage will be completed without establishing significant symbiotic relationships between the parents and the child that would lead to further problems in later years.

All of the above comments apply equally well to the psychotherapeutic relationship of therapist and client. The therapist who takes care of her own Child first will be more potent, offer better permissions, and provide a good model for her clients. The client can then feel safe and have no reason to take care of the therapist, and so be in a better position to change.

Symbiotic Relationships

Symbiotic relationships are always pathological, since by TA definition they involve the discounting of one or more developmentally available ego states. One way the groundwork for symbiosis may be established is when mother fails to meet the needs of her own Child ego state. When this happens she may become overly responsive to the needs of the infant. As the child grows older, mother may continue to provide and care for the needs of the child, rather than teaching and allowing the child to take care of herself. As a result, the young person does not learn to think effectively, since she is not allowed to develop or cathect her Adult or Parent ego states. When she grows up she may attempt, from her Child ego state, to manipulate others into gratifying her unmet needs and wants, failing to be aware of her own power to get her needs met in a direct manner.

On other occasions, a child learns to take the role in the symbiosis which was originally assumed by mother. For example, if mother is experienced by the child as very needy, enveloping, and overwhelming, the youngster might decide to exclude her own Child ego state and remain in Parent and/or Adult ego states in order to protect herself from being "swallowed up." Or if mother eventually tires of discounting her own needs and wants, she may later "pull a switch" on the child by putting her own needs first and refusing to adequately care for her child. The child then learns to take care of mother by ignoring her own needs and becoming a "little parent." She learns to assume the helper's role in symbiotic relationships, and goes through life thinking for others and telling them what to do while discounting her own needs and wants. When two persons are relating symbiotically, one person expresses a discounted version of feelings, wants, and needs (cathects Child) while the other assumes a discounted caretaking or persecuting position (cathects Parent).

Discounting

Whenever a person is attempting to establish or maintain a symbiosis, she is ignoring or distorting some aspect of her internal or external experience. This is called *discounting* [40]. Conversely, the purpose for discounting is to establish or maintain a symbiotic relationship which provides familiar strokes. All of this serves to manipulate or distort the person's experience so that she maintains her preconceived notions about herself, others, and the world, and thereby forwards her life script. When parents relate to their children symbiotically, they not only are involved in the process of discounting, but are teaching their children to discount as well.

Levels of Discounting

There are four levels of severity of discounting, and within these levels a person can discount in three areas: herself, others, and the situation. The four levels, along with examples, are presented below:

1. Discounting the *existence* of a problem (baby cries and parents go to sleep). This is a total discount and the most pathological. Since the awareness of the stimulus from the baby (others) is blocked, the problem cannot be defined or solved.

2. Discounting the *significance* of the problem (baby cries and parents say she is always fussy at that particular time of day). The baby and the cry are acknowledged as existing, but the situation is being discounted. Since the problem is not considered significant, the parents do not put energy into solving it.

3. Discounting the *change possibilities* of the problem (baby cries and parents claim that there is no way she will be satisfied). The parents are aware of a problem, acknowledge that it is important, but believe that it has no solution. They do not look for optional ways of responding and so discount the baby (others).

4. Discounting *personal abilities* (baby cries, parents know that it is a problem, that it can be solved, and that others could handle it, but see themselves as incapable of dealing with it). In this instance the parents are likely to get someone else to solve the problem, while discounting themselves.

In order to discount in any of these ways the parents must be operating (*a*) from a misinformed or uninformed Adult, (*b*) from a contaminated Adult, or (*c*) by excluding the Adult and cathecting an unhelpful Parent or Child ego state [58]. For example, mother may respond in a helpless, whiny Child ego state, failing to think. By doing so she excludes her Adult and fails to take in necessary information (baby is wet and cold) to help her solve the problem. Her Child insists that she is helpless and inadequate while her Parent calls her useless and no good. Or mother may be operating from a Parent-contaminated Adult, with Parent tapes masquerading as Adult information—for example, "It is better to let babies cry themselves to sleep than to pick them up." In both instances the parents may think they are gathering more proof that their behaviors are Adult-programmed when baby finally adapts, gives up, and stops crying. The exclamation at this point is usually "I knew nothing was wrong—see, she has stopped crying!" The child's adaptation thus reinforces the parents' discounting.

A person's need to make sense of her world and to get along with the "big people" around her leads to script decisions, including the establishment of a life position. Script behavior is directed by the

Adapted Child and involves a discount of at least part of one of the individual's ego states. She learns to get strokes in the only ways she believes are possible, and establishes symbiotic relationships which confirm her life position and script decisions. In order to establish and maintain these symbiotic relationships she develops a particular style and level of discounting. When a grown-up person relates symbiotically to others in the here-and-now, she must exaggerate some aspect of herself, the other person, or the situation in order to experience it similarly to the old scene in which she made her original script decision [40]. This distortion of thinking is called *grandiosity,* and includes such statements as:

> "You are just like my father!"
> "I'm helpless just like when I was a little kid!"
> "I can't stand it!"

Passive Behaviors

There are four styles of *passive behaviors* which a person may use to establish a symbiotic relationship [40]. None involve thinking through a problem to a solution while taking into account all of the ego states.

1. *Doing Nothing* means that psychic energy is used to inhibit responses and thinking. When Bob asked Pam to pick up something, she instead stood still and looked sullen. When Dan was asked by his boss to finish the report, he just sat still and stared blankly into space.

2. *Overadaptation* is psyching out what she thinks others want of her and adapting to this fantasy. She is anxious to please and identifies others as parent figures who are more important than her and whose needs and wants are her responsibility to figure out and resolve. Patsy wanted to be held, but would not ask because she assumed that no one would want to hold her. Bart, a manager, watched his boss pound the table as he gave orders, assumed that his boss was angry with him, and responded in a placating manner. These types of passive behavior are not the same as the nonpassive, conscious behavior called *adaptation,* which involves thinking and deciding to comply because it makes sense to do so.

3. *Agitation* involves the use of energy in purposeless, non-goal-oriented

activities (smoking, pacing, rocking, jiggling, hair twirling, talking incessantly, etc.). Mild and even moderate agitation can be alleviated by increasing the person's awareness of it, by identifying the message it is expressing indirectly, and by clarifying the positive intention of the behavior. More severe agitation frequently can be confronted by getting the person to respond to Parent direction or stroking ("Just sit down, no one is going to hurt you"). However, a confrontation without support for the person's Child may result in escalation to violence, since the severely agitated person is experiencing a threat to an important symbiotic relationship.

4. *Incapacitation and/or violence.* These behaviors are placed in the same category because they both involve an adamant refusal to think and solve problems and are immediate demands on the environment to take over all responsibility. The person's underlying experience is one of terror, and these behaviors are last-ditch efforts to protect the person from her fantasized catastrophic expectation. Behaviors may include getting sick, going crazy, attacking someone, and so on.

Redefining Transactions

People use redefining transactions to maintain an established view of themselves, other people, and the world (frame of reference) in order to advance their scripts [40]. *Redefining transactions* occur whenever someone discounts some aspect of a communication and *shifts the issue.* The shift may be obvious or subtle, and may come from any ego state. However, if the person doing the redefining is in her Adult ego state, she is operating from a contamination, without Adult awareness. When the redefining is subtle and agreed to by both parties, it may not be detected, allowing the communication to continue indefinitely without really addressing the original issue. Redefining transactions can be separated into two distinct types—tangential and blocking.

Tangential transactions occur when each person addresses different issues, or different aspects of the same issue. If both parties persist, they seem to "talk past" each other rather than communicate with each other. It is as if each person is having a separate parallel discussion without the other person's active involvement. The goal of the person doing the redefining is to establish a symbiosis which will reinforce her desired frame of reference. If the redefining is not confronted, the original issue is likely to be forgotten and a symbiosis established. Here are some examples of tangential transactions:

> Mother: "Who made this mess?"
> Daughter: "I didn't!" (Shift from *information* to *defense*)
>
> Therapist: "What are you feeling?"
> Client: "I don't think you can help me." (Shift from *feeling* to *thinking*)
>
> Husband: "Do you want to make love?"
> Wife: "I'm really tired tonight." (Shift from *want* to *feeling*)
>
> Boss: "When will the report be ready?"
> Employee: "Did you hear about the ball game last night?" (Shift from *report* to *ball game*)

Blocking transactions occur when a person attempts to avoid an issue by disagreeing with its purpose or meaning. These often occur even when there is a commonly accepted definition of the issue, and usually lead to hassles and arguments regarding the "true meaning" of the communication. All of this serves to block the communication and discount the originally intended meaning. Examples of blocking transactions include:

> Son: "Do you love me, mommy?"
> Mother: "What is love?" (Definition of *love*)
>
> Therapist: "What are you feeling?"
> Client: "Nothing . . . I'm just bored." (Definition of *feeling*)
>
> Wife: "Why are you ignoring me?"
> Husband: "I'm not! I was just thinking." (Definition of *ignoring*)

A person is likely to redefine whenever she experiences a threat to her frame of reference. A person's *frame of reference* includes her overall set of thoughts, feelings, and behaviors which comprise her personality structure and provide her with a means of understanding her world and getting her needs met. In other words, it is the way in which she has organized her ego states to work together as a unit in order to best get along in the world. The purpose of the redefining is to either (1) distort the stimulus so that it fits into her frame of reference, or (2) disallow the stimulus altogether by blocking its intended meaning. Confronting a person's redefinitions will invite her to explore and hopefully disclose her frame of reference—which stimuli she considers significant, how they are significant, and how she interprets the world to herself so as to meet her needs while maintaining her life script. The more confrontive the therapy, the more likely it is that the client will redefine in order to maintain her frame of reference. Successful confrontation occurs when the client becomes aware of her redefinitions and frame of reference and becomes motivated to change them.

Life Positions

The very early experiences of the infant play a deciding role in the establishing of that person's *life position* (also called *basic position* or *existential position*.) Once it is decided upon, a person's life position influences how she thinks, feels, acts, and relates with others. There are four basic life positions:

□ Position #1. I'm OK—You're OK.

□ Position #2. I'm OK—You're not-OK.

□ Position #3. I'm not-OK—You're OK.

□ Position #4. I'm not-OK—You're not-OK.

When an infant enters the world, she is probably in the healthy *#1 position,* I'm OK—You're OK, and as long as the child's basic needs are met, she will remain in this position. Persons in this position are winners. They reflect an optimisitc and healthy outlook on life, freely relate with others, and assume a "get-on-with" stance in their dealings with other persons and the environment.

If a young person is severely neglected or abused, she may eventually decide that it is others, not herself, who are not-OK. When this happens she assumes *position #2,* I'm-OK—You're not-OK. This is essentially a defense against a more basic feeling of being not-OK herself. Commonly, one of her parents modeled the I'm OK—You're not-OK position for her. For example, many child abusers were themselves abused as children. This position is often called the *paranoid* position, since persons in this position are often extremely distrusting or blaming. They may deny personal difficulties, feel cheated, and react toward the world with anger or frustration. Their general stance in dealings with others is a "get-rid-of" position.

Position #3, I'm not-OK—You're OK, is referred to as the *depressive* position, and is the most frequent in our society. If her needs are not met, the young person usually will decide that it is her fault and that she is inferior, ugly, or inadequate. Depression, guilt, fear, and distrust of others often accompany this position. These people have great difficulties accepting compliments and generally take a "get-away-from" stance in their dealings with others and the environment.

Position #4, I'm not-OK—You're not-OK, is taken by persons who were miserable enough at some point in their lives to have decided that neither themselves nor anyone else are worthwhile or valuable. This is the "give-up" or *futility* position, and persons who have assumed this position often wind up in prisons, mental institutions, or morgues. These persons generally have a "get-nowhere-with" attitude in their dealings with other persons and the environment.

Although a person may assume a basic life position at any time, she ordinarily does so during the first three years of life as a response to how parent figures react to her initial expressions of needs and feelings. Thus the "decision" to move into a not-OK position may even be preverbal and outside the person's awareness. For example, a child may be physically mistreated or consistently yelled at by her parents whenever they are around her. When she is alone she may comfort herself by touching herself, rocking, or just enjoying the temporary safety from their rough handling. As the child decides to be alone and avoid other persons whom she experiences as scary and hurtful, she moves into an I'm OK—You're not-OK position.

Once a person has assumed a basic life position she tends to selectively perceive the world in ways which will maintain that position and confirm her original decision. As a result she will spend the greatest proportion of her time in that life position. Someone who has adopted position #2, #3, or #4 may have a few pleasant experiences in which she feels OK about herself and others, but she will eventually manage to end up back in her life position. Very few people change their basic position without the aid of psychotherapy. However, since it is based upon a decision, that decision, like any other decision, can be changed. Since all persons are in fact OK, all the not-OK positions can be thought of as unhealthy delusions. Helping people to reassume a healthy life position is one of the major goals of Transactional Analysis.

The OK Corral

The fact that a person has assumed a life position does not mean that she will always relate from that position. It merely means that she will spend most of her time in that position and will manipulate or interpret most of her experiences in such a way that her basic decision is eventually confirmed. On a minute-to-minute basis she may appear to move from one position to another, depending upon her mood, her goals, and the situation. It is important that these *feeling states* not be confused with changes in her life position, which remains constant over time. Although these feeling states do not reflect changes in her life position, they are nonetheless important aspects of her personality. A person's feeling state reflects the attitudes which she is assuming at a given time and determines the kinds of strokes which she will exchange. This attitude then determines how she will relate to others in a specific situation. For example, Clara may assume a superior I'm OK—You're not-OK position as she berates her husband during breakfast. Later that day she may feel and act humble or stupid (I'm not-OK—You're OK) with her boss when he confronts her on being late for work. Still later she may feel rejected and misunderstood (I'm not-OK—You're not-OK) when she fails to understand the teachings of her tennis coach. Sooner or later

FIGURE 6-3. THE OK CORRAL.

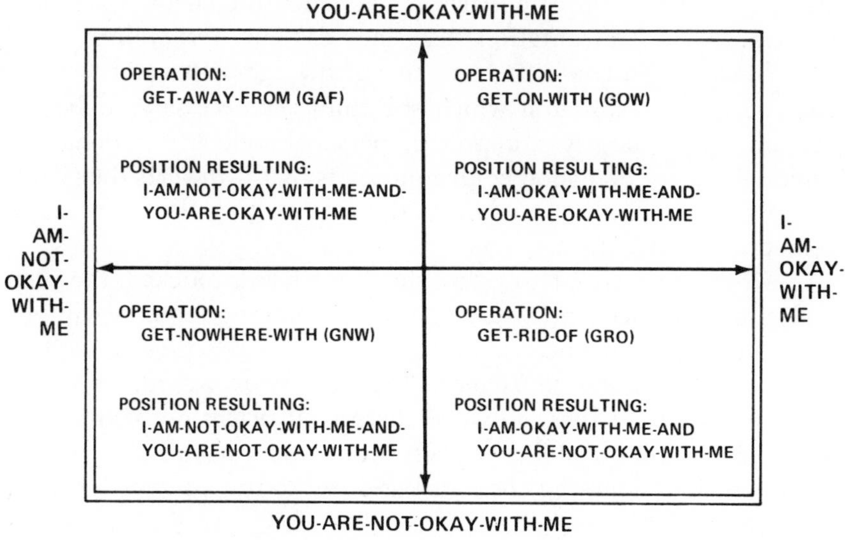

YOU-ARE-OKAY-WITH-ME

I-AM-NOT-OKAY-WITH-ME	OPERATION: GET-AWAY-FROM (GAF) POSITION RESULTING: I-AM-NOT-OKAY-WITH-ME-AND-YOU-ARE-OKAY-WITH-ME	OPERATION: GET-ON-WITH (GOW) POSITION RESULTING: I-AM-OKAY-WITH-ME-AND-YOU-ARE-OKAY-WITH-ME	**I-AM-OKAY-WITH-ME**
	OPERATION: GET-NOWHERE-WITH (GNW) POSITION RESULTING: I-AM-NOT-OKAY-WITH-ME-AND-YOU-ARE-NOT-OKAY-WITH-ME	OPERATION: GET-RID-OF (GRO) POSITION RESULTING: I-AM-OKAY-WITH-ME-AND YOU-ARE-NOT-OKAY-WITH-ME	

YOU-ARE-NOT-OKAY-WITH-ME

however, Clara will manage to end up in her life position, collecting her accompanying favorite payoff. Since Clara's life position is "I'm OK—You're not-OK," she eventually ends up angry and blames others for her miserable day.

The "OK Corral," shown in Figure 6–3 depicts the four life positions as well as the attitudinal stances which accompany each position [24]. It can also be used to describe the various feeling states which each person experiences at various times in her life.

Treatment Considerations

From the point of view of the material presented in this chapter, the purpose of therapy is to significantly alter the client's frame of reference, helping her give up her passive behaviors, redefining transactions, grandiosity, and other behaviors which indicate that she is discounting in an attempt to establish or maintain a symbiosis. If therapy is to be effective the therapist must successfully confront the client's discounting and invite her to find new and better ways to take care of herself.

A therapist (or group member) *confronts* the client's pathology whenever she refuses to support the latter's attempt to establish a symbiosis. A confrontation can be as mild as pleasantly crossing a transaction, refusing to answer a question when the client knows the answer, or even giving a positive stroke when the client is seeking a negative one. Confrontation also includes not responding at all. The therapist can confront from any of her ego states and to whatever degree of escalation which she thinks is necessary to be successful. This is largely a matter of personal style and training. The essential quality of a good confrontation is that it thwarts the client's attempt to establish a symbiosis, thereby inviting the client to do something different.

When the attempt to establish a symbiosis is blocked, the client will either (1) persist, (2) escalate by discounting more heavily, (3) leave and find someone else to be symbiotic with, or (4) accept the therapist's invitation to change. The first two possibilities can be confronted still further, provided there is sufficient protection available. The third possibility is best dealt with at the beginning of treatment by asking the client to agree not to run away or terminate treatment from a not-OK position. At the very least, ask her to agree to return to two more sessions following an announcement to stop treatment. Possibility 4, accepting an invitation to change, leads to further treatment contracts regarding how and what the client is discounting, how she wishes to change that, and how the therapist can assist her in redeciding and relearning new behaviors.

The purpose of therapy is to provide a new experience for the client which provides an opportunity for change. If the therapist is to be successful in inviting change in her clients she must avoid establishing symbiotic relationships with them. If she realizes that she has been relating symbiotically with a client, she should expose the symbiosis and avoid its reestablishment. If she is unable to do this because of her own needs, she should refer the client to a different therapist. Once again, it is important to distinguish between a *symbiosis* and *normal dependency.* In our opinion the former always supports pathology, whereas the latter may be healthy and therapeutic. The therapist can best avoid symbiotic relationships with her clients by making sure that all of her own ego states are taken care of, especially her Child, so that she is not using her clients to meet her own needs in or outside her awareness. Most therapists undergo personal therapy of their own to decrease the likelihood of this occurring.

It is also important that the therapist know when and how people establish symbiotic relationships so that she does not unwittingly support them. She pays keen attention to the various and sometimes subtle clues that this is occurring, and intervenes from appropriate ego states in order to confront it. This usually means that she responds from the same ego state as the one which the client is using to try to establish the symbiosis [40]. For example, if a client is attempting to establish a symbiosis from a Child position inviting the therapist into Parent, the therapist should usually respond with either (1) Adult statements which include her Child feelings, or (2) direct Child statements. Either of these confronts the establishment of the symbiosis. For example:

Client (from Child): "I just can't make it without you."

Therapist (Adult report of Child): "I hear what you're saying and I feel like you're wanting something from me now. Is that true?"

or

(Direct from Child): "Gee, I don't like it when you act like a Victim."

Conversely, if the client is coming on Parent inviting the therapist into Child, the therapist should usually respond with either: (1) Adult statements including Parent opinions, or (2) direct Parent statements. For example:

> Client (from Parent): "You should give me more strokes when I feel badly!"
>
> Therapist (Adult report of Parent): "I think you're giving me commands in order to avoid your feelings, and I think you should express them directly."
>
> *or*
>
> (Direct from Parent): "It's OK to be mad about it. Go ahead and tell me how you feel!"

The following series of questions provides a framework for assessing the level and frequency of symbiosis, passive behaviors, redefining transactions, and grandiosity. It is especially useful as a quick checklist when a client is not changing in therapy.

> Symbiosis: Does the client use all of her ego states to solve problems? Which ego states does she use? Which ego states are not used?
>
> Passive Behaviors: Is the client actively seeking a solution to her problems? Does she need to be pushed to get a response? Is she pleasing herself . . . or me? . . . or someone productively? Does she agitate instead of thinking? . . . instead of feeling? Does she incapacitate herself in any way . . . fainting, headaches, illness, etc.? Is she violent to self or others?
>
> Redefining Transactions: Does she answer questions? Does she change topics? Which issues does she avoid? Will she discuss feelings? . . . solve problems? Does she act confused? . . . question the meaning of questions?
>
> Grandiosity: How often does she use grandiose words and expressions? (such as "unbelievable," "overwhelming," "fantastic," "always," "all the time," "never," "can't," "can't stand it," "can't help it," "forever," superlatives—"best," "worst," "least," etc.)

Reparenting

Reparenting is a method developed by Jacqui Schiff that dramatically intervenes in symbiotic patterns [40]. It was first used with schizophrenic clients whose symbiotic tendencies and level of discounting are very high and require a major intervention to produce any far-reaching changes. The process of reparenting begins with a clear contract; then the client is allowed to regress and "redo" those areas of her childhood which were traumatic and led to destructive script decisions. With the therapist acting as a new parent, protection for the client is heightened and permissions for new and more normal behavior may be more effectively transmitted. The contract for reparenting may be for the major part of the treatment session or up to and including a lifetime. Such a contract should be entered into carefully, as strong transference and countertransference reactions tend to be brought out by the close, intense relationship that ordinarily ensues. Actually, with certain clients this treatment process may be quite difficult. It requires considerable time, effort, skill, and responsibility on the part of the therapist to effectively respond to and care for a very upset child who happens to be in the body of an adult. As a matter of fact, to enhance her effectiveness Schiff often took her clients into her home for a year or more and adopted them. The results are often worth the effort, however, and this technique is now being used effectively with nonschizophrenic clients as well.

7

Rackets and Games

"I'll trade you two 'gotchas' and an 'I'll be damned'
for one nervous breakdown."

We will discuss rackets and games in a single chapter, since they have a great deal in common. Both are learned systems that are substitute ways of getting strokes, and both require a discount of the self and/or another person. The Adapted Child substitutes these learned behaviors for spontaneous Free Child feelings or actions which were discounted or not permitted [21].

Rackets and games are somewhat different in that a game always involves an external process using ulterior transactions which lead to a racket feeling payoff [9]. A racket, however, may be either an internal or an external process which leads to or includes a racket feeling [4]. Also, one person may "run out" her racket without involving another person, whereas a game always involves transactions between two or more persons. As you read this chapter, keep in mind the following definitions:

□ *Racket:* An internal or external process (usually of complementary transactions) by which a person interprets or manipulates her environment as she justifies a not-OK, or discounted, position.
□ *Racket feeling:* A feeling which results from a discount.
□ *Game:* A series of duplex transactions which leads to a switch and a well-defined, predictable payoff which justifies a not-OK, or discounted, position.
□ *Stamp:* A feeling or a stroke which is collected to justify some later behavior.

Most people play a small number of favorite rackets and games with various persons and in varying intensities. Racketeers and game players intuitively seek out and find partners for complementary rackets and games, and it is in marriage and other close relationships that they are usually played the hardest. There are three degrees of intensity with which rackets and games are played.

☐ *First-degree rackets and games* are played in social circles with anyone willing to play and generally involve only a mild upset. A mild game of "Rapo" can be basically exciting and fun—a man and woman enjoy an evening of flirting with each other, he turns her down at the end of the night, and each feels slightly uncomfortable.

☐ *Second-degree rackets and games* occur when the players collect bigger racket feeling payoffs. The come-on in a "Rapo" game may even last for several days, until a blatant sexual advance is met with a strong rebuff. The "Rapo"-playing man leaves angry and justified that "all women are no good," while the woman, who is playing "Kick Me," feels hurt and rejected by another man.

☐ *Third-degree rackets and games* involve tissue damage, and the players may end up in the jail, hospital, or morgue—the man shoots the woman (or vice versa).

Rackets and games also vary in the length of time that passes while they are being played. A short version may take only a few seconds from start to finish, while longer versions may last weeks, months, or even years.

People racketeer and play games for the following reasons:

1. To structure time.
2. To acquire strokes—positive strokes may be acquired in the early moves of the game, and negative strokes always accompany the payoff. A "good" game is sometimes referred to as one in which the amount of pleasant strokes exchanged in the early phases of the game exceeds the amount of negative strokes which accompany the payoff. However, these games are not really "good," since they maintain a not-OK life position.
3. To maintain one's frame of reference.
4. To collect stamps.
5. To confirm parental injunctions and further the life script.
6. To maintain the person's life position by "proving" that self and others are not-OK.
7. To provide a high level of stroke exchange while blocking intimacy and maintaining distance.
8. To "make" people predictable.
9. (Game only) To keep others around when racket strokes are running out.

Rackets and Racket Feelings

Some families have rules against certain feelings while encouraging the expression of other feelings. For example, the Ironsides family may not allow its members to express sadness because they think it denotes weakness, but on the other hand think that it is all right to be angry. Children in this family may learn to suppress their sadness and to cover it with an angry facade. In contrast, the Grin family lives by the motto "Don't be angry, smile instead," and their children learn a quite different facade. By smiling, these people satisfy their Parent ego states by "being good children." These feelings are called *racket feelings* since they are an indirect way of getting strokes and avoiding the Free Child feeling.

Most Free Child feelings are indicators of wants, needs, or problems to be solved. A person's natural tendency is to have a feeling, express it, solve the problems which it represents, be done with it, and then go on to a new feeling. For example, if a person is sad, she will normally experience her sadness, express it, finish mourning her loss, and move on to something else. However, if she is sad, she will normally experience her sadness, express it, finish will substitute a racket feeling. This racket feeling may provide internal strokes, but since it will not easily satisfy or finish her original feeling, she will tend to continue indefinitely with the substitute feeling and/or behavior. A racket feeling can be any feeling which results from a discount, justifies someone's not-OK position, and does not successfully resolve the Free Child need or want. Racket feelings are Adapted Child–motivated, and are expressed from either the Adapted Child or the Parent ego state. When a person is expressing racket feelings she may be experienced by others as artificial, repetitive, stereotyped, or lacking in authenticity. However, a person who is experiencing a racket feeling is no less "real," "genuine," or "authentic" than a person who is experiencing a Free Child feeling. The difference between racket feelings and Free Child feelings lies in what the person does with her feelings. Free Child feelings are expressed directly and used as motivators to solve the problems and meet needs, while racket feelings are indirect expressions which involve a discount and maintain a not-OK position. The interested observer can diagnose whether or not the feeling is a racket feeling by asking the following two questions: (1) Which ego state is this person in as she expresses her feelings? (2) Is this feeling leading to an effective solution to the problem?

The psychopathology flow chart, originally created by Jonathon Weiss, illustrates the development of rackets and other substitute behaviors. A modified version of this chart appears in Figure 7-1. As the chart illustrates, the natural and healthy expressive process begins with a Free Child need, want, or feeling which is either met or not met. If it is met, the person remains in an OK life position and moves on to her next Free Child need. If it is not met, the child will react to her unmet needs with rage, fear, sadness, or some other escalated Free Child feeling. If the Free Child need is met at this point, the person may remain in an OK life position and recycle to her next Free Child need. If the need still is not met, she may or may not make a script decision. If a script decision is not made at this point, the person may substitute some behavior, but this will not become

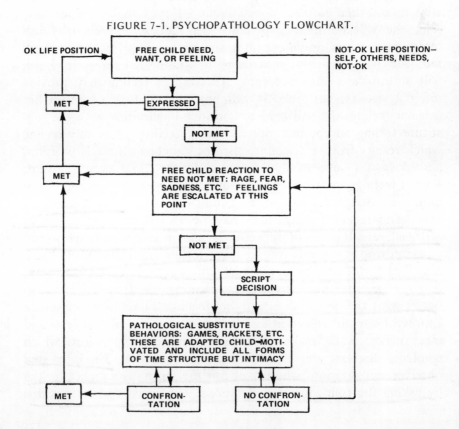

FIGURE 7-1. PSYCHOPATHOLOGY FLOWCHART.

ingrained as part of her life plan. If the person does make a script decision, she will also substitute pathological behaviors (rackets, games, etc.) to partially satisfy her unmet needs. These behaviors are Adapted Child–motivated and become a patterned response in future similar situations. Each time the substitute behavior is reinforced by the environment, the script decision is again reinforced. If the substitute behavior is confronted, the person may escalate or move to another form of the substitute behavior. However, if the confrontation is successful, the person may become aware of her original Free Child need and temporarily reassume an OK life position. If the substitute behavior is not confronted, the person is likely to continue with a series of substitute behaviors which only partially meet her underlying needs. These behaviors will maintain her not-OK life position, and she will continue to discount herself and others.

Racket feelings may be arrived at in several ways:

1. A racket feeling may be a substitute for a feeling which the person's Parent says is not-OK to express (recall the example given earlier in this section).

2. A racket feeling may be a substitute for the same Free Child feeling, but expressed in an adapted way. For example, a person who is very angry and has learned that it is not-OK to express anger in a straight way may deflect her anger as sarcasm, hostility, or cynicism.

3. A person may respond initially with a Free Child feeling to a given situation, but move into a racket feeling rather than solve the problem. For example, Jules tried to speak several times but was consistently interrupted by Ken. Jules became angry but was afraid to confront Ken's discounts by expressing his anger from his Free Child. He decided not to confront Ken, but instead used the situation to justify his belief that people are not-OK and held a grudge for several weeks without resolving the problem.

Racket Selection

Any feeling may become a racket feeling and be used to cover up a Free Child feeling: anger, sadness, confusion, fear, guilt, helpfulness, superiority, and so on. Most of us have a small number of favorite racket feelings, usually one in our Parent and one in our Child. We tend to switch from one to another depending upon the kinds of strokes we are seeking and the kinds of strokes that are available. To illustrate the wide range of racket feelings, consider how several persons may be experiencing different racket feelings while playing tennis. If seven such people were asked to report their feelings, each might report a different feeling, even though they are all in the same situation:

- □ Player #1 is angry at all the other players.
- □ Player #2 is disgusted about the condition of the courts.
- □ Player #3 is confused about how to keep score.
- □ Player #4 is afraid to play the net.
- □ Player #5 feels guilty about winning.
- □ Player #6 unnecessarily defers to her partner.
- □ Player #7 feels superior to all the other players.

When a person's feeling is a Free Child feeling rather than a racket feeling, that feeling will make sense for the situation and will motivate her to do something to finish the feeling—learn how to play better, petition to have the courts repaired, or take some other action which is reasonable for the situation. Free Child feelings lead to useful action and are finished when the problem is solved.

Racket feelings, on the other hand, are learned behaviors, and there are three ways to learn them:

1. When a parent *models* the racket feeling for the child—Mom shows her daughter that a woman should be quiet and sad by being quiet and sad herself.
2. By being *stroked* (reinforced or conditioned) into a person's behavior—a child may learn an anger racket because she gets most of her strokes when she is angry or obnoxious, especially if her parents do not pay attention to her when she is feeling good and doing well.
3. By a parent *telling* a child what to feel or think—an angry child learns a depression racket by being told, "You're not mad, you're just tired."

The Drama Triangle (Racket-Game Triangle)

An individual moves into a racket by discounting from any of the three major racket or game positions. She does this by either exaggerating or devaluating the worth of herself or the other person.

Persecutor (P): "I am better than you, you are inferior."

Rescuer (R): "I am OK only if I help others," or "I know more than you,
you are inadequate."

Victim (V): "I am helpless, you are better than me."

These racket and game positions can be demonstrated by using
Karpman's *drama triangle,* depicted in Figure 7-2. Some people
prefer to call this the *racket* or *game triangle* to emphasize the discounting aspects of the three positions.

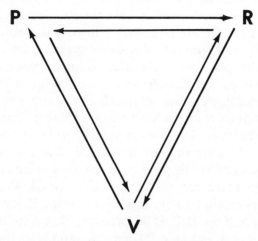

FIGURE 7-2. DRAMA TRIANGLE.

The *Rescuer* position is often used as the entry point into a
game. In these instances the Rescuer will eventually switch to Persecutor or Victim and collect a payoff. It is improbable that a
Rescuer consciously sets out to determine ways to prove that she or
others are not-OK. More likely she initiates her behaviors and transactions from a pseudo-nurturing Rescuing position, in which she is
attempting to stay OK and avoid being a Victim by "helping" others
to feel OK. Some Rescuers do experience others as inferior and will
report that they sense a need to take care of those poor souls. More
important than seeing others as inferior, however, is the Rescuer's
sense of *needing to be helpful.* This need to be helpful results from
an inner dialogue in which a person's Parent sends a message to her
Child, *"You're OK only if* you help [please, take care of, Rescue]
others." The Adapted Child responds with the decision "I'm OK
if . . ." and begins a Rescue transaction [34]. Rather than experi-

encing others as not-OK, she is usually so wrapped up in her own inner dialogue trying to please her internal Parent that she is not much concerned about other people at all; they merely provide the characters necessary for her to meet these conditions. Nonetheless, the Rescuer invites others to remain Victims and needs to keep Victims around in order to continue her racket or game.

The *Persecutor* position is assumed when a person makes another person not-OK. This is more blatant than the not-OKness invited by the Rescuer, and usually includes overt putdowns, sarcasm, and other negative strokes. Like the Rescuer, the Persecutor is trying to avoid the Victim position by inviting someone else into it, and the quantity and intensity of negative strokes is usually increased.

The *Victim* position is the most common payoff position in rackets and games. As already mentioned, most people take the Rescuer or Persecutor position in an attempt to either (1) temporarily avoid the Victim role, or (2) keep strokes flowing until they switch to Victim themselves. The Victim role is generally experienced as "I'm not-OK." Victims who are looking for Rescuers are usually in an I'm not-OK—You're OK position, while those who are looking for Persecutors are more apt to be in a I'm not-OK—You're not-OK position. An exception to the above statement is the Victim who experiences herself as OK while believing that not-OK people are Persecuting her—for example, "I am OK (and a Victim), but those others are not-OK and are picking on me (Persecutors)." These people are actually in an I'm OK—almost position.

Internal and External Rackets

A person may be in her racket, and therefore experience racket feelings, without interacting with others. For example:

Janes's Parent (to Jane's Child): "You goofed again."
Jane's Child: "I'll try harder."
Jane feels inadequate.

This is an internal complementary transaction between Jane's Parent (Persecutor) and her Child (Victim). If another person becomes involved, the transactions between the two are also complementary and may continue indefinitely.

Jane: "I goofed again."

John: "That's all right, you tried." Jane feels inadequate, and John feels helpful.

This is an external complementary transaction between John's Parent (Rescuer) and Jane's Child (Victim).

Rackets and the Drama Triangle

Each person has one or two favorite positions in the drama triangle and will seek out others who will exchange strokes from the complementary positions. If a Persecutor talks to a Persecutor they will likely pastime, but if the Persecutor finds a Victim they can exchange strokes of greater intensity.

Racketeers and game players usually spend much of their time in rackets, engaging in complementary transactions which stroke each others' not-OK positions. They may play games only when they believe that racket strokes are no longer forthcoming, that is, when other persons refuse to continue. At that time, they switch drama triangle positions and play games in order to keep the strokes coming in. Thus, a person may begin as a Victim, crying and moaning about how hard life is and how inadequate she is. So long as she has a sympathetic listener the transaction may continue indefinitely. However, when the listener tires of the Victim's Adapted Child whining and decides to leave, the original Victim might switch to Persecutor, castigating her listener for not really caring about her. By switching drama triangle positions she collects another stroke payoff and perhaps even influences her listener to stay [21].

Games

People are playing a game when they communicate on more than one level at the same time, and when the results of their transactions lead to racket feelings. A *psychological game* is defined by Berne as "an ongoing series of complementary ulterior transactions progressing to a well-defined predictable outcome" [4]. The predictable outcome, or payoff, consists of racket feelings for each player. Recall that a racket feeling is any feeling which results from a discount either of the self or someone else. These range from a Victim's sadness or confusion, to a Persecutor's anger or triumph, to a Rescuer's concern or pity. Games can be recognized by their repetitive occurrence, always beginning with a discount and always ending in racket feelings.

There are five different ways to understand and illustrate the dynamics of a game, and each of these methods is used to analyze a game from a different perspective. Some of these methods focus on fairly obvious behaviors which are readily apparent to the casual observer, while others focus on psychological maneuvers which are more difficult to recognize for anyone not trained to do so. With minor modifications, each of these methods can also be used to analyze rackets.

1. *Formal game analysis*—analyzes the various "advantages" of a game.
2. *Drama triangle*—focuses on racket and game positions.
3. *Transactional game diagram*—involves the diagnosis of ego states, including emphasis on psychological level communication.
4. *Symbiosis diagram*—focuses on identifying the preferred ego states of each player.
5. *Formula G*—describes the flow of a game, outlining the steps it will take once the initial moves are begun.

Formal Game Analysis

In *Games People Play*, Berne presents a formal analysis of games which includes the following six "advantages" [4]:

1. *Internal Psychological.* This refers to how the game contributes to internal psychic stability. For example, the person who plays "If It Weren't For You" (IWFY) maintains her belief that others control her destiny and that she is not responsible for her own unhappiness.
2. *External Psychological.* This refers to how or which anxiety-arousing situations or intimacies are being avoided. As the IWFY player blames others for her problems, she avoids having to deal with her own fears of inadequacy. For example, the housewife who complains that her husband will not allow her to take an outside job avoids her fears of not making it outside the home. She can also avoid intimacies with him by using their time together complaining, "If It Weren't For You."
3. *Internal Social.* This gives the characteristic phrase used in the game played with intimates—for example, "If It Weren't For You, I could work and fulfill myself."

4. *External Social.* This gives the key phrase used in the derivate game or pastime played in less intimate circles—for example, "If It Weren't For Him, I'd be happy."

5. *Biological.* This characterizes the kind of stroking which the game offers to the parties involved. IWFY provides two options—complaining from a whiny Child, or griping from a Persecuting Parent.

6. *Existential.* This states the life position from which the game is typically played. IWFY is commonly played from an I'm OK—You're not-OK position. ("I'm OK and could be happy if you weren't so oppressive.")

Drama Triangle Game Analysis

The drama triangle (Figure 7-2) depicts the racket and game positions which a person assumes when she is playing a game: Persecutor, Rescuer, or Victim. Any game player knows all the positions, and may switch from one side of the game to another. Most people, however, have a favorite position where they spend most of their time. A game switch occurs when either or both players initially assume or switch positions on the triangle, thereby providing a stroke payoff for each player in the game. The example in Figure 7-3 illustrates many of these switches, and shows how the final transaction of each game serves as the overt stimulus to the next game, which is played out when the next switch in drama triangle positions occurs.

A list of common games divided into groups determined by the three drama triangle positions is provided in Table 7-1. The first game in each column is the basic one for that position.

Transactional Game Analysis

The transactional diagram is used to analyze a game by diagraming the transactions, as in Figure 7-4. John and Jane are not comfortable relating straight, so with Adapted Child motivation and strategy they send dual or ulterior messages. While their Adult ego states are discussing a rendezvous (social message), Jane's Parent and John's Child are setting up a situation via covert or psychological messages which will lead to racket feelings. These psychological messages communicate which type of payoff each person is seeking, and signal others as to which games a person is available to play. These messages are called *sweatshirts,* since the observer's Little

A WIFE MAY BEGIN A CONVERSATION OSTEN-
SIBLY AS A HELPER (RESCUER) BY SAYING,
"WHAT'S TROUBLING YOU, DEAR?" TO HER
HUSBAND.

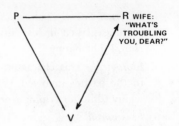

HOWEVER, WHEN HE TELLS HER THAT HE HAS
JUST LOST HIS JOB, SHE MAY SWITCH TO
PERSECUTOR AND PUT HIM DOWN FOR BEING
STUPID AND LAZY. HER GAME IS "NOW I'VE
GOT YOU, YOU SON OF A BITCH," WHILE
HIS GAME IS, "KICK ME."

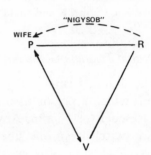

THE DRAMA TRIANGLE MAY ALSO BE USED TO
SHOW SWITCHES TO OTHER GAMES. TO
CONTINUE THE ABOVE EXAMPLE, IF THE
HUSBAND IS LOOKING VERY BADLY ("POOR
ME"), THE WIFE MAY SWITCH TO RESCUER
AND SAY, "I AM ONLY TRYING TO HELP YOU."

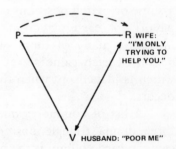

WHEN HE LOOKS BETTER, SHE MAY SWITCH
TO VICTIM AND SAY, "WHY DOES THIS AL-
WAYS HAPPEN TO ME?" THIS WILL LIKELY
INVITE HER HUSBAND TO RESCUE HER, AND
THE SWITCHES AND DRAMA CONTINUE.

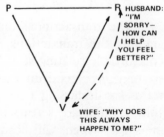

FIGURE 7-3. GAME SWITCHES IN THE DRAMA TRIANGLE.

TABLE 7-1. Games by Drama Triangle Positions

Persecutor	Rescuer	Victim
Now I've Got You, You Son Of a Bitch (NIGYSOB)	I'm Only Trying to Help You	Kick Me
		Why Does This Always
Blemish	What Would You Do With-	Happen to me?
Courtroom	out Me?	Stupid
If It Weren't for You	Cavalier	Wooden Leg
Rapo	Happy to Help	Harried
See What You Made Me Do	They'll Be Glad They Knew Me	Poor Me
Corner		Cops and Robbers
Schlemiel		Alcoholic, Addict
Why Don't You . . . Yes, But (WDYYB)		

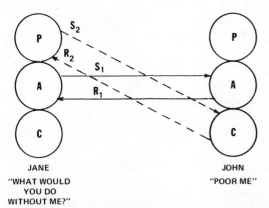

S$_1$ "I SUPPOSE YOU'LL NEED MY HELP AGAIN TONIGHT?"

R$_1$ "OH, YES . . . I CAN USE ALL THE HELP I CAN GET."

S$_2$ "WHAT WOULD YOU DO WITH- OUT ME?"

R$_2$ "POOR ME . . . I CAN'T MAKE IT ON MY OWN."

JANE
"WHAT WOULD YOU DO WITHOUT ME?"

JOHN
"POOR ME"

FIGURE 7-4. BERNE'S TRANSACTIONAL DIAGRAM OF A GAME. (S = STIMULUS; R = RESPONSE)

Professor "reads" the person's psychological communications as if they were embroidered on the front of her shirt [41]. In this example, Jane's sweatshirt reads, "I'm superior—You can't make it without me," while John's sweatshirt says, "Poor me—I'm helpless." In the early stages of the game, this communication is occurring outside of each player's awareness, so the game setup is not apparent to either person. The game is concluded when each person switches ego states, the psychological messages become overt, and racket feelings are experienced by each player. Jane is playing "What Would You Do Without Me?" while John is playing "Poor Me." The transactional diagram illustrates that if both partners are willing to play a game, then the game will continue. Robert Goulding has developed a streamlined version of the transactional game diagram, and lists five steps necessary for a game [26]. This is illustrated in Figure 7-5. Also, according to Goulding, a person can play a *single-handed game* by transacting with another person following the five necessary game steps. When the second person does not deliver the desired negative stroke, the game player merely uses her stroke filter to "counterfeit" the message, and takes her payoff anyway.

1. An ostensible stimulus, usually Adult to Adult (social stimulus)

2. A psychological stimulus (secret message) which includes a statement about the self (a con)

3. A response to the secret message which includes a statement about the second player (a gimmick)

4. A payoff of racket feelings

5. The game is played outside of Adult awareness (if the participant is aware of the psychological level of the communication, she is maneuvering the other, not playing a game)

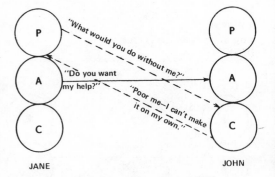

FIGURE 7-5. GOULDING'S TRANSACTIONAL DIAGRAM OF A GAME.

Symbiosis Diagram

Every game, as well as every racket, involves an attempt to establish or maintain a symbiotic relationship and begins with a discount. The symbiosis diagram indicates the preferred ego states and frame of reference sought by each game player [40].

In the example in Figure 7-6 Jane discounts her Child needs or feelings ("Let me take care of you" is stated verbally, while she suppresses that she is tired and wants to rest). John discounts his Adult's ability to solve problems and his Parent's guidance in taking care of himself when he says, "Yes, take care of me!" Jane is playing "What Would You Do Without Me?" while John is playing "Poor Me." Each individual is responding to a situation by ignoring the reality of what is happening and how each person feels, and by dealing exclusively from an internal frame of reference. Discounting can only occur when Adult thinking is avoided or Free Child needs or feelings are ignored.

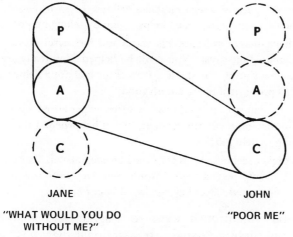

JANE   JOHN

"WHAT WOULD YOU DO   "POOR ME"
WITHOUT ME?"

FIGURE 7-6. SYMBIOSIS GAME DIAGRAM.

Formula G

Formula G, shown in Figure 7-7, was developed by Berne to describe the flow of a game [9] .

$$C + G = R \longrightarrow S \longrightarrow X \longrightarrow P$$

CON + GIMMICK = RESPONSE → SWITCH → CROSSUP → PAYOFF

FIGURE 7-7. FORMULA G. (THE UNDERLINING WAS ADDED BY THE AUTHORS TO INDICATE THAT THE LAST THREE EVENTS OFTEN OCCUR SIMULTANEOUSLY.)

Con: Jane's desire to play a game is initiated by a discount (her con). "Let me help you" is given verbally, while the nonverbal message is "You're inferior to me."

Gimmick: John also discounts, revealing that part of him is interested or hooked by the con—this is his gimmick—and responds to the secret message. His verbal response is "Help me." His nonverbal message is "You're right, I am inferior."

Response: A series of social messages follows, often ostensibly Adult-to-Adult—for example, Jane "helps" John by telling him what to do.

Switch: Each player switches ego states and the secret messages become apparent. Jane says, "You can't be helped. You really are inferior." She now shows that she is a Persecutor and not a helper. John says, "This proves it. I really am no good."

Crossup: A moment of confusion is often experienced by each player. John may momentarily wonder, "What happened? I thought she was trying to help me."

Payoff: Racket feelings are experienced by each player. Jane feels superior after having played "What Would You Do Without Me?" and John feels inadequate after having played "Poor Me."

All of the above-mentioned ways to diagram and analyze games (formal analysis, drama triangle, transactional diagrams, symbiosis diagram, formula G) are useful tools for the therapist, who may select among them depending on her clients' needs and goals.

Stamps

Rackets and games may be used to collect *stamps* [9]. Stamps are saved-up feelings or strokes which people use to justify some later behavior. These collected feelings or strokes are called stamps because they are saved up and cashed in for some prize, just like trading stamps. Stamps can be collected for upsets (brown stamps) as well as for good deeds (gold stamps).

Brown stamps may be accumulated whenever a person is in her racket feeling, such as when she receives a negative payoff at the end of a game. For example, a dominated woman refuses to express her anger when her husband criticizes her. Instead, she feels sorry for herself and collects brown stamps. After five years or so, she may "cash in her stamps" to justify beating him up, leaving the marriage, or some other behavior.

Gold stamps are collected when a person feels a need to justify her behavior by doing good things; for example, a hard-working doctor may work for many years before she finally justifies her need to take a short vacation. A collected stroke or recycled feeling is not a gold stamp if it is reused only for pleasure and not to justify any behavior or place a condition on OKness.

Some people save only one kind of stamp, but most people collect both kinds. For example, an alcoholic may justify a weekend binge by cashing in brown stamps—"I've had such a hard week, I need a drink"—or gold stamps—"I've done really well lately, let's celebrate and have a drink."

Stamps are collected by people who feel not-OK about their behavior. Some people cash in their stamps regularly for small prizes, like missing a day of work or failing a test. Others save them up for bigger prizes, such as divorce, suicide, homicide, or going crazy. Stamps are unnecessary and are used to keep a person from being autonomous by maintaining her racket and forwarding her script. The healthier the individual, the more she will directly and effectively express her feelings, wants, and needs as they occur, rather than collect stamps. One of the goals of TA treatment is to help the client give up her existing stamp collection and stop collecting them thereafter.

Summary and Example

When Free Child needs are not met, the young person learns to substitute Adapted Child behaviors which partially meet her needs. These substitute behaviors eventually become ingrained into the person's personality as part of her life script, or life plan, and function to maintain a *not-OK life position.* Let's take an example. Melanie grew up in a family where her natural pride and self-assertiveness were negatively stroked. Her family treated her as if she were inadequate and cute when she bumbled, pouted, and felt sorry for herself. As part of an overall *script,* Melanie decided upon a *life position* of "I'm not-OK—You're OK." She suppressed her Free Child feelings of self-satisfaction and assertion and developed *racket feelings* of inadequacy and depression. Her *racket* included all of the ways in which she interpreted the world so as to justify her frame of reference, including her not-OK life position. Sometimes she did this alone by pouting and feeling bad, or by telling herself that she was inadequate and would never amount to anything. At other times she found other persons who enjoyed putting her down, and engaged in complementary transactions with them while collecting negative strokes. Melanie also played *games* like "Kick Me" and "Stupid," in which she exchanged positive strokes with someone for a while before switching and taking her negative strokes and payoff. Occasionally, when she was communicating with someone who would not give her negative strokes, she played a *single-handed game* by interpreting the communication as one which reinforced her not-OK life position. Once Melanie had collected enough stamps, she cashed them in for the prize of quitting school at the age of sixteen, since she was convinced that she could not make it anyway.

Treatment Considerations

Rackets and games provide many strokes for some clients, and these life-long patterns of stroking are not easily given up. Initial confrontations of rackets or games often frustrate the client, who may escalate her patterns by crying louder or by threatening to leave or to hurt herself. When a client initiates a game in a treatment setting, the therapist has four choices of response: ignore the game, expose the game, play the game with the client, or play an alternate game [18]. It is best to ignore the game when you think that more can be gained by allowing it to continue. You can either confront it later when you believe it is more obvious, or you can sidestep the issue by inviting the client into OKness with an alternative technique. Exposing the game is a good idea if you think the client is ready to accept the information and respond appropriately. Therapists should avoid hooking into rackets and games with clients whenever possible. Unfortunately, even excellent therapists sometimes get hooked and find themselves in a racket or game with a client. When this occurs the therapist may still interfere with the game effectively by refusing to accept the payoff. This has the effect of spoiling the client's anticipated ending, and models new behavior which the client may decide to use for herself as a way to avoid payoffs. If the therapist "plays along" by providing the expected responses while remaining aware of the game, she is not in a game herself, but is carrying out an *operation* or *maneuver* as part of a plan to eventually expose the game. She may choose to do this when a client believes that no better alternative is possible, and is not yet ready to accept a confrontation. Some people suggest that therapists play alternate games with clients to teach them less harmful ways of getting strokes. We do not like this idea and encourage our clients to give up rackets and games and get-on-with getting strokes in straight ways.

If a therapist decides to intervene in a game, she may do so in a number of ways. Each of them serves to cross the transaction, either simply as in the first example, or in more complex ways, as in examples 2 through 8:

1. Cross the immediate transaction by sending a response either from or to a different ego state than expected.

2. Bring the psychological message to the client's awareness. The therapist provides the client with Adult information concerning the game she is playing, how it fits into her script, and how the moves of the game progress to a racket-feeling payoff. The therapist does this by allowing a game to be played out or described, asking the player how she feels after receiving the payoff, and then diagraming the moves. This is often facilitated by escalating the game in order to highlight the moves and payoffs, with double chairing, psychodrama, and encounter methods being especially potent techniques. With this information the client, especially if she is playing a first-degree game, can learn to avoid the payoff and can change how she relates to others.

3. Expose the intended payoff before it is reached.

4. Confront the discount(s). Then encourage the client to think and feel about what she is discounting; as she becomes aware of what is really going on within her, she may choose to stop discounting and go directly after what she wants, rather than continuing her usual game or racket.

5. Refuse the payoff (therapist).

6. Give the client permission to refuse the payoff.

7. Ask the client to take a posture incompatible with the discount and/or payoff (usually an Adult or Free Child position).

8. Help the client to satisfy her underlying Free Child need or want. The therapist exposes and works directly with the client's racket feelings, pointing out their repetitive nature and the client's responsibility for feeling the way she does. The goal is to help the client discover and express her suppressed Free Child want, need, or feeling. Once the client has attended to her Free Child needs and feelings, she will likely give up her racket feelings and the game moves which accompany them.

8

Scripts

"Momma said there'd be days liked this."

A *script* is a personal life plan which each individual forms by a series of *decisions* early in her life in reaction to her interpretation of the important things happening in her world. The most important decisions determine a person's basic character structure and are usually decided upon by age two or three. Most of the rest occur by about age six, while others may be made through adolescence and some even later.

It may be a surprise to some that such important decisions are made so early, but more and more observers are reporting how infants clearly react to and affect what is going on around them. For example, the four-week-old infant connects his mother's face with her voice and begins to differentiate between mother, father, and strangers; by six weeks he is smiling spontaneously, as well as in response to others; by twelve weeks he knows whether his mother is talking to him or to someone else, and as young as three months he recognizes when objects are unfamiliar, and may be fearful of strangers. Also during these early months the child quickly learns methods to influence his mother's behavior. He cries to be fed or changed or to be picked up and played with. If mother looks away, he starts fussing and whimpering until mother again pays attention to him. If she does not respond for three minutes, he tends to withdraw and turn away from her with a hopeless expression. By nine to twelve months he has some sense of who he is as a separate person; by fifteen to eighteen months his self-identity is fairly well established; and by the age of two both boys and girls have developed a concept of their own gender. So from the beginning infants gather data and make crucial decisions regarding their existence and basic personality patterns [48]. In general, the earlier a decision is made, the more far-reaching its influence and the more difficult it is to undo its effects.

Decision-Making Factors

Young children are essentially in a one-down position, living with people who have much more power than they. From this vulnerable status, a child reacts with feelings (C_1) to messages that come his way and then, after psyching out the situation as best he can (A_1), responds with decisions (A_1). When these decisions are reinforced by the message givers, they become patterned responses (P_1) and may eventually become integrated into an overall life script.

Vulnerability Quotient

The child makes script decisions because she thinks she must. Her primary needs are for strokes and caring, but her spontaneous behavior inevitably runs into some opposition. She experiences the power of negative strokes and senses that she is in a situation where she is extremely vulnerable to outside influences. Her Little Professor proceeds with safety as her primary concern, putting pleasure and other gratifications secondary. There are five factors which increase her vulnerability, which in turn increases the likelihood of her making decisions to constrict her Free Child. The interplay of these five factors results in a *vulnerability quotient,* which plays a determining role in each person's script decision [52].

1. **Lack of power.** A child is comparatively very small, like someone living in a land of giants. If you have forgotten what this is like, lie down on the floor in a room where other people are walking about. Notice how far away the ceiling is and how big the people are and how you must crane your neck to see them. Will they notice you? Will they step on you?

These other people are not only bigger, but they are also stronger. We can roughly determine the difference in physical strength between two people by taking the fourth power of the ratio of their heights. The height of the average adult female is twice that of the average two-year-old, and she is therefore sixteen times as strong ($2^4 = 16$)! Sibling comparisons are also enlightening. The average four-year-old, who unfortunately is often angry with a younger sibling, is three times as strong as a one-year-old toddler.

These differences in power are tremendous. Imagine wrestling or boxing with someone three times as strong as you, let alone sixteen times! Then keep in mind that the older person is also much better coordinated. Clearly, it would not take much anger from a parent or a sibling to terrify a small child. If the child is very frightened, she will likely respond with a major decision.

2. **Inability to handle stress.** The younger the child, the less anxiety she can handle at a given time. This, too, has a physiological basis. The infant's nervous system is like an electrical circuit which is not wired to handle large inputs—a strong charge from a major stress will cause a fuse to blow. When this occurs, the infant experiences unmanageable affect and essentially "blacks out." She will have no specific memory for the event, later recalling only an amorphous feeling of panic. Yet big people, with their huge power differentials, may get very frustrated, expect too much, and not notice or care that the infant is overwhelmed.

3. **Immature thinking capacity.** The young child is not yet able to think well. Her Adult ego state is rudimentary, so she is incapable of logical thinking. Her primary mechanism for responding to her environment is her Little Professor, which is intuitive and concrete, uses magical thinking, and has a poor sense of time. When she decides to carry out some Adapted Child behavior in order to get along, she does not think about how long she will keep behaving that way. It does not occur to her that she might continue doing it forever. Her Little Professor decisions are likely to be overgeneralized, global, exaggerated, and appropriate only for the short run, not the long run.

4. **Lack of information.** Children get most of their information from their parents until they are three, four, or five years old. As far as a child is concerned, her parents "own" the data about the world. Even worse, they may not even inform her about what is happening. For example, they may not reveal that mom is mad at dad, so the child may believe that mommy is mad at her, or that she has caused the problem between mommy and daddy. While she is thinking, "Why is mommy so mad?" mom and dad are thinking, "She wouldn't understand, so we won't upset her by talking about it."

Also, parents define reality for the child. If her parents say, "You are bad," the youngster has little choice but to believe it. It seems to her that her parents know everything, and her Adult ego state is not yet capable of figuring out what is really true. Thus, her early decisions are based on inadequate information. She especially does not know that it might be OK to behave differently later. Shirley, a preorgasmic client, recalled making such a decision. Her parents did not mean for her *never* to touch her genitals when they said, "Don't touch yourself there!" but she thought that they meant just that and decided it was always bad.

5. **Lack of options.** Most kids have no choice about where they live. If a child does not like her home or her parents, she has no option to leave and find a better place. She is stuck, and must figure out how to get along as best she can.

Message Styles

There are three different ways of sending messages to influence another person—modeling, attributing, and suggesting. Any of these messages, either singly or in combination, may lead to a script decision. Each may be sent *verbally* or *nonverbally,* and each may be sent *directly* or *indirectly.* Whether a message is sent verbally, nonverbally, or directly is fairly easy to determine, but the indirect mode may be difficult to distinguish since an indirect message is ostensibly aimed at one person but is received by a different person. Actually, the way any message is sent does not always correspond with how it is received. For one thing, people tend to use their stroke filters to distort messages which disagree with previous beliefs. For another, a small child's Little Professor may misinterpret what is meant. Messages that are both nonverbal and indirect are especially easy to misconstrue.

MODELING
Parents, older siblings, respected peers, therapists, and other important persons *model* how to be a person to anyone watching or listening. An interested observer may believe that the behavior is possible for him, take it in as a message, and respond to it with a decision. Here are some examples of messages received via modeling, along with the decisions made in response to them:

> A respected member of a group talks of his desire for closeness. A short while later another group member reveals his desire to be held, which he previously had thought was shameful. (Verbal, direct)

> The governor of a state says he will not let the races mix in his schools. People in other states stiffen in their resistance to integration. (Verbal, indirect)

> Father works hard and is self-sacrificing. Son decides that this is how to be a father. (Nonverbal, direct)

> A therapist tells his clients that it is OK to be open about how

they feel while appearing to keep a tight rein on his own emotions. Clients decide to open up very slowly about how they feel. (As usual, nonverbal cues take precedence over verbal cues.) (Nonverbal, direct)

Many television show heroes are unfeeling and violent while apparently being powerful and popular. A teenage viewer decides that this is the way to be a man. (Nonverbal, indirect)

Modeling is extremely important, since it is a process by which we transmit potential script messages all the time. Children, clients, and others watch and listen to persons whom they consider important and, depending on their needs and vulnerability, may take in script messages even when it is not intended that they do so. On the other hand, modeling provides an easy way to give positive messages. The more script-free we become, the more we serve as useful models.

ATTRIBUTING

An *attribution* is a message about what or who a person is. These messages are very powerful since they *define* or *label* the recipient in some way—irritating, slow, cute, and so on—and so the vulnerable child experiences little room for choice. A negative attribution has one or more discounts built right into the statement:

"You are bad!"
Decision: "No matter what I do, I'm bad. I must be evil inside." (Verbal, direct)

"You're just like your father!"
Decision: "Just like dad, I'm not trustworthy and no woman will ever want to get close to me and I'll die by the time I'm thirty-five from drinking too much." (Verbal, direct)

Father says to several of his adult friends, "People who speak poorly aren't worth much."
Son, overhearing, decides, "I'm not worth much." (Verbal, indirect)

Parents give daughter a baseball glove for her birthday.
Decision: "I'm a person who can use my body and play baseball and other sports." (Nonverbal, direct)

Father physically beats his child.

Decision: "I'm bad!" (Nonverbal, direct)

Man gets furious with his wife on many occasions and each time sullenly withdraws.

Daughter decides: "Women are bad. I will devote my life to making men happy." (Nonverbal, indirect)

Negative attributions invite a person to be a little crazy, since his own logical thinking is virtually precluded while someone else's reality is imposed on him. If a child is told *to be* like his father, he can try—and he knows what he is reacting to. But if he is told he *is* like his father, he does not know what to do about it. He must assume that some mysterious process over which he has no control is occurring inside his body.

Attributing is also an efficient way to get across a lot of information at once. In the second example above, "You're just like your father!" transmits a great deal of information, yet is sufficiently vague that the child may interpret it in unexpected ways. Mother might be referring only to her son's tendency to argue, yet he may decide all the things mentioned in the example and run away from home—just the way father had suddenly left some years before.

Some parents act as if their children should all be different from one another and use attributions as a way of dividing up potential characteristics in the family [47]. One child is regarded as smart, another as pretty, and another as creative. The first is also lazy, the second stupid, and the third homely. No matter what their actual potentials, each is limited to a few characteristics which do not overlap with those of another sibling.

Attributing is probably the most common as well as the most insidious and perhaps most powerful way that script messages are given. In light of this, keep in mind that the most powerful positive attribution is I'm OK—You're OK. Model it and say it!

SUGGESTING

Sometimes parents will directly or indirectly indicate to their children what they want or expect:

"Don't bother me!"

Decision: "I'll come around only when I've been especially good." (Verbal, direct)

"Keep at it and don't come back until you've done it right."
Decision: "I'll try real hard to be perfect." (Verbal, direct)

Mother, crying, says, "Nobody cares about me!"
Decision: "Even though I don't like it, I'll stay around and take care of mother. Other people's needs come before mine." (Verbal, indirect)

Father tells mother in a location where son can overhear, "He sure is cute when he's looking for trouble."
Decision: "I'm going to investigate carefully what trouble is. It sounds interesting." (Verbal, indirect)

When her daughter noisily bursts into the house, mother quickly and emphatically motions to be quiet.
Decision: "I'll be good [quiet] , especially when daddy is home because fathers are important and should not be bothered." (Nonverbal, direct)

Mother looks angrily at her husband but says nothing.
Son's decision: "I'll be very careful not to upset mother—she is dangerous and fragile." (Nonverbal, indirect)

The line between the three message styles is not always an easy one to draw, as you may have noticed in some of the preceding examples. Also, several message styles are sometimes sent simultaneously. Note the following example:

Father stomps into the house after work, slams the door, and sits down to dinner with an angry look.

Son's decision: "Men work hard, resent it, and can't share their feelings with anyone." (Modeling)

Daughter's decision: "Men must work hard and I will devote myself to helping them feel better." (Responding to father's indirect suggestion)

Wife's decision: "I'm no good." (Responding to husband's indirect attribution transmitted by his anger and silence)

Message Power

The power of a message to induce a script decision varies considerably. One important variable is the *type of stroke* used to deliver the message. As mentioned previously, negative strokes can be delivered more powerfully than positive strokes, so negative messages are more likely to be responded to than positive ones. The *timing* of a message is also very important. The same message given to a one-year-old and to a three-year-old may have very different results. For example, "Go away!" said to a one-year-old may be experienced as a Don't Exist message, whereas a three-year-old may understand it as a Don't Be Close message and make a different decision. A message given concurrently with a major life event also tends to have added power. Especially potent messages may be delivered at the time of parents getting a divorce, or at the arrival of a new sibling, or when one of the parents has died.

The power of a message may also be increased by the *frequency* with which it is given. If a parent gives the same message repeatedly over a short period of time, the child may believe that he has little choice but to accept it. The power of a script message is further increased if the messages from mother and father are very similar. Unfortunately, this is common, since two people who decide to live together usually have mutually complementary scripts and reinforce each other's messages. However, sometimes parents give opposite messages. If this occurs at about the same time, one may help to counteract the effect of the other. In such instances, each message will likely be responded to in some way, and the child will integrate his responses into a single decision.

> Mother says, "Leave me alone!" (The child hears the direct suggestion and interprets the attribution as "You are a nuisance.") Father then says, "Don't pay attention to mother, she is upset. Come over here with me."
>
> *Decision possibility 1:* "I'm a nuisance and I'll be real careful with mother, but father doesn't notice, so I'll spend more time with him."
>
> *Decision possibility 2:* "Father is right. Mom is always upset. I won't pay attention to women because they're always crabby. I'll just stay close to dad—men are easier to get along with."
>
> *Decision possibility 3:* "Father's right, there is nothing wrong with me. I'll come back to mother another time."

The *source* of a message is still another important variable. One parent is often experienced as more powerful, in which case his or her message will be more fully accepted. In the first few years of life, the primary caretaker will be experienced as more important. Since fulfillment of needs and personal safety are of primary concern to the infant, he will pay more attention to the person who spends the most time with him, and especially to the one who has basic responsibility for him. In most cultures, this is the mother, and so we regularly find that the most important and powerfully placed messages come from her. Father is also an important message giver, as are older siblings and any other people who live in the home. Cultural messages may also be very influential. These are mostly passed on by the parents and others in the home, but the fact that the child experiences them wherever he goes adds immensely to their potency. Cultural messages, like parental messages, are transmitted by all three methods—modeling, attributing, and suggesting—and leave most people little choice but to respond. However, if the individual has accepted parental messages that he is different from others, he may respond by deviating from the cultural norm. Usually he will then arrange to join another cultural group who have been labeled as misfits—for example, the "hippies" of the 1960s or the "freaks" of the 1970s.

The *emotional intensity* with which the message is given is yet another factor. The ego state which sends the message makes a substantial difference in its power. The Child can send messages with much more power than either the Parent or Adult, even when they are saying the same thing. Also, consider the difference in impact on a child between a firmly spoken "Go away, don't you see I'm busy" and the same words yelled angrily and accompanied by a hard slap. The latter is more likely to be responded to with a script decision.

Message Types

There are two basic types of messages which influence the formation of the script—*permissions* and *script messages.* Permissions (in some instances called *allowers*) are positive, or growth-inducing, and script messages are negative, or growth-inhibiting. Positive strokes given unconditionally are permissions and function to promote a relaxation or an avoidance of script decisions. Since permissions do not limit the child in any way, they allow for the natural growth of the individual, providing him with freedom of choice and the possibility of achieving his potential. However, some positive strokes are conditional and may lead to adaptations in getting along with people. The result is a limitation or scripting, albeit benign. We do not mean to imply that parents and others should not give conditional strokes. Conditional strokes are a vital way of letting others know what we like and want. When given with no more pressure than necessary, they are unlikely to provoke a script decision or limit future choices and responses.

Script messages from the Child are called *injunctions,* and those from the Parent are called *drivers.* (The latter have also been called *counterscript messages, counterinjunctions,* and *subscript messages.*) All of these lead to constriction of the Free Child, fewer choices, and destructive script decisions. Sometimes the injunction and the driver will say the same thing, in which case their source is differentiated by using the four methods for diagnosing ego states. More often they will be different statements implying the same message, since the Parent tends to give its messages in a more socially acceptable fashion than does the Child. For example:

> Parent: "Children should be seen and not heard."
> Child: "Damn you! You're always in my way!"

Traditionally, injunctions are discussed as if they were all phrased negatively and began with "Don't . . ." (Don't Make It, Don't Be Close, etc.), while drivers are discussed as if they were all phrased positively or began with an implicit "Do . . ." or "Be . . ." (Try Hard, Be Perfect, Please Me, etc.). In a therapeutic situation, though, it is best to use the client's language—"I wish you had never been born," "Do your best!" "Stay away," and so on.

Permissions and Injunctions

The permissions-injunctions are discussed below in chronological order corresponding with the major developmental issues each of us encounters in the process of growing up [1, 25].

First Permission and Injunction

The first and most vital permission needed for the infant is *to exist* and belong in the world. From the moment of psychological birth, the infant receives messages from her parents about whether or not they want her around. If she is ignored, kept at a distance, or handled perfunctorily, stiffly, or with rage, she will not experience much permission to live. Instead, she will receive a *Don't Exist* or *Don't Be* injunction.

Everyone alive has received some assistance or permission to live. Sometimes in very bad parenting situations, only the Adult of the caretaking person has been helpful. Figure 8-1 illustrates a typical set of messages received by a person who made only a tentative decision to live. The usual decision in these instances is for the infant's Free Child to go into hiding and for her Adapted Child to conform by not crying and asking for very little. If this person lives long enough to become a parent, she may pass on similar messages to her children.

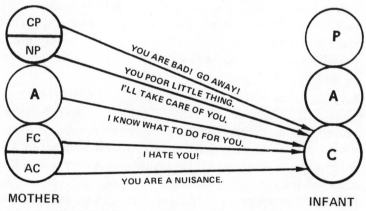

FIGURE 8-1. TYPICAL MESSAGES OF A SUICIDAL CLIENT.

When an individual is lovingly touched and cared for, she will not only decide to live and belong, but will also acquire a sense of *optimism* and *trust.* This basic trust is a trust in the self—not necessarily in other people. A person who automatically trusts someone else is discounting her own thinking. A person who trusts herself thinks about whom she will trust and under what circumstances she will trust them. She does not seek out reasons to distrust others, but rather is open to trust others or not, depending upon her experience with them. With effective parenting, the child learns that it is all right to be alive with needs, wants, and feelings, even when encountering someone who disagrees with her. Additional positive experiences from the other permissions will add to her sense of trust, her basic feeling of optimism, and her belief that she is OK.

The most important time to receive the basic permission to live is during the first year or so of life. If this permission is not received during this time, negative experiences tend to be interpreted by the Little Professor as a Don't Exist injunction. Don't Exist messages also can be given at later ages, often by more explicit means, such as saying, "Go away!" or "I wish you'd never been born!"

A person without a firm commitment to live has a poor foundation for dealing with other problems, since a foundation that tilts affects all later development. This holds true for changes later in life, too, so it is crucial for a client to resolve any reservation about his existence before seriously challenging other issues.

> Ron, a client with a Don't Exist injunction, was consciously working on getting close to other people, but at the same time, outside of his awareness, was using any poor experiences in relating to prove that he should not exist. He would not allow himself to get close to anyone until he decided that it was OK for him to live.

> Xavier's Mom and Dad were uncomfortable whenever people expressed feelings, so whenever Xavier expressed feelings they treated him as if they wished he were not around. It seemed to Xavier that they wished he were dead, so he took in a Don't Exist message. Later in his life, whenever Xavier would become aware of having strong feelings, he would get very frightened and would often go on to become preoccupied with thoughts of suicide. Before he could become comfortable with his feelings, he first had to decide to live no matter what.

Overt suicidal behavior is only one sign that a person may have a Don't Exist injunction. Others indicators include significant depression and its psychosomatic equivalents, family history of suicide or equivalent (dying from overwork, overeating, alcoholism, etc.), not changing in therapy even though apparently useful things are occurring, and getting worse in therapy.

Don't Exist is the primary injunction in all classification systems. Some people categorize secondary injunctions into three groupings: Don't Think, Don't Feel, and Don't Act (Do) [15]. Once the individual has decided to be alive, no matter how tentatively, then all other decisions will have to do with thinking, feeling, and behaving—either singly or in some combination. Notice how these three issues keep reappearing in the following developmental discussion of injunctions-permissions and later on with the allowers-drivers.

Second Permission and Injunction

Another permission especially needed at the time of birth and during the first year of life is *to have and be aware of sensations.* The infant needs permission to accept all of his basic bodily sensations, such as hunger, pain, temperature, and touch. The five sensory systems (visual, auditory, kinesthetic, gustatory, and olfactory) are all available to the infant. However, he may decide not to use parts of these systems if his parents are upset by them and impart a *Don't Feel Sensations* injunction.

For example, Adam's mother was very annoyed by his infant cries of hunger and disliked feeding him. He not only learned to stop crying, but also to suppress his awareness of hunger. Adam learned to eat only when other people were eating, or because he knew that people ate at certain times of the day. He also learned to eat frequently to keep his stomach full (mother fed him when he was not hungry) and to eat when he was scared (mother did not know how to solve a problem except by feeding herself or Adam).

Other people learn not to see certain things. They avoid looking or if they do look, they do not register internally what they are seeing. They may even make their eyes myopic so they can hardly see anything. Still others learn not to have a good awareness of hot, cold, or pain, and subsequently suffer frequent injuries.

Third Permission and Injunction

Permission *to feel emotions* is needed from the beginning of life and throughout the formative years. The newborn infant is able to express satisfaction, dissatisfaction, and severe distress. When the parents react to these displays as valuable pieces of information, they give important permission to the infant to continue expressing directly how he feels. He needs this responsiveness, particularly during his first year, in order to develop his ability to clearly express basic emotions such as happiness, fear, sadness, and anger. If his parents discount his feelings, they will transmit a *Don't Feel* injunction. As a result, the child may decide to discount his feelings and/or substitute other feelings which his parents approve of. These substitute feelings are called *racket feelings* and are discussed in more detail in the section on rackets.

Fourth Permission and Injunction

From the beginning of the Little Professor's development, the individual needs permission *to think.* It is important for the parents to respond reasonably, clearly, and with interest to the reactions, ideas, creativity, curiosity, and enthusiasms of the child. By doing so, they encourage her to develop her thinking to its full potential. Discounting by ignoring, misinforming, making fun of, or finding flaws in what she says or wonders about will give her the injunction *Don't Think.*

Fifth Permission and Injunction

Throughout childhood, permission is needed *to be emotionally and physically close to others.* If a parent is remote, fearful of touch, too busy, or uncaring, the injunction *Don't Be Close* is given. Another common way for this injunction to be transmitted is for a parent to die or to leave, in which case the child may decide, "I'll never get close to a man/woman. It hurts too much when they leave/die." In addition to these potent nonverbal messages, children often receive Don't Be Close injunctions as specific verbal directions:

"Stay away from men! They only want one thing!"

"Don't touch me!"

"Love 'em and leave 'em. Don't get tied down."

"You can't trust anyone." (This injunction also contains a Don't Think message.)

A child derives her sense of belonging from various aspects of her permissions to exist and to be close. These permissions are essential for her to conclude that there is a place for her and that she is secure.

Sixth Permission and Injunction

All people need acceptance of their physical attributes, which means permission *to be who you are*. This needs to be reconfirmed with every change in the child's physical development. All basic physical qualities need approval—a person's sex, sexual characteristics (size of shoulders, hips, genitals, breasts), race, body size, other structural characteristics (shape of nose, mouth, ears), color or shade of skin, eyes, hair, and so on.

Usually by the age of two and definitely by three, every child knows her sex and whether it is approved of by her family. Often a female is given the injunction *Don't Be You* because in her family or culture boys are seen as more valuable. On the other hand, a boy may be told by his mother that he is the wrong sex because she wanted a girl, or because he reminds her of someone that she hated, like her ex-husband or her father. Individuals whose structural characteristics were unacceptable in their family often have confusion rackets. In general, people with this injunction feel inadequate, as if there were something fundamentally wrong with them.

Don't Be You is the most common injunction used by one culture or group against another culture or group. Males have used this for centuries against females, and the same has been true of white versus black, French versus German, Gentiles versus Jews, and so on. Sometimes it will take a specific form within a family:

"Why don't you look like your father's side of the family, fair and handsome?"

"You don't look like me. Where did you come from?!"

"Your blood is mixed—black and white. You're no good!"

Seventh Permission and Injunction

The growing, rapidly changing child needs permission *to be your age*, with all the normal characteristics that accompany each age. Unfortunately, parents often become upset with small children and wish their child would grow up quickly and stop being a bother or a financial burden (because the parents want to be taken care of) and transmit that to their child. These are *Don't Be a Child* injunctions, since they instruct the child not to be needy or dependent, but to "hurry and grow up!"

Conversely, some parents do not want their children to grow up. These parents never feel better than when someone needs them, and they encourage their kids to be little, cuddly, and playful. They may especially prefer children who are clearly dependent, and lose interest when the kids become two or three. Some parents are bothered when their children pass puberty and become obviously sexual beings. Others do not get distressed until the children grow up and leave home. All these parents give *Don't Grow Up* injunctions. Some children get both messages—Don't Be a Child and Don't Grow Up. They are not supposed to be little and need to be taken care of, nor are they supposed to get too big and leave home. They are supposed to stay home and take care of mom and dad.

Not only do people need permission to be their age, but they also need permission to use all their previous ages without being called "childish." It is fun to have the option to be eight again and play at a party, or to be two and cuddle with someone. They are all good ages.

Eighth Permission and Injunction

Permission *to succeed* may be transmitted in many ways: approval and interest in the child's achievements, support for doing things, lack of jealousy, and behavior that models accomplishing things in a satisfying and enjoyable way. A child who receives these permissions experiences an inner sense of competency. She is a person who sets achievable goals, does whatever is necessary to meet those goals, and feels good about herself in the process. She experiences life as meaningful. It is hard for someone to feel successful when experiencing significant problems from any of the other injunctions. Some people try to make up for dissatisfactions in other areas by striving for worldly success. As a matter of fact, many people who appear very successful actually feel dissatisfied because no matter what they accomplish it does not meet the correct need. Making a million dollars or becoming a movie star does not make up for a lack of closeness or an inner sense of inadequacy.

There are several ways in which people receive *Don't Make It* injunctions. A parent may resent her child outdoing her and feel jealous because her child's success makes it clear how she, herself, has failed. Siblings, too, are often very competitive with each other. Parents sometimes add to this by telling younger siblings not to outdo the oldest, or the older siblings may be taught to feel guilty about doing better than the younger ones:

> "If it's good enough for me, it's good enough for you."
>
> "Just who do you think you are?"
>
> "Always share what you have with your little brother. It's not fair for one to have more than another."

Many Don't Make It messages are global, and their effect is to stop the individual from succeeding in most ways. Others apply only to specific areas, such as work or sex. Others just limit success, not stop it. Focusing on flaws while ignoring successes will slow most people down:

> "Be happy with what you've got."
>
> "You're just not the kind of person to be lucky in love."
>
> "You're stupid!" (said just after a mistake)
>
> "You're good for work, but that's about all."

Allowers and Drivers

The negative restrictive messages that come from the Parent of the parents are called *drivers*. Kahler has divided these script directives into five groupings: Be Perfect, Hurry Up, Try Hard, Please Me, and Be Strong [34]. Drivers contain socially acceptable moral judgments and value statements that parents would be willing to tell their friends and relatives about, making them especially inviting to accept. For example, Adam's parents wanted him to hurry. It even seemed like "Hurry Up" was their favorite phrase. When Adam did hurry, they were pleased and they all shared a momentary good feeling. Adam assumed an "I'm OK if" position at those times: "I'm OK if I'm hurrying." However, since neither Adam nor anyone else can respond to these kinds of messages all the time, they are not helpful in the long run. Underneath the social facade, they are restrictive in nature and lead to script decisions, just as the injunctions do.

Parents begin transmitting drivers soon after their children are born. Sometimes even before imparting an injunction, they let their children know from their Parent ego states what is expected and what will be tolerated. This process sometimes begins immediately following the birth of a child. If the infant is a boy, the parents and others may say, "My, what a *strong* boy!" If the infant is a girl, they may say, "My, what a *beautiful* girl!" These attributions are just the beginning of a long-term process, and are followed up with consistent reinforcing actions that set an early tone for the development of corresponding behaviors in the child. The boy is being taught to emphasize toughness, ignore his feelings, and ultimately become unresponsive to others—decisions in response to a Be Strong driver. The girl is learning that looking good to others is a way to get strokes—a decision in response to a Be Perfect or Please Me driver.

Anytime an injunction is transmitted, the child has a problem. However, he also may have experienced some drivers that offer a "You're OK if" solution. For example, when mother's Child says "Don't Be," her offspring ordinarily does not die. Instead the youngster remembers mother's message to Be Perfect, so she is very still and quiet and attempts to be the perfect child. The parents are pleased by this and as a result, the dictate of the injunction is temporarily avoided. Parents give off both messages at more or less the same time, reinforce both, and the child makes decisions in response to both. The result is one overall script with two major subdivisions— the *primary script* in response to the injunctions, and the *subscript* in response to the drivers. These are like two sides of the same coin— they may look a little different, but they are intimately interrelated and are in basic agreement. The chart below shows examples of the two types of messages from Wayne's parents and his respective decisions. Notice the correlations between script and subscript.

		Message	*Decision*
1.	Script	"Stay away from me!"	"I won't be close with people."
	Subscript	"Don't let them push you around."	"I will be strong." (Used as a way of avoiding people)
2.	Script	"You're terrible!"	"I'll kill myself if things go badly."
	Subscript	"You're all right when you don't cause problems."	"I'll try to be perfect." (Since being perfect is impossible, Wayne continually gathers proof that he is no good. This in turn results in recurrent depressions and increases the likelihood of suicide.)

On some level of awareness, Wayne blends these decisions together to form an overall life script: "I'll try to be perfect even though I know I'm not good enough to please people, and if all else fails, I'll just kill myself. Nobody really cares anyway."

As the child grows up, the injunctions and drivers are usually repeated verbally, and almost all clients remember hearing both. Since the drivers are more socially acceptable, they are usually repeated more often and are easier to recall. As a matter of fact, parents tend to update them at each age, passing on new versions which are merely modifications of the primary messages.

Any of the five drivers can come from either the negative Nurturing or negative Controlling Parent of the parents.

> Negative Nurturing Parent: "Now, sweetheart, if you will just work at it some more and get it done just right, then it will be OK." (Be Perfect)
>
> Negative Controlling Parent: "You'd better do it right! Or else I'll . . ." (Be Perfect)

The *allowers* are specific permissions that either prevent or relieve the effect of a driver. They may come from any of the parent's ego states. Drivers and allowers will be discussed in more detail in the section on miniscript.

Script Diagnosis

A person's overall script includes many components. To facilitate an accurate and complete diagnosis, Steiner organized these components into a *script checklist* [41]. He includes:

- ☐ Life course (besides an outline of the person's life, this also takes into account the decision, position, mythical hero, and physiological component or body manifestation of the script)
- ☐ Subscript (or, as Steiner put it, counterscript)
- ☐ Parental injunction
- ☐ Program
- ☐ Favorite game
- ☐ Pastime
- ☐ Payoffs involved in stamps, racket, and sweatshirt
- ☐ The ending, tragic or otherwise

The following sections provide methods for organizing and eliciting the information necessary to complete this checklist.

Decision Scale

People make script decisions in response to a combination of inputs, some positive and some negative. Even when both mom and dad experience closeness as scary, mom may be a little more comfortable with it than dad, and she will pass on to their daughter, Kim, a little more permission for closeness (or a little less injunction against it) than will Dad. Even if Kim lives alone with Dad, she is unlikely to receive an injunction totally against closeness. After all, Dad has lived for quite a few years, and during that time has done at least some relating which was not all bad. At worst he is likely to pass on to Kim a mixed message on the subject. Because there is always a mixture of messages, the script decisions made in response to these messages are rarely totally extreme. Kim is not likely to decide to completely avoid or to completely feel free to do a particular thing. After receiving a Don't Be Close message, she will not decide to avoid everyone under all circumstances. Instead, she will decide to do something short of that, letting herself associate with people, but with some limitations.

A *decision scale* may be used to illustrate the decisions a person makes in response to the mixture of positive and negative messages he receives about each issue that he faces [49]. The decision scale employs a 0-10 range, with zero meaning complete acceptance of the permission and 10 meaning complete acceptance of the script message. Thus, the higher the number, the more severe the problem. The client does the ratings with the help of the therapist and other group members. As in doing egograms, the Little Professor is the best judge of the proper number to choose.

Each permission-injunction or allower-driver pair (for example, OK To Be Close–Don't Be Close) may be scored in two different ways:

1. On an individual decision scale showing the responses to each important parent figure plus the composite decision made about the issue
2. On a composite decision scale showing all the composite decisions

As an example, the decision scale in Figure 8-2 depicts Napoleon's decisions about his personal physical characteristics made in response to their acceptance by each of his family members. Note that arrows mark the decisions and that separate decisions are listed for each message giver, plus another for his composite decision. Napoleon uses his composite decision when responding to most people. However, when someone is especially reminiscent of an old family member, Napoleon tends to respond with the specific decision he made in reaction to that particular person. Napoleon once said to this therapist, "My dad and brother sure gave me a hard time about being short. I'm still sensitive about it. Luckily, mom and sis thought I was OK. Women seem to accept me all right, but I sure feel self-conscious around the fellas!"

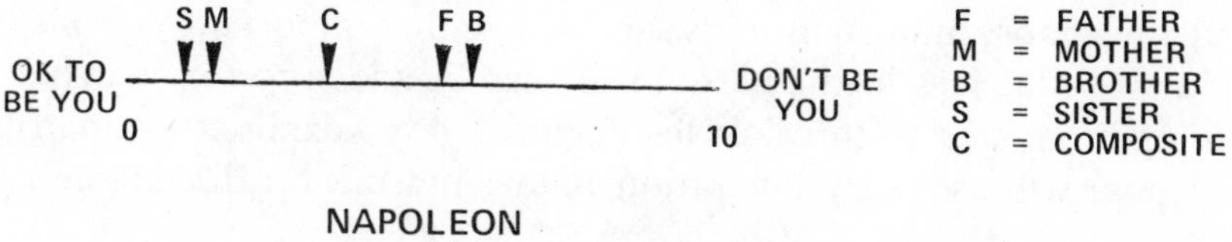

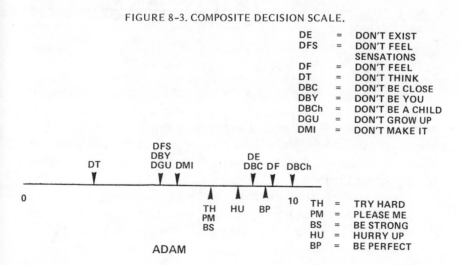

NAPOLEON

FIGURE 8-2. PHYSICAL ATTRIBUTE ACCEPTANCE DECISION SCALE.

To get an overall picture and organize treatment strategies it is useful to do a single decision scale showing all of a person's composite decisions, with permissions-injunctions above the line and allowers-drivers below. Figure 8-3 shows Adam's. Adam's composite

FIGURE 8-3. COMPOSITE DECISION SCALE.

decision scale shows that being a child, having feelings, and being close are definitely against the rules, with suicide a serious possibility. Thinking is his major strength, and trying to be perfect is his attempted route to salvation. Our treatment plan for Adam would utilize his good thinking and emphasize protection and permission for existence and imperfections. We would also encourage Adam to explore and express his Free Child desires and feelings, starting with sadness and fear, the two that are least enjoined for him.

Script Matrix

The *script matrix* is a diagram showing a person with his two parents and their most important messages [43] . Other important persons or cultural influences in the person's life can be added to this matrix by adding more sets of three circles. Figure 8-4 is Adam's script matrix, which we will use as an illustration and framework for discussion.

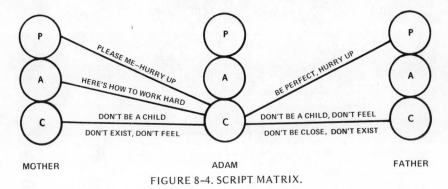

MOTHER   ADAM   FATHER

FIGURE 8-4. SCRIPT MATRIX.

Note that all the messages are directed to Adam's Child. This occurs for two reasons: (1) the script matrix, like a transactional diagram, shows the messages going to where the parents intend for them to go, and it is Adam's Child that his parents want to influence; and (2) Adam makes, directs, and carries out all of his script decisions from his Child [50] .

The messages from mother's Adult comprise the *program* or *pattern,* since they provide information used to carry out the script. Usually, but not always, these messages come from the parent of the same sex. Since the script messages are all recorded in Adam's Parent, he may at any time experience them again and continue to be influenced by them. No matter what his actual age, if Adam's Child is in doubt about proper behavior, he can quickly and simply replay his Parent tapes. The script matrix in Figure 8-4 illustrates the external sources of the messages, while Figure 8-5 depicts Adam's later internal replaying of these same messages.

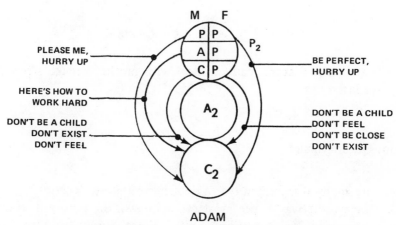

FIGURE 8-5. EXPERIENCING INTERNALIZED SCRIPT MESSAGES.

Permission Matrix

One problem with the script matrix is that it accentuates the negative, showing only the script messages and not the permissions. The decision scale, on the other hand, depicts both permissions and script messages, affording the opportunity to observe a person's strengths as well as the relative severity of her particular problems. This is important because in therapy we wish to build on strengths while changing the disabilities. A *permission matrix* may also be drawn to depict a person's permissions [55]. Adam's is again presented in Figure 8-6. Each of the permissions mentioned is a starting point for change. For example, the permission to exist which Adam received from his father's Parent can be used to clarify for Adam that part of his father knew that Adam was OK and did want him to live. When father's Child said, "Don't Exist," it was because father was upset and not because Adam was defective. When Adam becomes aware of this, it may be easier for him to make a firmer commitment

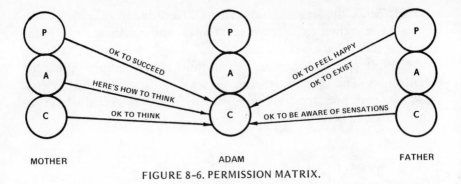

MOTHER   ADAM   FATHER

FIGURE 8-6. PERMISSION MATRIX.

to live and to feel more ready to deal with mother's much stronger negative influence.

Script Questionnaire

There are many different ways to determine a person's script. Sometimes the easiest way is the most efficient—ask the person directly. Script questions can be very unsubtle, "What is your life plan," or a bit more refined, "What do you expect will happen to you if things keep going the way they are?" or "What do you expect will happen if things go badly?" Jumping ahead into the future sometimes sharpens the focus. "If you keep doing what you are doing, what will be happening to you five, ten, or twenty years from now? If things go well? or badly?" A different angle may help. "What does your mother think will happen to you?" "What does she think when she is in a bad mood?" The same questions also should be asked about father and any other important people, since their messages, too, are part of the script decisions. One question that often elicits a great deal of information is "Describe your mother" or "Describe your father." The characteristics of mom and dad which are foremost in the person's mind are likely to be important—some because he thinks he should be like them but is not good enough, others because he is that way, and perhaps still others because he's trying very hard *not* to be that way. Other good questions are:

☐ What is your earliest memory?
☐ What is the family story about your birth?

- How were you named?
- What was/is your nickname?
- How old will you be when you die?
- What will it say on your tombstone?
- Describe yourself.
- What was mother's/father's main advice to you?
- What did your mother/father want you to be?
- What do you like most/least about yourself?
- Did you ever feel that something might be wrong with you? If so, what?
- Describe the bad feeling that you have had most often in your life.
- What was your favorite childhood story/fairy tale/book/hero/TV program?
- What would "heaven on earth" be for you?
- What do you wish your mother/father had done differently?
- If by magic you could change anything about yourself just by wishing, what would you wish for?
- What do you want most out of life?
- What famous person would you most want to be like?

Script Signs

Script signs are any behaviors which indicate that a person is in his script [9].

A *script signal* is a characteristic gesture, posture, or any kind of movement that occurs when a person is in script behavior. It may range from tightness in the face, to a "nervous" movement of the hand, to a smile of self-deprecation.

Vocal signals, an important subgroup, are listed below with examples of each type:

- *Breathing Sounds:* A sigh that says, "I'm hopeless, what's the use"
- *Accent:* Implying, "I'm better than you"
- *Tone of Voice:* A scolding Parent
- *Words:* "I need a *little* help"; "I *think* I *might* like to *try* that."
- *Types of Laughter:* Gallows laugh; "I always goof up, ha! ha!"; or the scripty laugh of the Child about to pull a fast one—"Hee! Hee! Hee!"

The *physiological component* is any physical symptom which signals scripty behavior—headaches, backaches, colitis, upper respiratory infections, and so on. A useful rule noted by Berne is to "think sphincter." The sphincters of the body are often used to express emotional reactions, resulting in such symptoms as diarrhea, vomiting, drinking, pursed lips, and so on.

Another script sign is represented by the favorite songs, TV programs, stories, fairy tales, or real life *heroes* that serve as sources for the elaboration of many people's scripts. Once a person's self-concept is formed, he may choose to model himself after someone to fill out the details of his script. Tyrone's hero was Albert Schweitzer, so he was trying very hard to become an expert in several fields at once. With the awareness that he was trying to match his hero's accomplishments, Tyrone decided to settle for less and still enjoy his hero. Rose, whose favorite story was Sleeping Beauty, kept finding fault with her husband while waiting for her real prince to come along and bring her happiness. Whatever her favorite story, or whoever her favorite person, have the client describe her hero and tell her tale in her own way. She will likely tell you either what she is doing or what she wants to be doing!

Fantasy

A person's fantasies can reveal a great deal about her script. What do the person's daydreams reveal? A great leader? A lover? A martyr? Successful in the beginning but a failure at the end? Or triumphant only after a great struggle? What happens when she makes up an unstructured story? Or a more structured one, like a story about what happens to a tree in each of the four seasons [46]. These are best told in the first person: "I am a tree . . . it is spring and I am growing," and so on.

In addition to the above, the *gestalt double-chair method,* which is basically an enactment in fantasy of a thought or body statement, may be used to investigate the script—especially when focusing the work by having the client state the issue in as direct a way as possible. (Paula plays Mother when she switches chairs.)

Paula: "I want to die and I don't know why."

Therapist: "Imagine your mother in that chair and tell her you want to die."

Paula: "Mom, I want to die."

Mother: "Now don't you talk that way. Let's go shopping."

Paula: "Mom! I want to die!"

Mother: "Now stop your fussing. You will upset your father!"

Paula: "Mom! Don't you care about me?"

Mother: "You be quiet now! Go out and play."

Paula: "If you don't care about me, I may as well not even be alive!" (sobbing)

The Don't Bother Me message that Paula had known about was really a Don't Exist injunction, as indicated by Mom's level of discounting. The empty chair confrontation with mother clarified this for her.

Use your Little Professor's intuition and creativity with these and other methods for analyzing scripts. Figuring out scripts can be fun—like doing a jigsaw puzzle; the pieces are all available to be found and put together in a harmonious way.

Script Types

Scripts can be compared to plays in that they may be comedies, tragedies, or merely dull. If the script resembles a comedy, it is called a *winner's script*. The strokes are mostly positive, some of them highly charged, and the ending is pleasant. A winner gets where he intends to go and has a good time doing it. Actually, the more a person is a winner, the less she has a script, and the more she does what she wants if it makes sense to her.

If a script resembles a tragedy, it is a *loser's script*. The strokes are mostly negative and the ending or payoff is unpleasant. Berne thought the payoffs could "be reduced to four alternatives: be a loner, be a bum, go crazy, or drop dead" [9]. This definition makes it sound more inevitable and extreme than we believe is usually the case. Many people do not get to the full expression of their payoff unless things go very badly. A script is usually more like an outline and a direction, and the worst possible outcome occurs only if enough stamps are collected to justify it. There are first-, second-, and third-degree loser's scripts, first-degree being the least severe and third-degree the most severe. The more severe scripts are sometimes called *hamartic* [44], referring to the hero of a Greek drama who commits a tragic error. In TA it means a person walking blindly, following a prescribed path to his own destruction. People with hamartic scripts often come to the attention of lawyers, therapists, or jailors.

Sometimes a script resembles a play which is not particularly interesting, or which is just plain dull. If so, it is called a *banal* or *nonwinning script*. The strokes are more or less evenly distributed between positive and negative and generally not highly charged. Nonwinners are "at-leasters" who say, "At least, I have this much to be thankful for." They "work very hard, not in the hope of winning but just to stay even" [6]. These people prefer to play it safe and avoid exciting situations, such as Child-to-Child intimacy. A typical male banal script is a hard-working businessman who primarily uses his Adult and does not get much closeness or fun for his Child. A typical female banal script is a hard-working housewife who functions a great deal in her Nurturing Parent with her children and her husband. She does not use her Adult except to run the house, nor does she meet her Child's needs for closeness.

Steiner and Wyckoff have written extensively on the subject of banal scripts for men and women [44, 61]. Some of the names they suggest for typical banal sex role scripts give their flavor:

MEN	WOMEN
Big Daddy	Mother Hubbard
Man in Front of the Woman	Plastic Woman
Playboy	The Woman Behind The Man
Jock	Poor Little Me
Intellectual	Creeping Beauty
Woman Hater	Nurse

Banal scripting is a subject of increasing interest and investigation, since the great majority of the population plods along with nonwinning scripts.

Life Determinants

There are three elements that determine the actual events of a person's life [53]:

1. *Script.* This refers to all the various aspects of the script that have been discussed.

2. *Effort.* This is the energy the person puts into taking charge of his life and altering his script. This energy comes from the drive for self-actualization, or life force, that everyone has. The person's script may influence the amount of such energy considerably, but it is always more than zero since no one is totally script-bound. Everyone has at least some freedom of choice and some opportunity to change because of his own efforts.

3. *Coincidence.* A great many things happen to people over which they have no control. Bad weather may ruin the crops, and good weather may bring a fortune. No matter how much energy a person expends, it may not be enough to overcome bad luck. Besides trouble with Mother Nature, it is always possible to bump unexpectedly into someone else's hamartic script. Likewise, even a very gamey person does not set up all his troubles. Some Victims are really victims. Lady Luck may allow some people with third-degree scripts to have lots of good luck and do very well—a rich uncle dies leaving Joe Loser a million dollars; Sally Shrewd marries him for his money, and they live relatively happily ever after. Everything is not determined by the person's script or by his efforts, although for most people those are major determinants. Chance is the joker in the deck, and should not be forgotten. Script, effort, and coincidence are always interacting in varying amounts. It is useful to be aware of all three when attempting to understand a person's life.

9

Redecisions

"Cats aren't the only ones with nine lives!"

What was once decided can be redecided [25]! Like the original decisions, redecisions are made by the Child. But why would anyone risk changing her script? First, she must be motivated, and second, she must feel safe enough [52].

Change Factors

Motivation

Motivation for change has three sources:

1. a *dissatisfaction* with present behavior, thinking, or feelings
2. a *desire* to behave, think, or feel a new way
3. a quest for *strokes*

The Free Child freely expresses her dislikes and wants, but in many people one or both of these have been discounted and suppressed. Understanding the four levels of discounting of problems is particularly important in marshaling these aspects of motivation. Take the example of a person who is unassertive:

1. *Existence of problem.* Does she know that being unassertive is a problem? . . . that it is all right to be unhappy about that and want to be assertive?
2. *Significance.* Does she know that it is a significant problem? . . . that it is not a small issue and is worthy of serious attention?

3. *Solvability.* Does she know that it is solvable? . . . that nonassertiveness is a learned behavior and that people can learn new behavior, including becoming assertive?

4. *Personal ability.* Does she know that she, herself, can do something about this? . . . that she is not bad or defective and so can change?

A therapy group can be especially helpful in confronting these four types of discounts. Invariably, some group member will actively demonstrate that being unassertive is a significant and solvable problem, showing the client that it is all right and possible for her to change.

The third motivational factor, the desire to obtain strokes, is extremely important. Strokes from the therapist or the group for different behavior is a powerful motivator. If strokes are available, the client may do almost anything (maybe even change!) to keep them coming. So when the therapist strokes with the desired outcome clearly in mind he will foster the achievement of the contract. Or perhaps it is as the experimental rat said, "Have I got that human trained! Every time I press that lever he gives me all the food I want."

Safety

The client is not vulnerable to the therapist in the same way as the child was to the parent, and these differences in the factors making up the vulnerability quotient cause a variety of effects on the process of changing.

POWER

The client is no longer so comparatively small, so the real childhood fear of physical assault is much less. There are definite differences in status and self-esteem, however, so the client may fantasize being smaller than the therapist, as though he were a child again. On the other hand, some clients may be bigger than the therapist and afraid of hurting her. More importantly, the client's Child may not view the therapist as being big enough to protect him from the giants of his past. The actual and fantasized sizes of both client and therapist are still pertinent—especially in therapies where people touch each other and physical activity is part of the treatment process. A stated rule against people getting hurt physically may increase each person's sense of safety and encourage risking new behaviors.

ABILITY TO HANDLE STRESS

Older children and adults have a nervous system which can satisfactorily deal with considerable amounts of affect and information—certainly much more than they could as infants. Many methods of therapy take advantage of this and have their clients reexperience old scenes and old feelings as part of a process toward making a redecision.

> During a double-chair confrontation with his mother, unassertive Milquetoast reexperienced an old scene that took place when he was three years old. With a great deal of fear and sadness Milquetoast recalled Mom spanking him for "talking back to her," and then remembered deciding not to ever again tell anyone how he really feels. With encouragement from the therapist Milquetoast told his mother he was angry with her. Soon he was yelling at her loudly, and went on to decide that he is not going to hold back his feelings anymore.

Reexperiencing such scenes may still be traumatic for the client's Child, and he should never be pushed to do more than he is willing to do. It is far better to stroke a client for what he has accomplished, even if he has not resolved the impasse. This invites him to feel good about himself, trust the therapist, and return to complete the work when he is ready.

It is also possible to avoid uncomfortable amounts of affect by dissociating the old feelings from the scene while working it through. In other words, the client is instructed to see and hear an old scene while *not* reexperiencing the feelings that accompanied it.

> Lou was abandoned by his father when he was four years old. As an adult he still became quite upset at any hint that someone would leave him. He believed that if he could feel better about father leaving he could handle present situations much better. However, he did not feel able to face the old feelings of abandonment. We asked Lou to visualize himself as a four-year-old standing a few feet in front of himself. He practiced for a few minutes seeing himself as a child, while simultaneously being aware of his present-day feelings where he sat. He reported that it was like watching a movie. When Lou was ready, he began to recreate a scene in which he watched and heard his

reactions as a four-year-old child when father abandoned him. He saw and heard young Lou go through the traumatic episode, while feeling OK in the present. After father was gone, grown-up Lou invited little Lou to come over and be held. Big Lou did this without getting upset. Instead he was very nurturing and supportive. Lou decided to remember the useful things that his Child knows, and to take care of himself.

MATURE THINKING CAPACITY

After the age of twelve or so, clients have a fully developed Adult, and so can think much better than when they were making their original script decisions. This is a crucial change, and is a major factor in decreasing clients' feelings of vulnerability. Many people change their behavior from new information alone. School, books, television, and movies help a great number of people change who never come to a therapist. Many first-degree scripts are changed this way, and many second-degree and third-degree scripts are significantly influenced by information to the Adult that the Child cannot refute. In these latter instances, once the client's Adult is decontaminated it is possible to find out what his Child needs in order for him to feel safe enough to change.

Even though the client now has this very useful Adult, he also retains his P_1 script decisions, his A_1 monitoring of what is happening, and his C_1 feelings. To be maximally effective, the therapist's interventions must appeal to the client's Child. If not, the client's Child may feel scared, discounted, or abandoned, and react as if given a Don't Be a Child injunction or a Be Strong driver. Protection and permissions for the Child are very important, and verbal interventions should be clear, concise, and simple enough so that a young child can understand them. Nonverbal interventions may be especially effective, since children are particularly aware of those aspects of communication—a timely reassuring touch on the arm may convey an unusually potent permission.

AVAILABILITY OF INFORMATION

The therapist, unlike the parent, does not control all the information. However, if the therapist uses a treatment model with a complex system of beliefs and language, it may appear that she has all the answers and the client may feel "one-down." Ordinarily, this does not happen with TA, since clients are encouraged to read and to understand TA concepts. However, a therapist who plays "Blemish" can operate in any system.

Clients should be allowed to get whatever information they need. Reading books like this one often helps. All the concepts and methods mentioned throughout this book are OK for clients to know about and understand. It is also all right for therapists to give specific information. Not only does the client then have the information, but he also has had the pleasant experience of a parent figure being spontaneously free with information. Some clients who had parents or previous therapists who were close-mouthed do not know this is possible, and think they must accomplish everything on their own. They sound very well trained when they say, "I sure would like to know if I'm making any sense, but I know you can't tell me." It is often all right to tell them!

The client has the option to leave and doesn't have to stay with a particular therapist. Knowing that he is able to leave may be an important factor for him to feel safe enough to stay. Many people have decided, "I'll never let myself be that vulnerable again!" and feel a need to be sure that they are in charge. Treatment contracts facilitate this, since the client is an active participant in the formation of treatment plans and the therapy is not just imposed on him. However, some clients may behave like stuck children and stay in treatment even though it is not going well. Then it may be helpful for the therapist to suggest to the client that he find someone who will be better for him. This does not imply that the therapist or client is incompetent or not-OK, only that a different combination of client and therapist might work better.

Table 9-1 summarizes the various factors which influence script decisions, as well as the complementary factors which promote growth and change.

Since the client is now less vulnerable, he is not likely to respond to messages from the therapist as readily as he did to messages from his parents. Furthermore, he still must overcome many years of relative powerlessness. This is why therapy sometimes takes a long time, especially for clients with second- or third-degree scripts. The client is scared to trust the therapist, or to accept the information and concern of this new person who is acting differently from

TABLE 9-1. Decision Factors

	Script Factors	Change Factors
Motivation:	Discomfort with Free Child behaviors	Discomfort with Adapted Child behaviors
	Desire to survive	Desire to meet Free Child needs
	Need for strokes	Need for strokes
Safety:	Lack of power	Power
	Inability to handle stress	Ability to handle stress
	Immature thinking capacity	Mature thinking capacity
	Lack of information	Availability of information
	Lack of options	Options

his parents. Before the therapist can be listened to safely, the client must believe that the combination of his own power plus the therapist's input is at least as powerful and believable as the original source of his script messages. Sometimes this takes a while!

Impasses

Resistance points in therapy usually reflect internal conflicts called *impasses* [27]. A *first-degree impasse* is a conflict between Child needs or wants and a driver message from the Parent in her Parent—for example, between "I want to get close" and "Be strong—don't trust anyone." A *second-degree impasse* occurs when the person experiences a conflict between her Child needs or wants and an injunction from the Child in her Parent—for example, between "I want to get close" and "Don't bother me—get away!" A *third-degree impasse* represents a conflict between two parts of her Child—for example, between "I want to get close" and "I'm afraid to reach out to people, so I won't."

Many impasses can be understood either by a structural or a functional analysis. For example, the third-degree impasse mentioned above can be described as a functional one between the Free Child and Adapted Child, or as a structural one between C_1 and P_1. However, there are many other instances where only a structural analysis of the Child will clarify just who the warring parties are. An

example of this is an impasse between two parts of the Adapted
Child, in this case between P_1 and A_1:

> Oliver's Little Professor wants to try out a new, more effective
> way of adapting to the people in his life. (This is Adapted Child
> because he is still thinking in terms of how to get along with
> others as his primary goal and he is not giving up his self-
> discounting). However, his familiar P_1 patterns resist changing.

Another common impasse which may only be understood structurally
is one which occurs between two different ages of the Child:

> Norman's two-year-old Child has been suppressed (home was
> very frightening when he was two) and he still wants to be
> taken care of. His five-year-old Child wants to maintain the
> status quo, believing that his two-year-old Child is a nuisance
> and will cause trouble. Both the two-year-old Child and the
> five-year-old contain Adapted Child and Free Child parts, so
> the impasse is not a functional split between Adapted Child
> and Free Child, but instead is a structural split between two
> different ages of the Child.

The three impasses are illustrated in Figure 9–1.
    First-degree impasses are usually easier to change than second-
degree impasses, since drivers are less potent than injunctions. However, these two types of impasse are also similar in that they refer to
a conflict between the Child and a part of the Parent. This contrasts
with the third-degree impasse, which is between two parts of the
Child. This sometimes results in different treatment approaches.
When the conflict is between the client's Child and her Parent, at
the point where she makes a redecision she might also say goodbye
to that part of her Parent. When the conflict is between two parts
of the Child, it is not advisable to try to get rid of either part, which,
unfortunately, is often the inclination of both the client and the
therapist. Often the client's Adapted Child wants to get rid of the
Free Child because she thinks the Free Child's wants and needs are
causing the trouble. On the other hand the therapist and part of the
client may want to get rid of the Adapted Child, thinking that the
Free Child needs to be left alone. However, whether the conflict is
between Adapted Child and Free Child, between two different ages

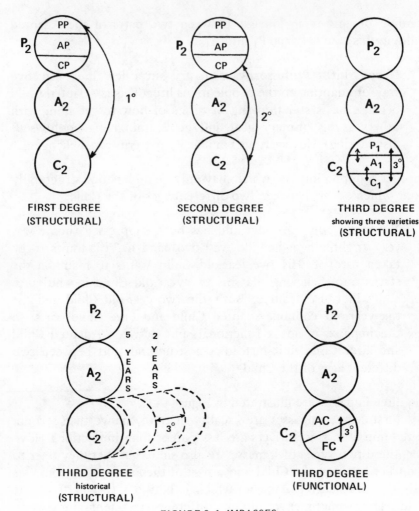

FIRST DEGREE
(STRUCTURAL)

SECOND DEGREE
(STRUCTURAL)

THIRD DEGREE
showing three varieties
(STRUCTURAL)

THIRD DEGREE
historical
(STRUCTURAL)

THIRD DEGREE
(FUNCTIONAL)

FIGURE 9-1. IMPASSES.

of the Child, or between any two structural parts of the Child, all the parts have valuable feelings, knowledge, experience, and skills for dealing with the world. Both contain good Child energy, and full functioning cannot occur when either part is split off from the personality. Both parts need to feel listened to and protected, and to be given space to make a joint redecision when they are ready. When both parts are appreciated and regarded as valuable, they will likely work out a new solution which satisfies both of them and resolves the impasse. For example:

FC: "I want strokes that feel good and not just because I work hard."

AC: "But I am bad and no one will give me good-feeling strokes. I must work hard or I won't get *any* strokes."

FC: "I appreciate your telling me what you think I must do, and now I understand that you are trying to help me. But I feel really terrible when you tell me I'm bad. Why do you do that?"

AC: "Because you never before would listen to me and I was afraid if you didn't pay attention to me that we would get in terrible trouble. Besides, lots of big people like mom and dad think you *are* bad."

FC: "I know they think that, that's why I don't want to be near them. And I've found some new people who feel good and say I'm not bad. Don't you believe them?"

AC: "I'm not so sure. You can't count on people who aren't family. [This was something he had heard many times.] What happens if you believe them and they leave? I think it's a good idea to be careful."

FC: "I agree. I'm scared about their changing their mind, too. But they do seem different from mom and dad. They don't change their minds nearly as much and they are a lot nicer. Will you listen real carefully just in case they change and let me know? I know you're real good at spotting that kind of thing and I'd appreciate your help."

AC: "OK, I'll do that 'cause I like how you sound about this and I appreciate what you've done about finding these people. They do seem different from mom and dad."

In the above example, if the client's Free Child had tried to push ahead alone, his Adapted Child would have used the energy of its concerns to undermine the eventual outcome. This might take the form of a game—the Free Child tries to get close while the Adapted Child "proves" that closeness is unsafe and ultimately collects a bad feeling payoff.

The Three P's

Effective treatment is faciliated when the therapist employs the three *P*'s of *permission, protection,* and *potency* [43, 16, 45]. A troubled person is more likely to try out a new behavior that is against the rules when he has sufficient permission to counterbalance his old injunctions. Therapeutic protection and potency provide a necessary framework for the redecision which may occur when the client accepts a permission. Each person knows best what permissions he needs and chooses which permissions he will accept. Since the client's sense of vulnerability helps to determine the level of risk he will take, the therapist's permissions must be given with protection and potency.

PERMISSION

All methods of therapy offer permissions. Some do this covertly, others quite overtly. A therapist who agrees to a contract and listens receptively to previously unmentionable secrets and fears is giving implicit permission to change. So is the group therapist when she brings together a variety of people offering many different examples of options of behavior. Stroking, or responding positively to changes for the better, is a very important permission for maintaining those changes and for fostering further changes. Therapists who suggest specific new behaviors also give considerable permission. The behaviorist who gives instructions for assertiveness, the gestalt therapist who says, "Speak for the feeling in your gut," the encounter leader who says, "Show her what you are feeling," and the TA analyst who says, "You are lovable even when you don't take care of me or anyone else" are all giving overt, strong permissions.

Permissions may be given from any ego state, including the Parent. Contrary to what some people think, not only is it all right for the therapist to have a Parent ego state, but it is also all right to use its opinions and power in therapy! The Child is also important in treatment. In fact, permissions delivered from the Child usually have the greatest impact—an enthusiastic Child is often very believable. Furthermore, a direct permission is a powerful tool to effect change. To tell a client, "It is all right for you to express your

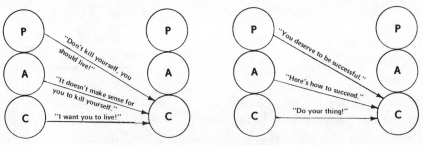

FIGURE 9-2. PERMISSION.

feelings!" will sometimes facilitate movement into a new behavior much faster than any other intervention. The most effective permissions are simultaneously communicated from all three ego states, as in the examples in Figure 9-2.

PROTECTION

All methods of therapy also offer at least some protection. The therapist is a high-status person who acts in the client's behalf with overt caring and concern. This unconditional positive regard is the foundation of good therapy, and other techniques and procedures built upon this foundation to enhance protection. Foremost among these is a mutually agreed-upon treatment contract. The client's active participation in the contracting process removes much of the scary magic from therapy. Carefully following the contract by giving only those permissions that fit clearly within the contract is also important. *Extraneous permissions are distracting and may be provocative.* It is also helpful to limit the scope of the contract, since doing so usually helps the client feel safer and more optimistic about succeeding, thus increasing her likelihood of success. The frequency and regularity of sessions and the therapist's availability by phone are additional contributors to the client's sense of safety, and are commonly needed before she will work on especially difficult contracts. The marathon leader provides similar protection by being available for a long time to help work through a problem.

Protection from physical harm during treatment is extremely important. The encounter group maxim that each person is totally responsible for what happens to himself during the session does not provide enough safety for some clients. Therefore, we have a rule against physically hurting anyone, and priority is given to help clients make decisions not to hurt themselves or others. If clients are allowed to be physically active by hitting pillows, breaking out of a circle, and so on, then the office should be designed and equipped to be a safe place for the client's Child to come out and do what he needs to do. All of this is done to minimize the possibility that the client's Adapted Child will use the treatment situation to break something or hurt himself or someone else and then proclaim, "See, I knew that expressing feelings was bad!"

Therapists who give strong behavioral permissions should also emphasize strong protection—not only physical but also emotional. Quick changes in behavior are sometimes followed by feelings of despair, pain, or fear. This is especially true at the time of any major redecision or change in behavior. The therapist should be available, encouraging the client to ask for what she needs—strokes, more permissions, reiteration of the facts, and so on.

> In a fantasied confrontation with mother, Iris yelled at her and said that she was no longer going to wait for her love. Instead she declared that she was already lovable. At that moment Iris felt great, but after she left the session she began to doubt what she had done and became very self-critical. She phoned her therapist, who assured Iris that her experience was not unusual and that she was not bad for having angry thoughts about her mother. Following this Iris felt much better and got-on-with her new program of assertiveness.

A few minutes on the phone will sometimes resolve a minicrisis and avoid the need for an extra session. We suggest the following guidelines for therapist-client telephone calls:

1. Be brief—five minutes is usually sufficient.
2. Emphasize protection.
3. Avoid rackets and games—if discounting persists, it is best to terminate the call.
4. It is best for the client to call *before* he escalates into a serious situation.
5. Use as prescriptions when extra protection is needed—for example, the therapist might say, "Call me at 9:00 P.M. tomorrow for some strokes for how you are carrying through with your redecision."

When these guidelines are followed, phone calls are infrequent yet very useful.

POTENCY

All methods of therapy require a potent therapist. The life script is a powerful force, decided under heavy parental pressures and reinforced by many years of games, rackets, and self-defeating behaviors. Permissions and protection must be given with potency to have lasting effect. Potency lies in the appropriateness and timing of the intervention, as well as the congruency and emphasis with which it is given. The potent therapist communicates her willingness and capacity to effect change and demonstrates strength in handling difficult therapeutic situations. She is not wishy-washy, ambivalent about change, or personally ineffectual. Instead she is strong, knowledgeable, clear, concise, and definite. All three of the therapist's ego states—especially her Child—believe in what is occurring.

When the therapist has Parent values which promote the client's well-being, Adult information about what the client needs, and a freed-up Child which allows her full use of her strength, creativity, and intuitive powers, she is capable of delivering permissions potently while offering protection. She will be an effective therapist!

Redecision Characteristics

A redecision is by definition a *positive* act. It is an undoing of an old decision and results in behavior closer to the desires of the Free Child. The client now has a new *option* for behavior—not another fixed pattern.

A redecision is an *intention*, not a promise. Many clients and therapists feel angry, disappointed, or some other racket feeling when new decisions are not perfectly carried out. It is essential to remember that the redecision is not a Child-to-Parent transaction after which the client is obligated to perform and should feel bad when he fails. Instead the client's Child, along with his Adult's assistance and perhaps the approval of a new part of his Parent, intends to carry out a new behavior and to put aside an old one. Like any new step a child takes, it will probably occur haltingly, and perhaps always with room for improvement. In no event does it become an obligation. Redecisions are not made to please a parent, a therapist, or anyone else. Redecisions are made only to please the self.

Conscious or Unconscious

Redecisions, like decisions, are sometimes made with little or no conscious awareness. This happens especially when there is some new input from the environment so that a person outside his awareness responds in reasonable comfort to an old situation with a slightly different pattern than usual. If the new pattern feels OK and is repeated enough times so that it becomes a freely available option, then a redecision has taken place. Some redecisions of this type might never get made otherwise, since the person's conscious mind is strongly opposed to any change.

> Harry is raised in a family with rules against physical closeness and decides not to risk much intimacy. He later marries Gladys who is spontaneously affectionate. Harry is uncomfortable with this for some time, but Gladys remains open and inviting. Eventually, without even really thinking about it, he becomes much more like her.

On the other hand, conscious redecisions also have advantages. The client can use his Adult to confirm the reasonableness of any new behavior, and so get reassurance for his Child. He can consciously practice new behaviors, both internally in fantasy and externally with others. He can ask others for approval. He can use his will power. He has all of his resources available to him.

Cure!?

A cornerstone of TA theory is the desire to effect cure. Like his father, Berne was a physician, and the medical model of curing patients was foremost in his mind. This probably increased his laudable aversion to the tendency of so many psychotherapists to settle for not being of much help to their clients. Berne wanted to be like a surgeon who precisely cuts out the offending lesion, thereby allowing the body to heal itself. A one-session cure was his ideal! TA therapists enthusiastically welcomed this permission and "got-on-with" curing their clients. They expected their clients to change and actively assisted them. This I'm OK—You're OK approach combined modeling, attributing, and suggesting all in one helpful package.

Groder suggests that "the 'cure' is facilitated by a mutually agreed upon verifiable contract" [28], which very helpfully reduces the grandiosity of the notion of cure. In the realm of emotional problems and characterological disorders, a total return to health is unusual. This is especially true if health is defined as that state which would have existed if the person had been raised on a diet full of love and permissions. We stress this because many clients and their therapists end up disappointed (or in some other racket feeling) with the results of therapy when, even after long effort and firm redecisions, they remain aware of a tendency in some circumstances to revert to old negative patterns. Individuals with Try Hard and/or Be Perfect as a primary driver are especially prone to this reaction. If the mutually agreed-upon, verifiable contract is emphasized, this will occur less often, since it is rarely appropriate to make a contract to do any new behavior perfectly.

Using the decision scale clarifies what actually occurs during the process of change: a client making a redecision moves closer to the full-acceptance-of-the-permission end of the scale. However, he probably will never get all the way there, since he cannot erase the memories of his traumatic past. Unlike a tape recorder that easily erases tapes, the brain records in protein that is most likely permanent. There is always room for new experiences, new memories, and new options, but it is not possible to eliminate the past and begin anew with a fresh start. The client's Adapted Child learning and Free Child fear cannot be obliterated, and will always be available to some extent.

When a client decides to take in new permissions, he acquires a new column in his Parent which is labeled for the source of the permission. This is true whether the permissions come from external sources or from the client himself. In a stressful situation, the Child may carry out the new decision while getting support from his new

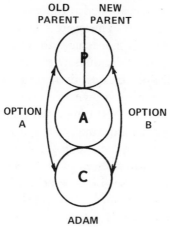

OLD   NEW
PARENT PARENT

OPTION   OPTION
A   B

P

A

C

ADAM
FIGURE 9–3. CHOICES AFTER
REDECISION.

Parent. If he gets too scared, he may revert to the old pattern and turn to the old Parent for approval. The amount of stress he will handle without going back to the previous system depends on the degree of comfort, safety, and familiarity with his new option. Figure 9–3 illustrates the choices.

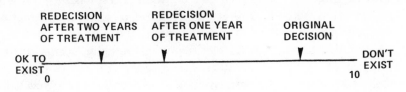

ADAM

FIGURE 9-4. EXISTENCE DECISION SCALE AFTER TREATMENT.

Another way to depict his potential choices is with a decision scale. Different scales may be drawn for each permission-injunction or allower-driver continuum that contains a redecision, or a composite scale may be used. For this example (Figure 9–4) we will use the Exist–Don't Exist scale. In practical terms this means that Adam is now less likely to react with thoughts or behaviors of suicide than before, and is less vulnerable to stress than he was previously.

Stress

A person's script decisions also function as indicators of vulnerability to particular stresses. The more severe the script decision, the smaller the stress that is necessary to elicit discounted, scripty responses. Therefore, an individual with a severe script notices and responds to many more stresses than a person who has a milder script. A stress scale can be drawn to better visualize these correlations [60]. We will use a 0–10 range, with the more severe stresses given a higher number. In a normal distribution of stresses, the more severe stresses are less frequent. The graph in Figure 9–5 illustrates the probable frequency of stresses of various intensities. In addition, note that two or more stresses in close proximity are equivalent to an even greater stress. For example, two level-3 stresses may be tantamount to a level-5, two 5s to 7, and so on.

The closer a decision is to the injunction or driver end of the decision scale (for example, at a 7), the more likely an individual will

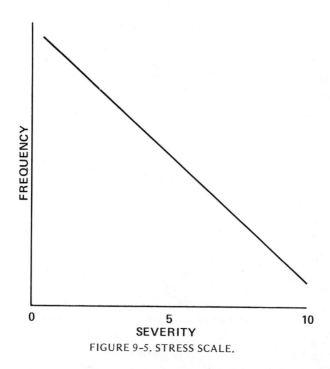

FIGURE 9-5. STRESS SCALE.

respond to a mild stress with scripty behavior. In this situation a level-3 stress might be noticed as meaningful, and result in discounting, racket feelings, and furthering of the script. Looking at this another way, the stroke filter, which is adjusted by the severity of the decision, would begin to distort strokes and information when stress is experienced as level-3 or above. Adam, whose original decision was an 8 on the Don't Exist scale, had to be ever alert to signs of displeasure from authorities. A level-2 stress was enough to get him to respond with scripty behavior. With his redecision he has moved to a 2 on the Exist side, and it now takes a much greater stress (perhaps a level-8) to evoke his old Adapted Child responses. When the stress is enough that he does go into his old patterns, it is helpful for him to have this information; otherwise he might become quite discouraged, undermine his new decisions, and discount his new options.

A redecision is rarely complete—that is, going to zero, or totally to the permission side of the scale. This is especially true if the original decision was significantly on the injunction side. However, the redecision allows for an increased ability to handle more severe stresses than before and to expeditiously use more positive options. Furthermore, a redecision increases the likelihood that a person will not even notice many of the stresses that used to bother him. The nearer the person is to the permission side of the scale, the less he notices stress, the better he handles it, the more he is reinforced for his decision, and the better he feels.

Winners and Losers

There are some important differences between winners and losers besides the style of their strokes and the content of their scripts. Basically, because of their more favorable position on the various decision scales, winners deal with stress differently:

1. Winners notice fewer stresses and handle bigger stresses more easily.
2. Winners tend to avoid stress and negative strokes. They do not stay in bad marriages that are not changing, or bad jobs that do not have pleasant psychic rewards or that are dangerous. Losers tend to stay in stressful situations that would upset almost anyone.
3. When winners do get into scripty behavior they have more and better methods for getting out and they do so more quickly.

Types of Treatment

With the help of the decision scales, it is possible to delineate two major types of treatment:

Supportive treatment helps a client to get back to feeling the way he was at his previous level of adjustment. He will not make any redecisions improving his position on any of the permission-injunction or allower-driver scales, so he will become upset at the same level of stress as before.

Reconstructive treatment helps a client to improve at least one permission-injunction or allower-driver scale with a redecision.

10

The Script in Action

"Do you think that
if I knew where I was, I'd be here?"

Process and Content

Once a person has decided upon a life script, she tends to live out the most important aspects of her life based on these preconceived notions. Her script influences how she will lead her life in two ways, providing both an overall *life plan* and a *life style* for carrying it out. A person's life plan is similar to a theatrical play and requires other persons to play specific roles within the context of a complete drama. This play has a beginning, a middle, and a climax, furnishing the *content* of a complete life story which outlines her destiny. A person's life style, or *process* of living, includes patterned behaviors that are consistent with her overall life plan, that reinforce it, and that provide subplots which help the life drama to unfold. She repeats these behaviors on a minute-by-minute basis in order to get strokes. These strokes, in turn, reinforce her beliefs, perceptions, feelings, and behaviors. Thus, a life script is both ongoing and repetitive. Certain messages are particularly significant to the formation of certain parts of the script. A person's life plan or content is mostly influenced by her injunctions, while her life style or process is mostly influenced by her drivers. The script program provides information in both areas: "how to" reach a final destiny as well as "how to" lead a life style.

Script content refers to messages, decisions, and payoffs, and can be uncovered by asking the question "*What?*" "*What* is missing from the person's life?" "*What* is the person's life plan?" "*What* is her goal in life?" "*What* is her chosen final payoff (including how tragic will it be)?"

Script process can best be determined by asking the question "*How?*" "*How* does the person set up her life to reach her goals?"

"How does she relate with others (patterned behaviors) in such a way as to reach her payoffs?" *"How* does she invite not-OKness in herself and others?" *"How* does she stop herself from being a spontaneous, autonomous person in the here-and-now?"

Scenario

The playing out of a life script in a specific here-and-now situation is referred to as the *scenario* [10] . The scenario has two possible outcomes: either (1) a person has a new experience which contradicts her script, in which case she may change it, or (2) she reconfirms her old beliefs and once again arrives at her script payoff. The positive aspect of the scenario is that it provides an opportunity for the person to alter her script by finding a new solution for the previously unmet needs. In fact, it is to provide this opportunity that many therapeutic techniques are designed to help clients reexperience old script scenes—that is, episodes that resulted in script decisions.

Miniscript

Taibi Kahler developed the concept of the *miniscript* to describe the process by which a person either furthers her script or maintains OKness [34] . The *not-OK miniscript* sequence describes the specific behavioral patterns which a person uses as she attempts to reenact her script on a second-by-second basis. Furthermore, it emphasizes the need to recognize and avoid those specific behaviors which a person uses to maintain and further her not-OKness. The *OK miniscript* describes the second-by-second process by which a person maintains a sense of OKness in herself and simultaneously invites OKness in others. A person is in *OKness* only when she is not in script, is not discounting, and is in an I'm OK—You're OK position.

Not-OK Miniscript

Script behavior begins when someone places a condition on her OKness by saying to herself, "I'm OK *if* . . .." She is now discounting, and therefore is actually in not-OKness. For example, let us assume that you are in an OK position as you are reading this sentence. In other words, you are feeling OK about yourself and are "getting-on-with" learning the information you are reading. To move into a not-OK position, some change must occur. Since you are an autonomous person and responsible for staying in an OK position, in order to move from your current OK position into some not-OK position, you must actively do something to change your feeling state. One way is to place a condition on your OKness—for example, "I'm OK if I were to . . ."

☐ . . . Be Strong

☐ . . . Try Hard

☐ . . . Hurry Up

☐ . . . Be Perfect

☐ . . . Please Me (Someone)

These five internal messages (drivers) represent the not-OK parts of subscript messages. A person turns on these drivers in an attempt to avoid the unpleasant feelings of her script, that is, she hopes to become or remain OK by being strong, trying hard, hurrying up, being perfect, or pleasing someone.

Drivers involve a discount, and are the first step in the racket process. While the person is in her driver, she may or may not experience racket feelings. If she is already experiencing a racket feeling, she may try to get out of it by going into driver behaviors. Unfortunately, she only succeeds in placing a condition on her OKness, and so sets herself up to feel badly once again. If she is not yet experiencing racket feelings, her drivers will open the gates which may lead her into them. Once a person moves into a driver, she is inviting herself and others into rackets and games. This does not mean that drivers will necessarily lead to racket feelings. Drivers may last only a short period of time, after which a person may return to nonscripty behavior, switch to another driver, or escalate into one or more racket feelings. The not-OK miniscript triangle in Figure 10–1 shows how the not-OK miniscript sequence may progress [7].

Note the following four components of the not-OK miniscript sequence:

1. The not-OK miniscript sequence begins with a driver. A person can move from OKness into driver behaviors by responding to an internal Parent message which places a condition on her OKness. Or, if she is already experiencing racket feelings, she may use a driver

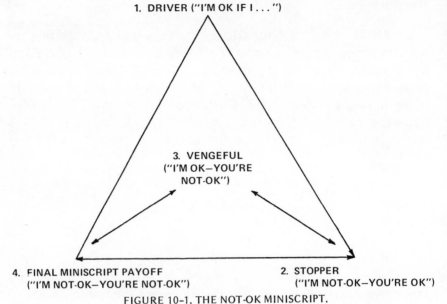

1. DRIVER ("I'M OK IF I . . . ")

3. VENGEFUL
("I'M OK—YOU'RE
NOT-OK")

4. FINAL MINISCRIPT PAYOFF
("I'M NOT-OK—YOU'RE NOT-OK")

2. STOPPER
("I'M NOT-OK—YOU'RE OK")

FIGURE 10-1. THE NOT-OK MINISCRIPT.

(Miniscript is shown for reference; a version expanded beyond transactional analysis
is included in Kahler, *TA Revisited,* Human Development Association, 1979)

to attempt to reestablish the conditions upon which she thinks she can return to OKness. In either case, her position is "I'm OK if . . . ." Although there are only five drivers which a person can use to initiate her not-OK miniscript sequence, there are many variations of behaviors within each category. For example, six persons with Be Perfect drivers may behave in the following ways:

> Person #1 is crisp, clear, and precise in her choice of words and the formation of her sentences. Even her casual conversation sounds like she is reading from a book. "I assure you that I understand the ramifications of your remarks, and that your concerns will be immediately forwarded to those persons whom they concern."

> Person #2 covers all the bases. She wants to make sure that her point is "crystal clear," but ends up muddying things instead. "The answer to your question is yes and no. On the one hand, if we look at it from this point of view, you are correct—assuming that you have checked out all possible alternatives. If you have overlooked something, then you are incorrect, unless you somehow have managed to make a correct decision despite your previous errors. On the other hand, if we look at it from a

different point of view, then you are also incorrect, or at least your answer is irrelevant to the question.''

Person #3 is definite and keeps ''hitting the nail on the head.'' ''The rain outside is falling from the sky downward onto the ground.''

Person #4 says very little, since she would rather not be noticed than risk a chance of making a mistake.

Person #5 sits in judgment of others. She is quick to point out the imperfections in what others say or do and stays in a one-up position. ''That's not quite right . . . here is a slightly better suggestion.''

Person #6 also sits in judgment but does so in a patronizing way. She saves her comments until last, then delivers them as ''stamps of approval'' from a wise sage to her loyal subjects. Looking down her nose, she says wryly, ''Very nice speech, Sally—now you're *beginning* to get it.''

The above examples only include verbalized statements, and are only a few of many possibilities of Be Perfect behaviors. The identification of driver behaviors is based on the recognition of seven factors. Two of these factors (physical sensation and internal discount) are internal and identifiable only the by individual experiencing the driver. The remaining five factors are outwardly observable behaviors (*words, voice tones* and *tempo, gestures, postures, facial expressions*). The driver behaviors of a client named Henry are outlined in Table 10-1. Avoiding these behaviors allows Henry to remain in OKness while inviting OKness in others.

2. If the not-OK miniscript sequence continues beyond a driver, the person moves to her *stopper.* The stopper is derived from the injunction and is any feeling state accompanying an I'm not-OK—You're OK position. These are the feelings which the person tries to avoid through driver behavior. She feels guilty, inadequate, stupid, or any other racket feeling which accompanies this feeling state for her. Once the not-OK miniscript sequence reaches the stopper level, the person may stay there, escalate to *vengeful* or *final miniscript payoff* position, return to a driver, or return to nonscripty behavior. This depends upon various factors, including her awareness of options, her life position, and the strokes available in each situation. Although all persons occasionally experience the last three positions

TABLE 10-1. Driver Chart: One Person's Driver Behaviors

Driver	Physical Sensation	Internal Discount	Words	Tones	Gestures	Postures	Facial Expressions
Be Perfect	Tense, robotlike	"You should do better"	"of course" "obviously" "efficacious" "clearly" "I think" (tells more than asked)	Clipped, righteous	Counting on fingers, cocked wrist, scratching head	Erect, rigid	Stern, ashamed, embarrassed
Try Hard	Tight stomach, tense shoulders	"You've got to try"	"It's hard" "I can't" "I'll try" "I don't know" (doesn't answer questions—repeats, tangents)	Impatient	Clenched, moving fists	Sitting forward, elbows on legs	Slight frown, perplexed look
Please Me (Someone)	Tight stomach	"You're not good enough"; "Make others feel good"	"You know" "Could you" "Can you" "Kinda" "Um Hmm" "Would you"	High whine	Hands outstretched, head nodding frequently	Head nodding	Raised eyebows, looks away
Hurry Up	Antsy	"You'll never get it done"	"Let's go" (interrupts people—finishes their sentences)	Up and down	Squirms, taps fingers	Moves quickly	Frowning, eyes shifting rapidly
Be Strong	Numb, rigid	"You can't let them know you're weak"	"No comment" "I don't care" (doesn't use here-and-now feelings)	Hard, monotone	Hands rigid, arms folded	Rigid, one leg over	Plastic, hard, cold

(stopper, vengeful, final miniscript payoff) and their accompanying feeling states, an individual will spend most of her time in the position which corresponds to her life position, since that is where she collects her favorite racket feelings. For example, a person with a life position I'm not-OK—You're OK will likely spend much of her time in the stopper position feeling inadequate. A person with a life position I'm OK—You're not-OK will likely move to the vengeful position, feeling angry, righteous, or triumphant. The person with a life position I'm not-OK—You're not-OK is more apt to escalate to final miniscript payoff, collecting racket feelings of rejection and futility. Racket feelings are experienced and stamps are collected at each of these three positions, and may be collected in any order (note the arrows in the not-OK miniscript triangle) and to whatever intensity is called for by her script. The various moves around the not-OK miniscript triangle can also be used to illustrate switches in rackets and games. These switches provide emotional intensity and various types of stroking, and illustrate an ongoing compromise between the type of payoff which a person desires and what is available in a given situation.

3. The *vengeful* position is an attempt to avoid painful feelings by blaming someone else. Here the person's feeling state is I'm OK—You're not-OK, and she feels angry, righteous, triumphant, etc.

4. The *final miniscript payoff* position is one of futility, and the person's feeling state is I'm not-OK—You're not-OK. She may feel unloved, hopeless, rejected, and so on. The term *final miniscript payoff* refers to the fact that this is the last payoff position in the not-OK miniscript triangle. Payoffs are also received at the stopper and vengeful positions.

Children learn driver behaviors from parents and other authority figures. The child learns these behaviors as she attempts to "be OK" in the eyes of the "big people" around her. Paradoxically, by placing a condition on OKness, these drivers begin the not-OK sequence and actually open the door into racket feelings. This happens especially when the person believes that she has not carried out the dictates of her driver—when she is not "being perfect" or not "pleasing someone," for example. Everyone experiences each of these drivers on some occasions; however, they are rank-ordered differently among different people. The one or two drivers which a person experiences most commonly are called her *primary drivers*. In general, friends of the same sex will have the same primary drivers—for example, two men may spend a great deal of time pastiming while "being perfect" for each other. On the other hand, sexual and marital partners are most often attracted to each other when their primary drivers are complementary—for example, husbands who are "being perfect" are often paired with wives who want to "please someone" [34].

In addition to maintaining the script process within an individual, drivers invite others into their scripts. If a person goes into driver behavior, the person with whom she is talking will usually respond with driver behavior of her own. Either or both may then escalate to racket feelings. If the first person stays out of script behavior, the second will usually do likewise. A person's primary drivers can be useful in helping to identify her script pattern, since these are highly correlated [31]. This will be discussed in more detail in the section on script patterns.

The OK Miniscript

Whenever a person is experiencing OKness and therefore demonstrating OK behavior, she is occupying one of the four position on the OK miniscript triangle depicted in Figure 10–2.

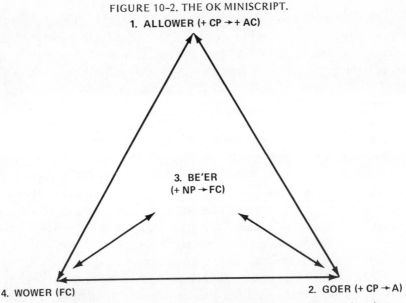

FIGURE 10-2. THE OK MINISCRIPT.
1. ALLOWER (+ CP → + AC)

3. BE'ER
(+ NP → FC)

4. WOWER (FC)   2. GOER (+ CP → A)

(Miniscript is shown for reference; a version expanded beyond transactional analysis is included in Kahler, *TA Revisited*, Human Development Association, 1979)

Each of the four OK miniscript positions (*allower, goer, be'er, wower*) represents an OK behavior diametrically opposed to the corresponding scripty behavior in the not-OK miniscript. Any person, at any given time, is occupying one of the eight positions represented in the OK and not-OK miniscript triangles (Figures 10–1 and 10–2). It is possible for an observer to diagnose, on a transaction-by-transaction basis, which of these eight positions are being assumed by her clients, as well as by herself. Just as the not-OK miniscript can be used to gauge a person's movement into scripty behavior, so can the OK miniscript be used to gauge her movement into OKness. Each of the four OK miniscript positions represent the cathexis of different functional ego states, and each sequential position invites more OKness and a greater sense of self-worth. In the following paragraphs we will describe and give examples of the various positions in the OK miniscript. The OK miniscript triangle shows only those functional ego states which seem to be most actively involved when a person moves into a particular position. Other ego states may also be used, either as part of an internal dialogue or externally to transact with others. This is especially true in cases where Nurturing and/or Controlling Parent functioning is involved. The distinction between nurturing and controlling is not always a clear one, and sometimes they overlap; for example, "Take good care of yourself!" could provide either or both functions. The most important variable is the responding ego state (Adult, positive Adapted Child, Free Child), since this provides an observable measure of OKness and good feelings which can be verified by the individual's experience.

Position 1, the *allower*, usually involves an internal message from the positive Controlling Parent to the positive Adapted Child. As this message is played, the person maintains OKness by responding to a Parent tape which "allows" her to meet her needs in an OK way, without a great deal of Adult thinking and sometimes even without Adult awareness. Examples of allower behavior include:

- Brushing your teeth
- Smiling and saying hello as you greet someone
- Doing chores

An allower may be demonstrated transactionally by cathecting an active positive Parent ego state and sending a message to someone else's positive Adapted Child, or by transacting from positive

Adapted Child to positive Adapted Child. For example:

> Therapist (leading a double-chair exercise) to client: "Stop holding back, and feel your power as you do!"
>
> Mother to child: "Be careful not to hurt youself."
>
> Clerk to customer: "Please have a seat until I finish with the lady in front of you."
>
> Customer to clerk: "Thank you."

All of these are examples of OK behavior, since none of them involves discounts and none of them invites scripty behavior. Each is said from an I'm OK—You're OK position and is intended to "get-on-with" solving a problem or meeting a need.

Position 2, the *goer*, usually involves an internal message from the positive Controlling Parent to the Adult. This message may also be received by the Little Professor, in which case the person is invited to use her creative and intuitive thinking, as well as her rationality. The person responds to the Parent directive by solving a problem, figuring out a solution, and taking action. Since the Adult and/or Little Professor is cathected, the person is aware of her actions and senses that she is "taking charge" of the situation and assuming responsibility for what she is doing. She may transact with others from either Adult or positive Parent, and aims her communication toward her partner's Adult, inviting her partner to take charge, think, and respond in the here-and-now. The range of OK feelings experienced in the goer position is quite wide, and many people spend a great deal of their OK time in this position. The examples below are representative of goer behaviors:

- ☐ Enjoying putting together a jigsaw puzzle
- ☐ Resolving a misunderstanding with a friend
- ☐ Searching through an address book to find a friend's telephone number

Examples of goer transactions include:

> Therapist to client: "Let's stop now, while you figure out what you need to do to solve this problem."
>
> Mother to child: "I won't do it for you, but I'll teach you how."
>
> Clerk to customer: "Tell me what the problem is."

Position 3, the *be'er*, was originally called the *Affirming Free Child.* A person in the be'er position is experiencing her OKness more fully than a person in either an allower or a goer, is more in touch with her Free Child, and directs her communication to the Free Child of others. The internal message is usually from positive Nurturing Parent to Free Child, and the person responds with a direct expression of Free Child wants, needs, or feelings. At the same time, her experience is here-and-now as she accepts the permission from her Nurturing Parent to fully realize what is occurring within and around her. Here are some examples of be'er behaviors:

☐ Laughing heartily at a funny story

☐ Lying in the sun and enjoying its warmth and the gentle sounds of the waves reaching the shore

☐ Crying openly while grieving over the death of a pet

A person who is in the be'er position transacts with others primarily from her Free Child. The be'er position is also demonstrated in a person who cathects a positive Nurturing Parent ego state in order to send permission, support, or encouragement to another person's Free Child. This differs from a Rescue transaction (negative Nurturing Parent) in that the receiver wants and needs the permission. Examples include:

Therapist to teary-eyed client: "It's OK to cry." (Client cries openly.)

Mother (enthusiastically) to child: "I'm very happy to be with you!"

Friend to friend (over telephone): "I miss you and I'm really looking forward to seeing you again."

Position 4, the *wower*, is experienced infrequently by most people. The wower is akin to what some call a "peak experience," and what Eric Berne has described as *true intimacy.* Berne believed that intimacy is a shared experience in which two persons mutually reach peak sensations of closeness, well-being, and euphoria. We have defined *intimacy* more broadly, and believe that it is possible to experience the wower position without the presence of another person. Nonetheless, this state of being is most often reached by two persons sharing an intimate experience, and the unilateral wower experience is the exception. A person who has moved into a wower position is in her Free Child, fully open to herself and her experience.

She is completely centered in the here-and-now, and if her experience is one of shared intimacy, she is simultaneously open and responsive to the Free Child of her partner. A person in the wower position undergoes a powerful emotional experience, and if she remains in the wower position for very long she is likely to experience distortions of time, space, and perception.

Script Patterns

There are six script patterns which people tend to follow: *never, always, until (before), after, almost (over and over),* and *open-ended* [6, 31]. Most of us follow a single script pattern in all of the major aspects of our lives. However, some people follow one pattern in their personal life and a second pattern in their public or professional life. The script pattern is manifest both in the person's overall life plan (destiny) and in her life style. For example, a person with a *never* pattern is apt to live out her life in such a way that she "never" gets what she wants most. At the same time, her *never* pattern will manifest itself on a daily and even second-by-second basis. She "never" finishes her tasks, reaches her goals, or completes her sentences. These script patterns are all found in Greek myths, which provide prototypes for human existence. The six script patterns are described in the following paragraphs, along with the primary drivers that accompany each.

Never

The *never* script is illustrated by the myth of Tantalus, who was forced to spend eternity bound to a rock with food and water just beyond his reach. Like Tantalus, Paul has a *never* script pattern and "never" seems to get to do or have what he most wants—his Parent forbids it, saying, "You'll never amount to anything!" His overall life plan calls for him never to enjoy sex, never to experience intimacy or closeness, and never to succeed professionally. On a day-to-day basis, Paul begins many projects and behaviors and never manages to finish them. Sometimes he never seems to get started at all, and presents himself as a desperate loser. His *never* script is reflected in a sentence pattern which is disjointed, contains many tangents, and never seems to finish (see Figure 10-3). For example, "Have you heard about, um, did you know that—well, maybe I shouldn't tell you this, but um, I don't know, um, let me see—um, I wonder if you've already heard this anyway, um, then again . . . . " Paul's primary driver is Try Hard, and other drivers are seldom used.

SENTENCE PATTERN **PRIMARY DRIVER**

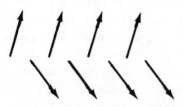

TRY HARD;
OTHERS SELDOM SEEN

FIGURE 10-3. *NEVER* SCRIPT.

Always

A person with an *always* script is in a position opposite that of the person with a *never* script. A person with an *always* script has decided that she must keep on doing the same thing, such as working, moving about and never settling down, living with a particular person, or whatever. The *always* script is demonstrated by the myth of Arachne, who angered the goddess Minerva and was forced to spend eternity as a spider, always weaving a never-ending web. Cheryl is an example of a person with an *always* pattern; as an adolescent, she enjoyed sex in spite of her parents' admonitions, became pregnant, got married, and decided that she must always live with her mistake. Her Parent says to her, "You made your bed, now lie in it!" Cheryl's *always* script is manifested on a day-to-day basis by her need to always be right, to stick to her guns, and to be very careful not to make mistakes to which she will be always committed. Although there is no clearly defined sentence pattern which indicates an *always* script, Cheryl's vocabulary includes an abundance of cautious quali-fying words: "maybe," "sometimes," "perhaps," "kind of," "sort of," "could be," "might," "we'll see," "I'm not sure," "I don't know," and so on. Her primary drivers are Be Strong and Hurry Up.

Until

An *until (before)* script insists that the person wait until a certain time or until a certain act has been performed before she can have her reward. "If you're real good and get all your work done, then you can play." It is described in the myths of Jason and Hercules, who were forced to perform monumental tasks before they could achieve happiness. Similarly, Mary's overall life plan calls for her to spend virtually her entire lifetime working hard to raise her family, after which she may enjoy her "sunset years" or receive her reward in the hereafter. In other words, Mary is scripted to do certain things and to discount herself until a certain time or deed has occurred. On a day-to-day basis, Mary follows her *until* pattern by not allowing herself to enjoy things until after she has done her work or taken care of others. Her *until* script is manifest in a sentence pattern which is not completed until some other matter has been covered. She inserts additional material in the middle of her sentence as additional pieces of information. Consider the following examples and Figure 10–4:

> No-script sentence pattern: "There are six types of script patterns: never, always, until, after, almost, and open-ended."
>
> *Until*-script sentence pattern: "There are six types of script patterns: never, always, until—*and that's the one that we are discussing now*—after, almost, and open-ended."

The primary driver for persons with an *until* pattern is Be Perfect, with Hurry Up and Be Strong also frequently used.

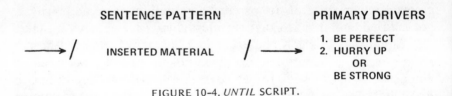

SENTENCE PATTERN		PRIMARY DRIVERS

FIGURE 10–4. *UNTIL* SCRIPT.

After

The *after* script pattern is consistent with the myth of Damocles, who was forced by the gods to live his entire life with a sword suspended above his head. Since the sword was hanging by a single thread, Damocles' fate was to be forever unsure when the thread would break and the sword behead him. A person with an *after* pattern has decided that although things may be going well for awhile, eventually some event or time will occur, after which she will encounter troubles or difficulties. For example, Lulu decided that "After forty, life is over." Once she turned forty, Lulu got fat, forgot about sex, and became depressed. Another example is Cal, who decided "After you're married, life is full of obligations." Cal got married, then collected obligations such as mortgages, in-laws to care for, and children whom he considered burdens. On a day-to-day basis, the *after* script is illustrated by a consistent pattern of fun, then atonement; joy, then misery; or pleasure followed by pain. Each time the person enjoys some success or happiness, she follows this with some negative payoff or atonement. "If you're going to dance, you have to pay the piper." The *after* script is manifest in a sentence pattern which begins with a positive statement, particularly with regard to feelings, hopes, or aspirations, and ends with a negative statement. Consider the following examples and Figure 10-5:

"Gee, I really had a great time last night, but boy, I sure am pooped out today!"

"I'm really happy to see you . . . it's too bad we can't get together more often."

"I want to succeed and be happy, but I guess I probably never will."

The primary driver for persons with an *after* pattern is Please Me (Someone), and Hurry Up is commonly number two.

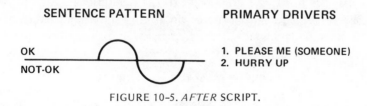

SENTENCE PATTERN	PRIMARY DRIVERS
OK	1. PLEASE ME (SOMEONE)
NOT-OK	2. HURRY UP

FIGURE 10-5. *AFTER* SCRIPT.

Almost

The *almost (over and over)* script pattern is illustrated by the myth of Sisyphus, whose destiny was to spend eternity rolling a large boulder to the top of a hill. Every time he would almost reach the top, the boulder would slip and roll back down to the bottom of the hill again. Sisyphus would begin anew, "almost" reach the top, and repeat this process over and over. A person with an *almost* script never quite reaches her goals. The script plan may call for the person to strive to become the president of a large corporation; however, once she makes it to vice-president, she will set herself up for failure. On a day-to-day basis, the *almost* script pattern is illustrated by the person who "almost" finishes her work, or by someone who watches a movie "almost" in its entirety but falls asleep during the final scene. A more subtle version of the *almost* pattern is depicted by Lester, who listens intently to the lectures of his professors, but does not quite understand what they are saying.

There are three types of sentence patterns which illustrate the *almost* script (see Figure 10-6). In the first instance, the person "almost" finishes her communication or "almost" delivers her message. For example, if her intent is to positively stroke another person, she may say something like this: "I like your painting, especially its artistic quality, overall design, and color scheme, but I think you should have picked a better subject." (Note that it is the process or pattern of communication which depicts the script pattern, not the content of the message.) The second type of almost sentence pattern may actually be more of a paragraph pattern. In this case, the person never quite makes her point, but instead starts over again from a different direction: "I'm really glad to see you here . . . I mean, I'm surprised that you came to visit me . . . that is, I wasn't expecting you today . . . you know what I mean . . . anyway, here we are. . . ." (This *almost* pattern differs from the *never* sentence pattern in that each statement or sentence is almost completed, but the message is not quite conveyed, so the person begins again from a new direction.) The third type of an *almost* sentence pattern occurs when a person begins a sentence, pauses, and completes her state-

FIGURE 10-6. *ALMOST* SCRIPT.

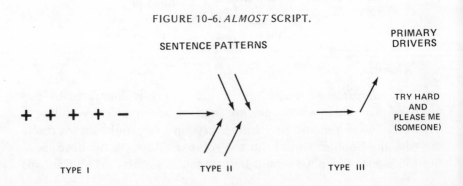

SENTENCE PATTERNS

PRIMARY DRIVERS

TRY HARD AND PLEASE ME (SOMEONE)

TYPE I   TYPE II   TYPE III

ment from a different position. For example: "Excuse me, sir, where is . . . that is, can you tell me what time it is?" (This *almost* pattern differs from the *until* pattern in that the tangential second statement is finished. Unlike the *never* pattern, a single tangent is taken and completed.) The primary drivers for persons with *almost* patterns are Try Hard and Please Me (Someone).

Open-Ended

The *open-ended* script pattern is illustrated in the myth of Philemon and Baucis, who were forced by the gods to spend their eternities as laurel trees. The *open-ended* script does not tell a person what to do after a certain time; instead, without giving options for later on, it stresses what the person is supposed to do earlier in life. For example, a woman's life plan may be to dedicate herself to raising her children. Once her children are grown up and gone, she does not know what to do with herself. Another example is a person whose life plan is to work hard and who becomes lost or disoriented when she retires from work. The person with an *open-ended* script may demonstrate a different script pattern early in her life, in which case the open-ended aspect of her script pattern will become apparent only after a certain time or event is reached. Once this time or event has occurred, her script runs out and she is left without a life plan. She may experience confusion, lack of orientation, or despair.

There is a great deal of variation in the life styles of persons with open-ended scripts, since the emphasis is on how long the script lasts rather than how it unfolds. There are no consistent sentence patterns or primary drivers which apply to these persons as a group, although each person will display her own patterns and miniscript sequences. Although the *open-ended* script pattern and the *after* script pattern may seem similar at first, there are important differences between the two. The *open-ended* script calls for a person to live out a particular life plan until a certain time or event occurs, after which she has no life plan and feels lost or confused. The *after* script allows the person a great deal of freedom until a particular time or event occurs, after which she experiences her script payoffs. Consider, for example, Joan and Carol. Joan had an *open-ended* script and dedicated her life to raising her children, as her script called for her to do. Once they were grown up and had left home, she experienced despair, confusion, and a general sense of not

TABLE 10-2. Script Process, Sentence Patterns, and Drivers

Script Pattern	Mythical Hero	Thesis	Life Pattern	Content	Sentence Pattern	Drivers
Never	Tantalus	"As a child, I was forbidden by parents to do things I most wanted to do."	Daily, monthly, yearly, setups to never make it in important ways, e.g., orgasms, promotions	"I just can't find time to finish books I start." "I've never met a man I'm satisfied with."		Try Hard (Others seldom seen)
Always	Arachne	"Well, if that's what you want to do, you can spend the rest of your life doing it! You've made your bed, now lie in it!"	"Blah"—few highs or lows experienced	Love, but no sex Sex, but no love	None consistent Many qualifying words	Be Strong Hurry Up (Sometimes others)
After	Damocles	"Things can be going well now, but afterward something will happen. If you have a high, you'll have to have a low to pay for it."	Starts by doing OK from an adapted position, then sets self up to not make it or to finish poorly	"I like you—why couldn't we have met sooner?"	+ feelings /"but . . ."/ – feelings OK / not-OK	Please Me Hurry Up

					→/Inserted material/→	
Until (Before)	Jason; Hercules	"You can't have fun until ... you've got your work done ... you have achieved."	Sees self as more OK than others Achievement and goal-oriented	Work now, play later: "I'll talk about that as soon as I take care of this" (especially if repeated).	+++++–	Be Perfect (Hurry Up, Be Strong also ranked high)
Almost (Over and Over)	Sisyphus	"I almost make it, but not quite"; "... if only, if only?"	Almost gets there, then falters and repeats process	"I almost finished the book." "That was a great book ... what did the last chapter mean?"		Try Hard Please Me
Open-Ended	Baucis and Philemon	"I've made no plans for ... when I retire ... When I grow old ... menopause."	Programmed by duty	Life revolves around a particular issue	None evident	None consistent

knowing how to lead her life. She came to therapy saying, "I just feel lost . . . I don't know what to do with myself anymore." Like most people with *open-ended* scripts, Joan was open to suggestions from the group and readily accepted their invitations to explore new interests and opportunities. Carol, on the other hand, had an *after* script. She enjoyed raising her children and derived much benefit from motherhood. However, once her children were grown up and gone from home, she experienced severe depression and became suicidal. She came to therapy saying, "My kids were everything to me, and we were so happy together. Now I have nothing to live for." As is usually the case for someone with an *after* script, Carol would not accept encouraging strokes from the group, nor would she consider alternative interests—she had more invested in remaining a Victim and collecting her script payoff. Both Joan and Carol can be contrasted with Bobbi, another dedicated mother who had an *until* pattern. Bobbi was convinced that she had to be miserable until she had raised her children, and only then could she begin to enjoy life. When Bobbi came to therapy, she complained, "I can't stand raising children . . . I'll be so glad when they are gone so that there will finally be some time for me." It took a lot of work before Bobbi redecided to stop waiting "until" and to enjoy her life in the here-and-now.

Table 10-2 summarizes script patterns and correlates them with the primary drivers with which they are most often found.

Treatment Considerations

In order for therapy to be effective, it is crucial that the therapeutic situation be a new experience for the client, rather than just another arena in which she lives out her script. The therapist assumes the responsibility of maintaining her own OK behavior while inviting OKness in her clients. Identifying script process enables her to quickly ascertain how the client will live out her script on a second-by-second basis. Without this information leading her to appropriate ways of crossing transactions, she might unwittingly support the process of her client's script while attempting to change its content. For example, a therapist could support a client's *almost* pattern by suggesting that she "stop working and think about it for awhile," rather than encouraging her to finish her work. Or a therapist could support a client's "Hurry Up" driver and her ensuing script process by not confronting her when she continuously interrupts the therapist's sentences. On the other hand, the therapist who is aware of script process can invite OKness in her clients and increase her therapeutic effectiveness, regardless of the treatment style she uses to deal with script content.

One way to help clients change their script process is to directly provide them with information regarding how they maintain their not-OKness. For example, clients may be given specific information regarding their drivers, sentence patterns, and various miniscript positions. Furthermore, clients can learn to monitor themselves and to identify their own script processes. Once any client has done this, she can make contracts to change her behavior, including her drivers and her sentence patterns, so that she will no longer reinforce her script on a second-by-second basis. As she spends less time in script behavior, she will spend less time in racket and game behavior and more time in OKness. Since she does not reach her script payoffs as often, she may eventually extinguish a large number of script behaviors.

Such direct teaching of script process information may provide some relief to clients. However, this method of therapy by itself is relatively inefficient for those whose scripts are severe and intense. Most clients need to work directly from their Child ego states in order to redecide those script decisions which they are using to control their lives. Many experiential techniques have been developed which are effective in assisting clients to reexperience their Child ego states and to become aware of their script decisions. To achieve this, the therapist may borrow methods from various schools of psychotherapy: gestalt, encounter, scream therapy, bioenergetics, fantasy, dream work, reparenting, and so on. Any of these methods may be effective, and the correct choice depends upon the skills of the therapist and the needs of the client in a particular situation. However, all of these methods can be diluted or sabotaged by the therapist who is unaware of the ongoing process between herself and her client and how this process is reinforcing the client's life script. A potent therapist is one who uses effective intervention strategies *and* maintains a process which invites OKness in her clients.

We all spend a great deal of time in driver behavior, and the impact of our drivers on both ourselves and our clients depends on several factors:

1. *Frequency.* A driver which is frequently repeated will have more impact than one which occurs less often.

2. *Severity.* Drivers vary in terms of their severity. For example, a Be Perfect driver may be experienced as a slight push or as a powerful message supporting a Don't Exist injunction.

3. *Racket.* Driver behaviors which accompany racket feelings have more impact, since clients tend to respond to all the messages being sent.

4. *Escalation.* Drivers do not necessarily lead to racket feelings, and their impact is lessened when they are not backed up with not-OK Child energy.

5. *Life Position.* A therapist whose basic position is I'm OK—You're OK will convey that belief to clients even when she slips and commits a driver, while a therapist who is in a not-OK life position will convey that position despite her attempts not to. A therapist who accepts her driver behaviors and works to change them without kicking herself models how to grow and change for her clients.

There are a number of specific ways in which a therapist invites OKness by remaining aware of drivers and script patterns. First, she monitors her own behaviors and avoids drivers while she is doing therapy. Second, she remains aware of the drivers which her client is demonstrating while she is working. By doing so, she can intervene in the client's work in such a way as to invite the client out of driver behavior and into an OK ego state. This can be done without labeling driver behavior as such. For example, a client who is using a Be Perfect driver and an *until* sentence pattern to give a long-winded answer to a question can be asked to repeat her answer in a short sentence from her Child ego state. Or, a client who is using Try Hard and Please Me drivers with an *almost* sentence pattern can be asked to look at the therapist and "take a guess" rather than continuing to belabor the issue. Third, the therapist can remain aware of sentence patterns which indicate script process and intervene in such a way that script disruption is achieved. *Script disruption* refers to a process by which the usual script pattern is interfered with and the client is invited into an OK position. Table 10–3 gives examples of various forms of script disruption which are effective with specific script patterns.

If a person changes the order of her drivers, she will reinforce a process which is inconsistent with her script pattern. Changing certain scripty sentence patterns may speed up the redecision process by helping a person to eventually extinguish these aspects of her script pattern.

TABLE 10-3. Script Disruptions

Script Pattern	Script Disruption
Until	1. Do the work *now* (don't let client ramble first, work later). 2. Keep work short. 3. OK to work *before* it's all figured out.
Almost	1. Finish the work (if not finished, ask client to summarize progress and state future direction). 2. Finish each sentence (no *buts*).
After	1. Give permission and get contract not to use work to invite bad feelings later (especially with hamartic scripts and psychosomatic clients). 2. Stroke after positive statements (before negative statement follows). 3. End work on positive note—watch for escalations later.
Always	1. No hedging or disowning: —OK to make decisions ("What do you want?") —OK to make commitments ("What will you do?") —OK to state feelings, thoughts, opinions ("What do you feel/think?") 2. Encourage and stroke risk taking—OK to make mistakes, change mind.
Never	1. Stroke (lavishly) each step toward OKness, no matter how small. 2. Confront Try Hard by inviting into Adult. 3. Stroke Free Child spontaneity.

Drivers and script patterns are learned behaviors which, like rackets, games, injunctions, life positions, and so on must be redecided and replaced with new behaviors before treatment is completed.

Potent therapy results from effective and appropriate intervention strategies *combined with* script-free process.

Parent Continuum

The more a therapist invites OKness in herself and her clients, the more effective she will be. One way to roughly gauge the amount of OKness which a person invites in herself and others is to observe how she uses her OK functional ego states. Her use of her Parent ego state is especially revealing, since a person's Parent sends messages in two directions—actively to another person, and internally to herself. Therefore, her Parent can be used not only to maintain her own script, but also to support someone else's. On a more positive note, the Parent can also be used to support and reinforce OKness. The *parent continuum* in Figure 10-7 shows the various functions of the

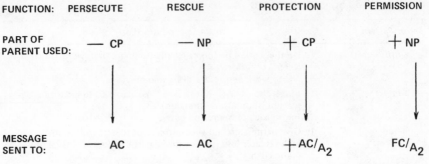

FIGURE 10-7. PARENT CONTINUUM.

Parent ego state [33]. The amount of OKness invited increases as you read from left to right.

Not-OK Controlling Parent statements are usually received by the not-OK Adapted Child, who experiences them as Persecution. A persecution transaction occurs when the therapist directly or indirectly puts down the client in such a way as to reinforce the latter's Victim position. This is usually accomplished via negative strokes or discounts.

Not-OK Nurturing Parent statements are also usually received by the not-OK Adapted Child, and are experienced as overpermissiveness (lack of protection) or as Rescues. Rescuing occurs when the therapist offers help which the client does not want or need. A common example of this is when the therapist persists in delivering "permissions" to a client who is in an Adapted Child ego state refusing to accept them.

OK Controlling Parent statements are most often received by the OK Adapted Child and/or Adult and are taken in as Protections. Sometimes the Free Child is also listening and feels safe to move ahead. One form of protection transaction occurs when the therapist directs the client to do, say, or feel something which is consistent with the client's wishes but contrary to the client's Parent tapes. In effect, the therapist is saying, "Go ahead and do what you want to do. Don't listen to your Parent." This may occur when the therapist gives commands or instructions or in some other way directs the client's experience—"Get louder," "Let it out," applying bioenergetic pressure techniques, and so on. A second type of protection transaction also occurs when the therapist provides the environment and support necessary for the client to risk going against her script decision, but does so without directing the client's experience. In effect, the therapist is saying, "Go ahead and do it when you're ready."

Telling the client what to do may be an especially potent intervention when Parent tapes are very harsh, and may be important during the initial stages of treatment. In fact, for many clients this type of protection is needed before permission to change will be accepted. However, the second type of protection is generally preferable, since it allows the client to change at her own pace, invites less resistance, and may be taken in by the Free Child as a permission. The therapist who repeatedly tells her clients what to do without noticing their Adapted Child responses will often fall short of inviting autonomous script-free behavior. Instead, her clients may terminate therapy as soon as they begin to carry the therapist around in their heads. Rather than integrating the therapist's messages and "making them their own," they merely respond to this new Parent ego state from an Adapted Child position. Although it is true that this Adapted Child position is usually better than their previous spot, it is nonetheless short of redecision and autonomy. This does not mean that it is bad for a client to carry the therapist around in her head, that is, hear and respond to various messages which she received from her. In fact, any therapy which is successful includes the client's establishing new Parent tapes which are more appropriate to her needs and wants. However, the more autonomous the person, the more she will exercise her freedom of choice in responding to any of her Parent messages. Her Little Professor will select options which are good for her, rather than those which merely pay off with others, including her therapist.

OK Nurturing Parent statements are usually received by the Free Child and/or Adult as permissions. A permission transaction occurs when the therapist states directly or indirectly to a client *who is ready to receive it* that "it's OK to. . . ." Permission also differs from protection in that it never carries an expectation or an obligation. There is no command, no directive, and no coercion (covert or subtle) in the therapist's statement. Eric Berne compared the permission transaction with a fishing license—the license allows the person to fish, but does not expect, direct, command, or coerce her to do so [9]. If there is expectation on the part of the therapist, then the client may respond from an Adapted position and not fully accept the permission. True permission is something which is *taken* by the client rather than *given* by the therapist. Therefore, it is essential that the client's Free Child and/or Adult ego states be available to take the permission and make the redecision. If a permission is taken, the client will make the decision under her own steam and using her own energy. The therapist, the client, and the group members will all experience a sense of autonomous decision and commitment, rather than adaptation to the therapist or group. The redecision will usually be stated verbally, without drivers or scripty sentence patterns, and in a congruent manner.

11

Transactional Analysis Treatment

". . . with a little help from my friends."

What is Transactional Analysis Treatment?

In Transactional Analysis, *treatment* or *therapy* refers to a relationship in which at least one person is working on a contract for personal change and another person, the therapist, is using a TA frame of reference to facilitate those changes. The therapist uses the concepts of ego states, transactions, discounting, rackets and games, and script components to formulate and carry out this change process.

One of the most appealing aspects of TA to the practicing clinician is its versatility, which allows the individual therapist a great deal of freedom in choosing her particular style and technique of therapy. Transactional Analysis can be thought of as a large umbrellalike structure which provides guidelines under which many treatment techniques and methods can be effectively employed; within the field of Transactional Analysis itself, there are many "schools" which emphasize different aspects of TA theory and practice. Additionally, TA provides a framework within which many other therapeutic modalities can be integrated.

Even though TA is flexible and allows much freedom to the individual therapist, it nonetheless provides a framework for treatment which is consistent among all Transactional Analysts. Perhaps the most obvious of these consistencies is a *common TA language.* Transactional Analysts may vary somewhat in terms of how much TA vocabulary they speak out loud, but all of them think TA and can explain what they do using TA concepts. Transactional Analysis words not only appeal to the Child, but also accurately identify the various parts and processes of the personality, so that therapists and clients alike can readily understand what these terms mean.

Since basic TA terms are easily learned, clients can use them effectively to understand what they are doing and use this understanding to help themselves change. This cognitive structure allows the client to work actively between sessions, encouraging her to think for herself without the continual aid of her therapist. Although the basic TA vocabulary is simple and straightforward, it also includes additional terms to describe more complicated aspects of the personality. It is not vital for clients to understand all of the information which therapists know. However, it is certainly OK for clients to have and use information to whatever extent they find it beneficial in helping themselves change. The basic minimum for effective TA therapy is for clients to have a working knowledge of a few TA concepts—*Parent, Adult, Child, game, racket, discount, decision, script, stamp, stroke,* and *contract.*

One of the disadvantages of TA vocabulary is that some of the words sound like putdowns, especially to the uninitiated. Words like *game, racket, driver, Persecuter, Rescuer, Victim,* and *gallows* are meant to be descriptive, not evaluative. The therapist has a responsibility to use these words to help clients, not to criticize them. She should also be alert to the possibility that her clients may be using these concepts to maintain not-OKness rather than to "get-on-with" changing—"Oh, there I go again! I'm in my racket [driver, etc.]. I'll never change!" If this is occurring, it needs to be changed to a positive approach—"Oops, there I go again. Now I wonder why I turned on my racket. Oh, yes, that's what was upsetting me. Well, I'll do this instead." It is also important that clients not use TA vocabulary to escape into a head trip as a way of avoiding personal change.

A second thing which Transactional Analysts have in common is that they all work with *ego states and life scripts.* The concept of ego states is so essential to TA treatment that Eric Berne was prompted to say that when a therapist is working with her clients' ego states, she is practicing Transactional Analysis; and when she is not dealing with ego states, then she is not practicing Transactional Analysis [5]. At first, this may appear to be an oversimplification. However, when we consider that virtually all of TA theory is built upon the concept of ego states, then this statement becomes more meaningful. The same can be said about scripts. Ego states and scripts are the essential ingredients of TA theory and practice, and all other aspects of TA theory can be considered offshoots of these two main branches.

Third, Transactional Analysis is *contractual*. This means that the client is responsible for determining her treatment goals and is an active participant in the treatment process. Contracts will be discussed in more detail later in this chapter.

Fourth, Transactional Analysts work with a *decisional model*. TA therapists assume that their clients' emotional disturbances result from early childhood decisions which can be changed. Ideally, these changes are integrated into all aspects of the client's personality—cognitive, affective, and behavioral. With a redecision the client moves to an I'm OK—You're OK position. She is in touch with her feelings (affective), uses them to figure out what she wants and needs (cognitive), and then goes ahead and does what is necessary (behavioral) to meet those needs in OK ways. Furthermore, clients are encouraged to change their behaviors first and analyze the causes only to the extent necessary for a redecision to be reached.

Last, and in many ways most important, TA emphasizes a treatment approach which is based on the assumption *I'm OK—You're OK*. This means that each person has a lovable part and is capable of change. The therapist does not consider the client to be inadequate, defective, or incapable of modification, no matter what the diagnosis. On the other hand, it does not mean that the therapist or the client should just smile benignly at whatever the client does. Transactional Analysts maintain the position of I'm OK—You're OK even though they may feel and verbalize concern or dissatisfaction with their clients' behaviors and suggest areas for change. However, when the therapist does this, she also assumes the responsibility to communicate that information in such a way that she does not "lay her trip" on her clients or imply that they are defective or not-OK.

Contracts

A *contract* is an agreement between the therapist and the client which outlines the goals, stages, and conditions of treatment. Whenever two or more people are relating, there is always some expectation on the part of each person regarding what she wishes to get out of that relationship. The purpose of a contract is to make those intentions explicit in order to avoid covert transactions which may lead to scripty behaviors. There are actually three types of contracts which are commonly made between therapists and clients: *business contracts, treatment contracts,* and *working agreements.* These will be discussed in the order that they most commonly occur.

Business Contracts

The business contract outlines the boundaries of the professional relationship between the therapist and the client. As such, its purpose is to make clear what can be expected from each person in terms of services offered, time of sessions, financial arrangements, and availability. Steiner has written extensively about this type of contract and outlines four components which he considers to be essential: mutual consent, valid consideration, competency, and lawful object [42].

Mutual consent implies that both therapist and client are entering into this agreement voluntarily. In other words, the client is requesting treatment from the therapist, and the therapist is agreeing to treat the client. Moreover, this means that the specific issue the client wants to change is acceptable to both parties.

Valid consideration means that each person is putting something of value into the relationship. For the therapist, this signifies that she will use the full force of her skills and expertise to assist the client in meeting her treatment goals. Generally, the therapist also provides office space, furniture, and any other equipment necessary for treatment to occur. For the client, this usually means payment of fees. If the client is unable to afford financial payment, it is sometimes advisable that she pay for treatment in other ways. These may include an exchange of services, the writing of essays or poetry, or any other form of payment which is agreeable to both the client and the therapist. Regardless of the method of payment, the client should not be exploited by requiring her to pay more than what the treatment is worth, and the therapist should avoid the Rescuing position of treating more low-fee clients than is comfortable for her. Additionally, both the client and the therapist are expected to attend each session and to be on time.

The *competency* requirement stipulates that both the client and therapist must be competent to undertake the goals of treatment. This means that both the client and the therapist use their Adult ego states in the process of making the contract and during the course of treatment. Competency also means that the therapist has the knowledge and expertise to effectively treat the client. Examples of contracts which do not meet the requirements of competency include:

- ☐ A contract made with a psychotic person who is not using her Adult.
- ☐ A contract made when either person is high on drugs or alcohol.
- ☐ A therapist agreeing to treat a client whom she is incompetent to treat because the therapist has either inadequate training or inadequate supervision.
- ☐ A therapist agreeing to work with a client on issues which are not resolved for the therapist herself—for example, a therapist who does not enjoy sex is probably not competent to work with clients on sexual issues, and the therapist who does not allow herself to be close is not likely to be effective with clients who are working on establishing close relationships.

Lawful object means that the therapist and client will work together using legal and ethical means to obtain legal and ethical results.

Treatment Contracts

A treatment contract is an agreement between the client and the therapist to accomplish a clearly stated goal. The client states an intended change, and the therapist agrees to work with the client to help to effect that change. All of the client's ego states are involved in the establishment of the treatment contract. Her Adult is needed to provide accurate information regarding what she is doing and what she wishes to change, while her Free Child provides energy and motivation. Her Adapted Child and Parent are investigated to clarify how she maintains her present not-OKness and how she is likely to sabotage her efforts to change. As a matter of fact, either or both the Adapted Child or Parent may already be at work undermining a positive outcome by suggesting contracts which are not for the benefit of the Free Child, but which instead subtly reinforce old script decisions. For example, a contract to get better grades in school might be made either to satisfy a Free Child desire for success or to placate Parent demands. If it is the latter, the client will be without Free Child motivation and likely to repeat old Adapted Child patterns with the therapist. After these possibilities have been thoroughly checked out, the client may make a clear contract from her Adult. The contract should be brief, straight to the point, and stated in words which are clearly understandable to the Child. It should also be as behaviorally specific as possible so that its attainment can be readily ascertained, at least by the client and preferably also by outside sources.

All of the therapist's ego states also are involved in the establishment of the contract. Her Adult processes the contract for internal consistency, achievability, and whether or not it makes sense. Her Free Child intuitively responds about the "feel" of the contract. Does the client's goal feel good and worth attaining? Is it the kind of thing that would "turn on" someone's Free Child? If not, it may be that the proposed contract is not really from the client's Free Child, but instead is from her Adapted Child. The therapist's Adapted Child may also have a response. If, for example, the client wants to be assertive with her husband and this scares the Adapted Child of the therapist, it might be better to refer the client to someone else. Finally, the response of the therapist's Parent is important. The Parent's approval of the contract will allow for consistency and increased potency on the part of the therapist, while disapproval may produce ambivalent responses which would undermine her success. Ideally, all of the ego states of the therapist should be in favor of and interested in the accomplishment of the client's contract.

When a client considers how she wishes to change, she has four general options:

1. She can continue to do what she is doing now and feel not-OK about it.
2. She can continue to do what she is doing now and feel OK about it.
3. She can do something different and feel not-OK about it.
4. She can do something different and feel OK about it.

An acceptable treatment contract is any desired change in which the client ends up at one of the OK options (numbers 2 and 4 above).

Some examples of treatment contracts include:

□ To get and hold a job for at least a year.
□ To stop withdrawing from people and to make three new friends.
□ To express myself assertively with men (women, people, etc.).
□ To finish my dissertation.
□ To stop having headaches prior to making a public speech.

The last contract is exemplified by Jody, a person who was satisfied with her behaviors but wanted to change her affective response which accompanied them. Jody held a professional position which required that she do a great deal of public speaking. Each time she was to address a group of people, she would experience a great deal of anxiety for several hours prior to her speech and would have headaches. However, once she began speaking she would cathect Adult, remain in charge, and do a very effective job. Jody's treatment contract was to stop hassling herself and to be rid of her anxiety prior to speaking. She knew when she had accomplished this because she was no longer uptight or nervous and no longer had headaches.

It is important to have the treatment contract clarified as soon as possible, since the contract is an indication that both the client and therapist are actively working toward the same goal. When the client is not clear about where she is going, she is less likely to get there or to know when she has arrived. The treatment contract also assures that the client is actively involved in changing. This is crucial, since only the client, not the therapist or anyone else, can provide the energy and motivation needed in order to change. The therapeutic relationship begins with the first contact between the client and the therapist, and the process of change and the activity of therapy is clearly outlined once a treatment contract is established.

However, sometimes other issues need to be resolved first. In all cases, the client must have the opportunity to generate her own motivation and to feel safe in a working alliance with the therapist. It is also warranted to work without a contract during an emotional crisis, when the client's feelings are very intense. It is often more useful to allow her to express them freely than to break in and ask her to make a treatment contract. After this energy has been released from her Child, her Adult is more available to accurately assess and communicate what is happening with her. At the same time, the client is receiving a powerful implicit permission from the therapist that it is OK for her to remain in touch with and express her Free Child feelings.

Working Agreements

From time to time throughout the course of therapy, a client may be asked to do a specific thing or to perform a specific task. These requests are made by the therapist and/or group members, and are intended to help the client reach her treatment goals. On other occasions, the client herself may suggest subcontracts which she thinks will help her reach her goals or provide her with some extra protection while she is trying out new behaviors. These working agreements are frequently referred to colloquially as *contracts* or *subcontracts*. When these agreements call for behaviors to be performed outside the treatment session, they are called *homework assignments*.

Working agreements are contracts in the sense that they are stated intentions of behaviors. However, they differ from treatment contracts in that working agreements may come from any ego state, including the Parent or Adapted Child, and sometimes appear to contradict the treatment contract in order to provide short-term protection. Whatever the immediate purpose of the working agreement, its long-range goal should benefit the Free Child's treatment contract, as the following examples illustrate:

> Therapist: "Will you agree not to hurt yourself again, and if you feel scared that you are going to, will you call me or one of the group members and ask for protection?"
>
> Emily: "I'm really afraid to do that, but I will do it anyway."
>
> Bob: "I've been feeling really suicidal since I've started changing. I want to make a contract that I won't hurt myself in any way for six months, no matter how much I feel like it."
>
> Therapist: "That's an excellent idea. Will you also agree to use the next six months to work on a permanent decision never to kill yourself, no matter what, and to bring up this issue again before the six months are over if you haven't yet made a redecision?"
>
> Bob: "Yes, I will do both of those. I feel much better with that."
>
> Jennifer: "I've been asserting myself much more lately, but I've been really scared and having lots of nightmares. I want to keep changing, but I also want to assure my scared Child that I won't push her any faster than she's ready to move. I'm going to make a contract to pay attention to my scared kid, and back off when she's getting too panicky."
>
> Therapist: "Good thinking. It's OK for you to try new behaviors without pushing yourself so that you keep resisting. Now I'm wondering, what are you saying to yourself after you have been assertive?"

Working agreements are most likely to succeed when they are obtained from the client's Free Child and Adult ego states, with recognition of her Parent and Adapted Child positions. When the client is not willing to make a protection agreement from her Free Child or Adult, the therapist may choose to accept one from her Adapted Child or Parent. However, these are less likely to work. For example, if a client is actively suicidal, it is most useful to help her to arrive at a redecision, that is, a new decision from her Child ego state that she will never kill herself under any circumstances. If she is not ready or willing to make such a redecision, then the next best thing is to ask her for a working agreement from her Adult ego state that she will not hurt herself for a specified period of time while she works on making a redecision. If she is still unwilling to do this, the therapist may settle for a promise from the client's Adapted Child that she will not hurt herself, but will call the therapist if she needs extra protection. This type of working agreement is tenuous and dangerous, and should only be accepted as a last resort. The therapist's task is to invite the client to move from a working agreement to a treatment contract and then to a redecision as soon as possible.

Three-Handed Contracts

Many therapists are not self-employed, but instead work for agencies on a salaried basis. Whenever you have a situation in which a third person or group is involved, that person's or group's roles and expectations should be clearly defined as part of the contracting process. For instance, some agencies dictate rules about the length of sessions, fees, types of treatment provided, and even the number of sessions allowed. Sometimes an agency or organization such as a court, school system, prison, or drug program pays the therapist to treat the client according to its expectations, rather than according to the needs of the client. The client has the right to know the effects of these three-handed contracts, and these are best handled by openly admitting that they exist and discussing their ramifactions. Similar problems may arise when a parent brings her child to a therapist for treatment, or when the therapist is treating different members of the same family. In these instances, it may be a good idea to secure contracts in a family session, where all members are present and can comment on each other's contracts. Whether arrived at this way or separately, the contracts should outline the expectations regarding confidentiality in order to avoid three-handed games [5]. When doing this, be sure not to make promises which you will not keep. For example, if there are conditions under which you will break confidentiality in order to increase protection (suicide attempt, drug overdose, etc.), then say so when the issue of confidentiality is initially raised.

In summary, TA therapy is an active process between the therapist, the client, and sometimes a group. The client may be an individual, a couple, a family, or any group of persons who wish to change the ways they interrelate. Each person involved in the treatment process is considered responsible for her actions and behaviors throughout the course of treatment and makes her own individual contract for change.

Stages of Treatment

Treatment progresses more smoothly when its various stages are worked through consecutively [11]. Some issues need to be resolved before later issues can be successfully faced. It is the therapist's responsibility to make sure that each of these stages is worked through sufficiently so that the client is ready to take on the next stage of change. Many snags in the treatment process result from the therapist's lack of awareness that stages have been skipped. The client may feel unresolved or sense a lack of protection which precludes her working toward redecision and new behaviors.

Stage One: Motivation

In order for the change process to begin, the client must feel a need or desire to change. One particularly unmotivated client, Betsy, was so out of touch with her Free Child feelings that she was not aware of her own unhappiness or discomfort. In order to get along in the world, Betsy had decided to discount her Free Child and listened to a Parent ego state which told her to ignore her discounted needs. Finally, in order to keep her frame of reference intact, she discounted Adult information regarding problems, change possibilities, and ways to take care of herself.

Most clients become motivated to change when they become aware of their own unhappiness or discomfort. However, this stage is not completed until the client also realizes that change is possible. Many clients learn about TA and other methods of therapy by talking with friends, reading books, or attending lectures and/or workshops. These are all sources of new information which contradict the old script decisions. Clients in this stage of treatment usually need this information as well as support for their new-found Free Child needs and feelings.

Some clients are satisfied with their present state of affairs but are encouraged, pushed, hassled, or cajoled by others to change. For example, a sociopathic client may not care about changing, but may be pressured to do so by parents, school officials, courts, probation officers, and so on. These clients require a great deal of work before they are ready to make a commitment to change. Motivating these persons requires special skills and training. In fact, in settings where unmotivated clients are commonly treated, the therapist who is skillful at motivating them to change is more sought after than one who is only competent when working with already motivated clients [13].

Stage Two: Awareness

Once the client has decided that she is dissatisfied with her present state of affairs and wishes to change, she needs to clarify for herself what it is that dissatisfies her. Stage Two is largely a process of decontaminating her Adult, and usually involves helping the client identify her thoughts and feelings. Stage One is reached when a client decides she wants to change, while Stage Two is the process by which she learns what she wants to change.

Stage Three: Treatment Contract

Establishing a treatment contract is an ongoing process which includes periodic refinement. Often the original contract is merely an opening gambit to determine if the therapist is trustworthy. Or it may be only a way station en route to the major destination as the client's awareness, motivation, and sense of safety change. It is important that the contract be reviewed and updated periodically to make sure that it is still relevant. Throughout the course of treatment, the contract should feel right to the therapist's Child and make sense to her Adult. Anytime the therapist experiences resistance from the client, it is a good idea to review the contract. Sometimes the treatment may have strayed from the contract and the resistance indicates the client's unwillingness to continue working in this new direction. Reviewing the contract often rekindles the client's Adult and Free Child desires to change, providing new energy for getting through the impasse. Once the treatment contract is established, the client is ready to move to Stage Four.

Stage Four: Deconfusing the Child

Stage Four includes the various techniques, methods, and experiences which are used to help the client arrive at a redecision and change her script. She learns to accept responsibility for her decisions and discovers how she uses her present behavior to maintain her script. This stage of treatment may take place in a single piece of work or it may continue over a long period of time. There are two goals during this stage of treatment: (1) to deconfuse the client's Child by helping her to get in touch with and express unmet needs and feelings; and (2) to help her develop an internal sense of safety sufficient to make a redecision. Here are some questions for therapists and clients to keep in mind during this work on the way to a redecision:

1. What was the original decision that is causing the present problem? (Here is where all methods for script diagnosis are used.)
2. What is the client doing *now* to maintain her old decisions?
3. What are the advantages of her present behavior?
4. How does she carry out her old decisions with the therapist? with other group members?
5. At what level is she discounting?
6. What does she need to make a new decision?
7. What is she lacking in terms of permission, protection, information, stroking, and so on?
8. Are there any other issues that she needs to deal with in order to make a new decision?

A client rarely goes from contract A to redecision Z. Usually, she must resolve problems around B, C, D, and so on before she feels safe and ready to move on to Z.

Stage 5: Redecision

Redecision occurs when the client changes some aspect of her script. We wish to emphasize that redecisions often occur gradually over time, rather than as one-shot statements. If a client is not ready to make a new decision, it is necessary to go back to one of the previous steps and find out what is missing. When the client does make a redecision, she still may need to continue working to integrate her new decision into a more satisfying life style.

Stage Six: Relearning

Many therapists believe that the redecision is the goal of treatment. We agree with this statement, but at the same time realize that it is oversimplified. A redecision opens the doors for change and new behaviors. However, if the redecision is to be lasting and meaningful, it must be integrated into the client's life style. Most clients need additional time, practice, and information before they are satisfied with their new decisions and regularly following them. The relearning process occurs as the client integrates her redecision into her overall life plan and is answering such questions as:

□ How will I carry out my new decision?

□ When?

□ How will I arrange to get strokes from myself and others for my new behaviors?

□ How do I block myself from carrying out my new decisions?

□ How will I work through these blocks?

During the relearning stage the therapist remains available as a source of information, strokes the client for her changes, and continues to confront her residual script behaviors. The therapist and group members also provide feedback to the client regarding how they think she is doing as she experiments with new behaviors. It is important not to expect the client to do a perfect job just because she has made a redecision. She will probably make mistakes and needs to talk about any problems she is having in learning new ways to take care of herself. Once she is regularly carrying out her new decision, she is ready to decide whether she wishes to work on a different issue or to terminate treatment.

Stage Seven: Termination

Each client must eventually face the issue of termination. The question of when termination is appropriate is not an easy one to answer. No one ever reaches perfection, and people always have issues to work through and ways to improve themselves. At some point, however, clients reach a point of diminishing returns: the time, energy, and money spent for treatment outweighs the benefits which the client is receiving. One option is to continue treatment on a less frequent basis by coming only periodically, attending an occasional group session, or scheduling an individual session or marathon when she feels the need. Another option is to terminate treatment for a specified period of time and then reevaluate the situation. Still another option is to terminate with the idea of not returning. The final decision about whether or not to terminate treatment usually rests with the client. The therapist's responsibility is to give feedback regarding how she sees the client doing, especially with regard to the client's treatment contract. If termination seems scripty, then the therapist should confront the client with this information. Both the therapist and group members can provide helpful feedback to the client regarding how they experience her, but the client still makes the final decision regarding whether she terminates or stays.

We have several rules of thumb which we follow when a client indicates that she is ready to stop treatment. First, we ask clients to agree to attend two extra sessions after they announce that they wish to terminate. This provides extra protection for the client to experience how she feels while contemplating termination and to deal with the process of saying goodbye. It also gives her some time to think about and clear up any unresolved issues before leaving, as well as to change her mind if the original decision proves hasty. Second, we request that clients announce their intent to terminate in the group rather than in an individual session or via phone calls, letters, or third-party messages. We consider all of these behaviors to be indicators that the client is avoiding dealing with the therapist or group in a straight manner, and therefore that the client is not ready to terminate. Third, we like to hear from all of the client's ego states about how each of them feels regarding her desire to quit treatment. Does it make sense to her Adult? Does her Child feel satisfied with her present ways of taking care of herself? Does her Parent provide adequate nurturing and protection for continued growth? Sometimes a five-chair exercise in which the client talks about terminating therapy from each of her functional ego states provides a great deal of insight and motivates her to stay around and finish some unresolved issues. Finally, before a client terminates, we ask her to review her contracts. Has she met her treatment goals as outlined in her treatment contract? If not, why not? Is terminating at this time a way to avoid her contract? Has she met the financial obligations agreed to with the therapist? If not, how does she plan to do so?

Sometimes termination is initiated by the therapist rather than the client. When this occurs, the therapeutic reasons should be very clear in order to avoid a gamey situation, and differences of opinion regarding whether or not a client should terminate should be resolved in a mutually acceptable way. If a therapist suggests that a client terminate treatment because the two of them are involved in rackets and games which are interfering with the treatment process, it is very important for the therapist to accept her share of responsibility in that process, as well as giving feedback regarding the client's role. Above all, the client should not be told that she is untreatable or incurable. Instead, she should be referred to someone who will not hook into her games and who can provide the treatment which she needs.

The Four Rules of Therapy

The process of therapy sometimes seems to offer a baffling array of choices about what to do next. The client sends off many different stimuli contained in a myriad of issues, but which are the crucial ones? The therapist has at her disposal many different techniques, but how does she choose which to use? The treatment contract partially answers these questions, and remembering the stages of treatment also helps to keep the work focused. In addition to these guidelines, there are four rules of therapy which, when followed, provide a direction for the therapist when further problems arise [52]. Although the treatment contract provides the overall focus, other issues must sometimes take precedence before satisfactory progress can be made.

The first rule is by far the most important and sets the foundation for good therapy, since it creates the warm positive atmosphere conducive to change. The remaining rules are about certain priorities in therapy and can be carried out effectively only when the first rule is being followed. The first rule of therapy is: *The therapist should remain in an OK position both during and after therapy.* This rule contains several elements. Primarily it means that the therapist is aware of being lovable and important regardless of how well she is performing. Therefore, she takes good care of herself and does not discount any of her ego states; she does not accept contracts which she does not understand or which she feels uncomfortable about; and she does not Rescue, or Try Hard, or feel guilty and become a martyr. When a therapist follows this rule, she provides a good model for her clients. As she experiences her own OKness, she does not discount the people she works with, but instead invites their OKness. She is more likely to stroke the OK parts of her clients and help them flourish. In short, she is probably doing good therapy!

Many problems in therapy stem from not following this rule. Countertransference reactions occur because the therapist is discounting herself in some way. Therefore, when in doubt about any problem or impasse in therapy, the therapist should check to see if she is discounting herself, such as striving to do a perfect job, or feeling impatient because she is hearing from her Parent that she should have already cured this client. No therapist is fully immune from the effects of her own script, and so on occasion will fall prey to some of these problems. The first rule is a reminder of what is possible, even though no one follows it perfectly. Stroke yourself and enjoy your OKness even though you are not a perfect therapist. This will not only be delightful for you, but also helpful to your clients. This rule and admonition to stroke yourself applies equally well to all people-helpers—teachers, parents, policemen, consultants, and so on.

The second rule of therapy is: *Deal with the structure of the relationship between the therapist and the client before dealing with the content of the contract.* This is true not only at the beginning of therapy, but at all times. When and where does the session meet? How much do the clients pay and when? What are the guidelines for relating during the session? For example, in our groups no one hurts anyone; otherwise, it is OK to touch. These kinds of issues must be handled before much that is useful will occur. The therapist is the leader of the session and must set the conditions and framework for the relationship. This provides a safe situation and, when done potently, helps to establish an environment conducive to change. If any of the conditions of the structure are violated, further testing of the limits is likely to follow, and the client's sense of safety is reduced. If one person in a group breaks the rules, the other members may also digress from working on their contracts in order to check out the structure. Following are several examples of violations of structure which demand immediate attention:

1. Missing a session
2. Throwing a hard object
3. Running out of the session
4. Not paying the agreed-upon fee
5. The therapist breaking or not enforcing any of the rules

The looser the structure, the more a client needs to provide her own protection. This may be useful for some clients, but a client with early developmental problems and a loose internal structure needs a secure external structure with clear boundaries. If a client is not changing in therapy, this may be because she does not believe that the structure of the therapy situation can handle her and provide the protection she needs. She may need to transfer to a therapist who uses a different style of therapy.

The third rule of therapy is: *Deal with transference or counter-transference issues before dealing with the content of the contract.* The third rule overlaps somewhat with the second rule, inasmuch as transgressions from the structure are often due to transference issues. Transference occurs when a client "puts the face" of someone from the past onto someone in the present, often the therapist. She then proceeds to relate to the person as if he were the significant other from her past. Countertransference occurs when the therapist relates to a client in a similar way. If a client is not changing—although ostensibly working on her contract—two likely possibilities are that either she is in an unrecognized transference bind or that the therapist is in a countertransference bind and so is not responding to the client in appropriate ways. George's work on the content issue of taking in positive strokes from people important to him is an example of a transference problem. He was not able to achieve his contract while he unconsciously experienced the hated image of his mother on the therapist when she was stroking him. This transference distortion had to be resolved before he could meet his treatment goals. The therapist may elect not to deal overtly with the transference at the time it is occurring, preferring to let it intensify so that when it is pointed out, it will be clear. The important thing is that the therapist be aware of what is going on and select a way to deal with it.

The fourth and last rule of therapy is: *Deal with here-and-now problems that exist between the participants (including the therapist) and with other major life events before dealing with the content of the contract.* This is especially important if the therapist's treatment style is one-to-one therapy within the group, and so she tends not to focus on interaction between members. Many new groups need a period of time when the interaction among the members is the primary focus. This gives everyone a chance to get to know each other and the leader without revealing too much too fast. Examples of here-and-now problems in the therapy situation include feelings of rivalry or jealousy, resentments, love affairs, concerns regarding confidentiality, reactions to new members entering the group or old members leaving, and any frictions between coleaders. Important life events include death in the family, marriage, separation or divorce, illness or injury, and birthdays. When the therapist pays attention to these, energy is not wasted in discounting, and the therapist makes clear her belief that the real-life events and concerns of her clients are important.

What To Do When a Client Does Not Change

Review the *stages of treatment.* What is being overlooked? Go back to an earlier stage and begin again. Perhaps there is a problem with the contract. For example, Al contracted to stay out of trouble with authorities, but really wanted to work on getting close to people. He kept resisting change until he revealed what he really wanted.

Sometimes the problem stems from *ambivalence* in the therapist. The therapist may not approve of the outcome, or may be frightened of it in some way. Marcia had a treatment contract to be assertive with her boss, but her therapist was afraid of his own boss. The therapist communicated this fear to Marcia on a psychological level, and she did not receive from him the protection and permission which she needed.

Still another common problem is with *transference* issues. In other words, the client will have generalized her original script decision into the therapeutic relationship. Gail had originally decided, "I'm a nuisance and I'll be careful with mother." Later, she assumed that she was still a nuisance and needed to be careful with everybody from whom she wanted something, including her therapist. Dawn was following a similar pattern when she spoke pleasantly to her therapist for five minutes, but did not go anywhere in particular. When questioned about this, she recalled that her mother approved of pleasantness more than anything else and did not like to hear about Dawn's problems. Transference problems are very common, and this possibility should be checked out whenever treatment is not progressing well.

People are sometimes slow to change because change means *giving up* familiar and certain *strokes.* They may need to establish new stroking patterns to replace the old ones, or learn to accept fewer strokes as a normal pattern.

Working at the wrong *level of discounting* is another common reason for an impasse. Ed was working on various options for being assertive and getting nowhere. The problem was that he had not really allowed himself to be clearly aware of what he wanted, so he had nothing specific to be assertive about.

Another reason a client may not change, or may even get worse, is because of an undiscovered *Don't Exist message.* Ted was working on feeling comfortable getting close to someone, but instead became more upset every time he was somewhat successful. Upon further investigation, we learned that Ted had a Don't Exist message which was triggered whenever he went against mother's injunction to Don't Be Close. Sometimes, a troublesome Don't Exist message might even be a well-known one that the client and therapist believe has long ago been redecided. If the old Don't Exist injunction was very potent, the client may revive it at each major step in therapy, since each step is experienced as a new stressful situation. Also, when a client redecides that "I will never kill myself, no matter what!" he may not be thinking about all of the eventual possibilities. He is speaking like a child who promises something, but then does not carry it out because he does not understand all that the promise entails. As an example, Allison redecided that "I will never kill myself, no matter what" and felt very good about this redecision. Later, her therapist went on vacation, and Allison again experienced thoughts of suicide. Her explanation was, "I never thought about your leaving. I can't

live without you!" Some people, especially those with early developmental problems, erect rigid boundaries between different parts of
themselves. They feel "split" into sections that do not communicate
with one another, and so a decision from one part may not influence
another part. Howard once redecided from his suicidal five-year-old
Child ego state that he would never kill himself. However, his two-
year-old Child was not listening, which became apparent after
another suicide attempt. Eventually, the two-year-old Howie decided
to live. Following yet another suicide attempt, he learned that his
one-year-old Child had not been in touch with what had been going
on, and that part also needed to redecide.

Sometimes messages must be worked on in a specific *sequence*
for a redecision to occur. If a client is not changing, look for the
influence of messages coming from a different part of the script
matrix. Patty was aware of a strong Don't Exist injunction from her
father, and in spite of what looked like a lot of good work on her
part, was not making an effective redecision. She was asked to tell
her mother (in a double-chair exercise) that she was going to inform
father that she would not kill herself. Her mother responded by
saying, "Oh, dear! Now, don't you upset your father! What will
happen to me?" Patty then realized that she was not dealing with
father's message because of the strong decision to take care of
mother, made with the hope of getting some nurturing from mother.
Before Patty could confront father and decide to live, she needed to
decide not to take care of mother and work through that issue.
Constructing a decision scale noting each family member separately
can help with these problems, since each person giving a Don't Exist
injunction must be dealt with. Mother gave Patty a Don't Exist injunction when she told her that her own (mother's) feelings were
more important than Patty's deciding to live.

Sometimes the *injunction* which is most essential to work on is
missed because it is *covered up by a socially acceptable message* from
a different ego state. Do not immediately accept the first message,
since it may be only superficial. Look for the message that is supporting the feeling, thought, or behavior. It will be there! One way
to find the script message is to have the client behave in some unusual way. This will often cause an internal crossed transaction and
result in a different response from her Parent, bringing out information that was previously hidden. Once again, it may be helpful to
intensify this internal confrontation by having the client increase her

assertion or exaggerate her behavior. For example, have the client be even more of a Victim than usual, or louder, or more argumentative, or ask her to say the unthinkable. The client may not spontaneously figure out how to do any of these, since her frame of reference may not include such possibilities. Here the therapist can be helpful with suggestions. Once the script message is found, the client will be more open to learning options for changing.

> June was a very passive client who always deferred to her husband and other male authority figures. In a double-chair exercise with her mother, June asked what she should do. Mother replied, "Whatever you want, dear." Since mother's response seemed evasive, it was suggested to June that she tell her mother that she would therefore assert herself with her husband. Upon hearing this, mother became upset and exclaimed, "Oh, no! You can't do that! He will leave you!" Now June was aware of the source and power of the message that was influencing her and directed her efforts accordingly.

When the Client Does Change

What does it mean when the client changes? Has she made a redecision or not? There are many possible explanations for any change, and only one involves a redecision.

1. He may have switched from one aspect of his script to another. Earl was a hard-working, dutiful husband who revealed very few feelings. His contract was to get in touch with and express more feelings. A few weeks after making his contract, he went on a weekend binge and had an affair with his wife's best friend. It turned out that his father, when drunk, had often said, "You can't keep a good man down" (Don't Succeed). Instead of making a redecision, Earl was following his father's slogan.

2. She may be in the process of collecting proof that her script decision was correct. Bobbi, who was afraid to get close to men, began a torrid love affair but expected ultimately to be left in the lurch. She got what she expected!

3. He may have a specific message to rebel. Every three of four years, Fritz left a close relationship that seemed to be going well. He mixed up his

desire to avoid being passive with his father's message, "Don't let them push you around."

4. She may be switching from the message of one parent to the message of another parent. Helen decided to leave her unhappy marriage (mother had never left hers) and become an independent woman who did not need anyone (father's example).

5. He may have been in script and shifted to subscript, as when Brian came out of his depression and began working very hard.

6. She may have been in subscript and shifted to script. Monica stopped doing what everyone wanted, told them all to "go to Hell," and left. A few weeks later, she attempted suicide.

7. He may have found the spell-breaker, or escape hatch, which allows him to get away from his script. Terry made a serious suicide attempt, but miraculously survived. After his recovery, he resumed living without his previous self-doubts and "Kick Me" sweatshirt.

8. Finally, she may have made a redecision. If she has, the new behavior will likely make sense to the therapist's Adult, feel right to his Child, and follow reasonably from what was transpiring in the treatment. She will still need support and may not carry out her redecision perfectly, but she will still want to do it. When she does, her face and body will usually relax so that she looks younger, perhaps even childlike, and more beautiful than ever.

Appendix:

Experiences for Learning

The following exercises may be done in a group or in some instances alone. Ordinarily they will provide interesting and pleasurable learning experiences, and on occasion they will facilitate getting into feelings connected with earlier life scenes. If at any time you do not wish to go further, sit or stand with an erect posture, look around the room, and allow yourself to be aware of three things in your environment. This will likely bring you out of the experience. If an exercise proves too scary for you, stop until you figure out a way to proceed safely.

Ego States

1. Do a five-chair exercise around any topic you choose. Examples: How do you feel/think about food, sex, or closeness from your CP, NP, A, FC, AC?

2. One group of five people, with each member labeled as one of the five functional ego states (and so together comprising one person), talks with another similar group of five people. The first "person" is a thirty-year-old woman and the second "person" is her husband, who has just stated that he wants a divorce. As with actual people, the ego states talk both among themselves and to the other person, directing their comments to the specific ego state they wish. Do this for three minutes, then have the participants switch ego states. Switch every three minutes until each person has been each ego state.

☐ Were you more comfortable in a particular ego state?

☐ Were you especially uncomfortable in a particular ego state?

☐ Did you step out of your designated role while being a particular ego state?

☐ Which ego state would you like to be in more?

☐ Which ego state would you like to be in less?

3. In groups of one to five, brainstorm any subject you like for three minutes. Example: all the different uses for flowers. Allow your thoughts free rein without any evaluation, censoring, or concern for practicality. After three minutes, suggest that the participants think further about the subject by now bringing into mind what a Nurturing or Controlling Parent would think about the topic.

After two more minutes, have the participants evaluate the ideas and pick out the three best.

The first two sections are accomplished best by the Little Professor, and the last by the Adult along with the Little Professor.

Premature evaluations and criticism tend to shut down the Little Professor and limit the number of ideas. Each person should be praised for her ideas.

4. Fantasize that you are the object which you would most like to be in the whole world. Describe yourself for two minutes. Afterwards, tell your partner.

> "I am a bird. I fly and soar through the sky to wherever I wish. I am beautiful and graceful," etc.

Now fantasize being the object you would least like to be. Describe yourself for two minutes. Afterwards, tell your partner.

> "I am a rock. I am thick and hard and dense and can't feel. People sit on me and chip at me," etc.

Now fantasize for two minutes being the parts of your favorite object that you do not like. Afterwards, tell your partner.

> "I am a bird. I cannot talk or communicate well. I can't think very well, and have the same kind of thoughts each day," etc.

Now fantasize for two minutes being the parts of your least-liked object that would be good for you. Afterwards, tell your partner.

"I am a rock. I am strong, and it is hard for anyone to hurt me. No one knows what is inside me," etc.

This exercise not only brings out the creativity of the Little Professor, but also encourages expression from other ego states, sometimes unexpectedly. The favorite object often brings out Free Child behaviors and desires. It also may bring out Adapted Child characteristics—those behaviors which please other people. The unliked parts of the liked object may represent Free Child aspects unacceptable to parent figures, or they may be Adapted Child features. Similarly, the least-liked object may bring out either Adapted Child or Free Child. If Free Child, they are usually well suppressed, so few people see them. The liked aspects of the least-liked object may be features of the Adapted Child which are approved of by the Parent or hidden strengths of the Free Child. The above discussion is not meant to be exhaustive, so you will undoubtedly find other possibilities. Also, sometimes a fantasy is just a fantasy and does not necessarily represent anything. If so, just move on to something else, rather than struggle for a hidden meaning. Even Sigmund Freud agreed that "sometimes a cigar is just a cigar."

Strokes

1. Do a stroking profile on yourself. Which scale(s) would you like to raise? If you are in a group or working with a partner, how does their profile of you compare with yours? If there is a significant difference, you may not be letting yourself know what you are actually doing.

2. Practice *giving* a stroke you do not ordinarily give. Example: Tell someone, "I like you." How do you feel doing that? Do you wish to add that behavior to your repertoire?

Do the same with *taking* a stroke you do not ordinarily take. Example: Accept and believe someone telling you, "You're nice to be with."

Do the same with *asking for* a stroke you do not ordinarily ask for. Example: Ask for someone to tell you, "You're smart."

Do the same thing with *refusing to give* a stroke you do not ordinarily refuse to give. Example: Refuse to help or stroke someone when they ask, even though you believe they need it. Is there a part of you that is glad you did not do it?

3. Brag about yourself for thirty seconds in a group and feel good about it. If you are not ready for this, practice by yourself first. When you do that successfully, fantasize that the group is present. After you have done that successfully, do it in the group itself, or with a friend.

4. Ask someone you like to hold you and practice enjoying that while not feeling obligated.

Transactions

1. Select a partner. One person will be seeking some facts, while the other avoids answering. Choose either position and any topic you wish. The first person asks questions from Adult while the second person avoids the issue and responds from Child. Do this for ten or twelve transactions, before ending with an Adult-to-Adult transaction. Then switch roles and choose a different topic. This time, one person seeks information (Adult) and the other responds from Parent. Do this ten or twelve times, before ending with an Adult-to-Adult transaction. Then discuss both experiences.

2. Select another partner. This time, use your words to talk about one thing while your nonverbal cues communicate something else. Your partner is free to respond as she wants. Change roles after each topic. You can use some of the following examples—or be creative and make up your own. Carry on each conversation for ten to twelve transactions, then discuss.

SOCIAL (VERBAL) MESSAGE	PSYCHOLOGICAL (NONVERBAL) MESSAGE
"Do you know where Fifth Street is?"	"Would you like to get it on?"
"Will you come and visit me sometime?" (At PTA meeting)	"I don't really want you to."
"Aren't kids different nowadays?"	"I like you—let's be friends."
"What is your opinion about . . . [fill in]?"	"What do you know, anyway!"

3. This time, one partner will talk about something important to her. The other partner responds by saying nothing and remaining stonefaced. The first person continues to try to get a response. The second person remains stonefaced. After two minutes, switch roles. Then discuss your reactions.

4. Repeat number 3, only this time the second person smiles or laughs, but still says nothing. After two minutes, switch roles, then discuss your reactions.

Time Structuring

1. This exercise was developed by Eric Berne, and is referred to in his reports on intimacy experiments. Select a partner with whom you feel comfortable. Sit in chairs facing each other or cross-legged on the floor. Sit so that your heads are between twenty-two and thirty-six inches apart. You may hold each others' hands if you wish (a good idea), and follow these instructions:

1. *Avoid withdrawal.* Maintain eye contact throughout the duration of the exercise. Do not "pull down the shades" by going inside your head; share the entire exercise with your partner.

2. *Avoid rituals.* Do not exchange verbal ritual strokes such as "Hi," "Hello," "How are you," or nonverbal ritual strokes such as winks or social smiles.

3. *Avoid pastimes.* Do not chitchat or make small talk. Do not talk about anything which is not occurring here-and-now. Do not talk about this exercise.

4. *Avoid activities.* Do not make this a project. Do not be concerned with how well you are doing—there is no right or wrong way.

5. *Avoid rackets and games.* Do not get into feelings which do not concern your present experience. Do not send ulterior messages. Do not monitor what you are experiencing.

6. *Share intimacy.* Stay in touch with your Child. Share what you feel openly with your partner. Use sentences that begin with "I" and "You."

After a few minutes, stop and cathect your Adult. Discuss your experiences with your partner. Do not be concerned if you experience temporary alterations in your sense of time, perception, or mood, since this sometimes occurs.

2. In a group of six persons, have each person select a time structure from the list below. (If you have fewer persons, eliminate Withdrawal and Ritual first.) Fantasize that you are discussing a camp-out together. Continue the discussion for twelve minutes, switching roles every two minutes; then discuss your experiences.

	TIME STRUCTURE SOUGHT	ACTIVITY
Person #1	Withdrawal	Has nothing to say
Person #2	Ritual	Wants to chitchat ritualistically—speaks in clichés
Person #3	Pastime	Wants to "talk about" past experiences, future plans
Person #4	Activity	Wants to make solid plans, with all details worked out
Person #5	Racket/Game	Wants to feel left out or unwanted
Person #6	Intimacy	Wants to stay here-and-now and share present experience

3. For one week, say only what you mean. For example, do not say, "How are you." or "How have you been," unless you really want to know. If you do want to know, make sure you get an answer to your question—if not, ask it again. If you still get no answer, drop it. Notice the difference in how you ask and how the other person responds. Conversely, when someone asks you how you are and so on, answer with a true statement. Notice how you feel as you do, and how the other person responds. For another week, pastime only about things you really want to talk about. If you are uninterested in a conversation, tell the other person(s) what you want to talk about or change the subject gracefully. Ask yourself if the strokes you are getting through rituals and pastimes are the ones you really want. If not, how can you structure your time so as to get the kinds of strokes you want?

Rackets and Games

1. Choose a partner. Person #1 sits or stands comfortably and merely responds that she is content and needs nothing from her partner at

the moment. Person #2 needs to be "helpful," however, and sets out to Rescue the first person; Person #2 will not be satisfied until she "makes Person #1 more comfortable," but the latter does not accept her "help." Continue for about five minutes, then switch roles. Discuss your experiences.

2. Select another partner. Imagine that you are attending a meeting and discussing an issue before a large audience. Choose any issue, such as bussing school children, raising funds for a charity, or deciding if pets are to be allowed in the neighborhood. Person #1 remains in a relatively OK position while Person #2 is a *subtle* Persecutor. Person #2 must remain one-up and superior to Person #1, but does so very carefully so as not to appear nasty or rude in front of the larger group. Discuss your experiences.

3. Draw the drama triangle on a blackboard in front of the room. One person role-plays a husband while a second role-plays a wife, and they discuss an upcoming holiday weekend.

Each of the discussants selects a "coach" who stands on either side of the blackboard. When the wife's "coach" points to a drama triangle role (Persecutor, Rescuer, or Victim), the wife assumes that position and continues the discussion from there. The husband's "coach" does the same. The "coaches" decide when the discussants switch by pointing to different drama triangle positions, and the role players switch positions each time. Continue for several minutes, then discuss your reactions.

4. Recall the last time you were very upset. With someone guiding you, recreate the scene, "playing" the various roles of the people involved. After five or ten minutes, stop and discuss with your guide the drama triangle positions of the people involved.

Scripts

1. Answer any or all of the questions mentioned in the questionnaire section of the chapter on scripts (Chapter 8). Do this with a partner if possible. Pick out the answers that apply to your script.

2. You have been granted one wish to change anything about yourself that you would like. What is it? Is it something that is possible? Assuming it is possible, how is it that you are not already doing it? How did you learn not to do it? What are the disadvantages

of doing it? If what you want is not possible, what are the advantages for you to be wishing for something that cannot happen?

3. Write down what you would like to accomplish in the next year and in the next ten years. Are you presently acting in such a way to succeed at meeting your goals? If not, what do you have to do? Starting when? What are the disadvantages?

4. Imagine you are one hundred years old and you decided to reflect back upon your life. Are you satisfied? If not, what would you change? What would your mother say about your life? What would your father say? What would your siblings say? What would your spouse and children say? What will you do about it now?

Reference List

1. Allen, James, and Barbara Allen, "Scripts: The Role of Permission," *Transactional Analysis Journal* 2, No. 2 (April 1972): 72–74. Our list of permissions and corresponding developmental stages is somewhat different from the Allens'.

2. Bandler, Richard, and John Grinder, *Patterns of the Hypnotic Techniques of Milton H. Erickson, M.D.*, vol. 1 (Cupertino, Calif.: Meta Publications, 1975).

3. Berne, Eric, "Away from a Theory of the Impact of Interpersonal Interaction on Non-Verbal Participation," *Transactional Analysis Journal* 1, No. 1 (January 1971): 6–13. The January 1971 *Transactional Analysis Journal* is a memorial issue for Eric Berne and contains articles about Berne, a biographical sketch, and an annotated bibliography of Berne's writings.

4. Berne, Eric, *Games People Play* (New York: Grove Press, 1964).

5. Berne, Eric, *Principles of Group Treatment* (New York: Oxford University Press, 1966).

6. Berne, Eric, *Sex in Human Loving* (New York: Simon and Schuster, 1970).

7. Berne, Eric, *The Structure and Dynamics of Organizations and Groups* (New York: Grove Press, 1963).

8. Berne, Eric, *Transactional Analysis in Psychotherapy* (New York: Grove Press, 1961).

9. Berne, Eric, *What Do You Say After You Say Hello?* (New York: Grove Press, 1972).

10. Boyd, Harry, "Scripts and Scenarios," *Transactional Analysis Journal* 6, No. 3 (July 1976): 278–80.

11. Boyd, Harry, "The Structure and Sequence of Psychotherapy," *Transactional Analysis Journal* 6, No. 2 (April 1976): 180–83.

12. Brown, Michael, and Taibi Kahler, *NoTAtions: A Guide to Transactional Analysis Literature* (Dexter, Mich.: Huron Valley Institute Press, 1977).

13. Brown, Michael, *Psychodiagnosis in Brief* (Dexter, Mich.: Huron Valley Institute Press, 1977).

14. Bruce, Ted, and Richard Erskine, "Counterfeit Strokes," *Transactional Analysis Journal* 4, No. 2 (April 1974): 18.

15. Costello, R. Kennon, "Consolidating Injunctions," *Transactional Analysis Journal* 6, No. 1 (January 1976): 52–56.

16. Crossman, Pat, "Permission and Protection," *Transactional Analysis Bulletin* 5, No. 19 (July 1966): 152.

17. Dusay, John, *Egograms* (New York: Harper & Row, 1977).

18. Dusay, John, "Response," *Transactional Analysis Bulletin* 5, No. 18 (April 1966): 136–37.

19. Edwards, Mary, "The Two Parents," *Transactional Analysis Bulletin* 7, No. 26 (April 1966): 37–38.

20. English, Fanita, "Strokes in the Credit Bank for David Kupfer," *Transactional Analysis Journal* 1, No. 3 (July 1971): 27.

21. English, Fanita, "The Substitution Factor: Rackets and Real Feelings (Part 1)," *Transactional Analysis Journal* 1, No. 4 (October 1971): 25–26.

22. Erickson, Milton, Ernest Rossi, and Sheila Rossi, *Hypnotic Realities* (New York: Irvington Publishers, 1976), pp. 276–79.

23. Ernst, Frank, "Psychological Rackets in the OK Corral," *Transactional Analysis Journal* 3, No. 2 (April 1973): 19–23.

24. Ernst, Franklin. "The OK Corral: The Grid for Get-on-With," *Transactional Analysis Journal* 1, No. 4 (October 1971): 231–40.

25. Goulding, Robert, and Mary Goulding, "Injunctions, Decisions,

and Redecisions," *Transactional Analysis Journal* 6, No. 1 (January 1976): 41–48.

26. Goulding, Robert, "New Directions in Transactional Analysis: Creating an Environment for Redecision and Change," in *Progress in Group and Family Therapy*, edited by Clifford J. Sager and Helen Singer Kaplan (New York: Brunner/Mazel, 1972), pp. 105-34.

27. Goulding, Robert, "Thinking and Feeling Transactional Analysis: Three Impasses," *Voices* 10, No. 1 (Spring 1974): 11-13.

28. Groder, Martin, "Guest Editorial," *Transactional Analysis Journal* 6, No. 4. (October 1976): 365.

29. Holloway, William, "The Intrapsychic and Interpersonal in Personality Development and Script Formation," *Monograph Series Of Midwest Institute For Human Understanding, Inc.* (Medina, Ohio, 1974), p. 56.

30. James, Muriel, and Dorothy Jongeward, *Born to Win* (Reading, Mass.: Addison-Wesley, 1971).

31. Kahler, Taibi, "Drivers: The Key to the Process of Scripts," *Transactional Analysis Journal* 5, No. 3 (July 1975): 280-84.

32. Kahler, Taibi, "Scripts: Process and Content," *Transactional Analysis Journal* 5, No. 3 (July 1975): 227-79.

33. Kahler, Taibi, "Structural Analysis: A Focus on Stroke Rationale, a Parent Continuum," *Transactional Analysis Journal* 5, No. 3 (July 1975): 267-71. Modified by authors.

34. Kahler, Taibi, with Hedges Capers, "The Miniscript," *Transactional Analysis Journal* 4, No. 1 (January, 1974): 26-42.

35. Karpman, Stephen B., "Fairy Tale and Script Drama Analysis," *Transactional Analysis Bulletin* 7, No. 26 (April 1968): 39-43.

36. Karpman, Stephen, "Options," *Transactional Analysis Journal* 1 No. 1 (January 1971): 79-87.

37. Mart, Larry, Teal Nichols, and Margaret Cantrell, "Parent Shrinkers Revisited," *Transactional Analysis Journal* 5, No. 3 (July 1975): 259-63.

38. McKenna, Jim, "Stroking Profile," *Transactional Analysis*

Journal 4, No. 4 (October 1974): 20. Copyright 1973, Jim McKenna, M.S.W., St. Louis, Mo.

39. Samuels, Solon, "Stroke Strategy: 1. The Basis of Therapy," *Transactional Analysis Journal* 1, No. 3 (July 1971): 23-24.

40. Schiff, Jacqui Lee, et al., *The Cathexis Reader: The Transactional Analysis Treatment of Psychosis* (New York: Harper & Row, 1975).

41. Steiner, Claude, "A Script Checklist," *Transactional Analysis Bulletin* 6, No. 22 (April 1967): 38-39.

42. Steiner, Claude M., *Games Alcoholics Play* (New York: Grove Press, 1971).

43. Steiner, Claude, "Script and Counterscript," *Transactional Analysis Bulletin* 5, No. 18 (April 1966): 133.

44. Steiner, Claude, *Scripts People Live: Transactional Analysis of Life Scripts* (New York: Grove Press, 1974).

45. Steiner, Claude, "Transactional Analysis as a Treatment Philosophy," *Transactional Analysis Bulletin* 7, No. 27 (July 1968): 63.

46. Stevens, John, *Awareness: Exploring, Experimenting, Experiencing* (Moab, Utah: Real People Press, 1971). Contains many excellent fantasy trips and other exercises for self-exploration.

47. White, Jerome, "Adapted Child Complexes," *Transactional Analysis Bulletin* 9, No. 36 (October 1970): 150-53.

48. White, Jerome, and Terry White, "TA Psychohistory," *Transactional Analysis Journal* 4, No. 3 (July 1974): 5-17.

49. Woollams, Stanley, "Decision Scale," *Transactional Analysis Journal*, forthcoming.

50. Woollams, Stanley, "Formation of the Script," *Transactional Analysis Journal* 3, No. 1 (January 1973): 31-37.

51. Woollams, Stanley, "Formation of the Script—II," *Transactional Analysis Journal*, forthcoming.

52. Woollams, Stanley, "From 21 to 43," in *Transactional Analysis after Eric Berne,* edited by Graham Barnes (New York: Harper's College Press, 1977). pp. 366-67. By permission of Harper & Row, Publishers, Inc.

53. Woollams, Stanley, "Life Determinants," unpublished manuscript, 1977.

54. Woollams, Stanley, and Kristyn Huige, "Normal Dependency and Symbiosis," *Transactional Analysis Journal* 7, No. 3 (July 1977): 5.

55. Woollams, Stanley, "Permission Matrix," unpublished manuscript, 1977.

56. Woollams, Stanley, "The Internal Stroke Economy," *Transactional Analysis Journal*, 8, No. 3 (July 1978): 194–97.

57. Woollams, Stanley, and Michael Brown, *Transactional Analysis* (Dexter, Mich.: Huron Valley Institute Press, 1978).

58. Woollams, Stanley, Michael Brown, and Kristyn Huige, *Transactional Analysis in Brief,* 3rd ed. (Ann Arbor, Mich.: Huron Valley Institute, 1976).

59. Woollams, Stanley, "When Fewer Strokes Are Better," *Transactional Analysis Journal* 6, No. 3 (July 1976): 270–71.

60. Woollams, Stanley, "Cure!?" *Transactional Analysis Journal,* forthcoming.

61. Wyckoff, Hogie, "The Stroke Economy in Women's Scripts," *Transactional Analysis Journal* 1, No. 3 (July 1971): 16–20.

Index